Screening Morocco

This series of publications on Africa, Latin America, Southeast Asia, and Global and Comparative Studies is designed to present significant research, translation, and opinion to area specialists and to a wide community of persons interested in world affairs. The editor seeks manuscripts of quality on any subject and can usually make a decision regarding publication within three months of receipt of the original work. Production methods generally permit a work to appear within one year of acceptance. The editor works closely with authors to produce a high-quality book. The series appears in a paperback format and is distributed worldwide. For more information, contact the executive editor at Ohio University Press, 19 Circle Drive, The Ridges, Athens, Ohio 45701.

Executive editor: Gillian Berchowitz
AREA CONSULTANTS
Africa: Gillian Berchowitz
Latin America: Brad Jokisch, Patrick Barr-Melej, and Rafael Obregon
Southeast Asia: William H. Frederick

Screening Morocco

CONTEMPORARY FILM
IN A CHANGING SOCIETY

Valérie K. Orlando

Ohio University Research in International Studies
Africa Series No. 89
Ohio University Press
Athens

To obtain permission to quote, reprint, or otherwise reproduce or
distribute material from Ohio University Press publications, please
contact our rights and permissions department at (740) 593-1154 or
(740) 593-4536 (fax).
www.ohioswallow.com

Printed in the United States of America
The books in the Ohio University Research in International Studies Series
are printed on acid-free paper. ∞

20 19 18 17 16 15 14 13 12 11   5 4 3 2 1

Library of Congress Cataloging-in-Publication Data

Orlando, Valérie, 1963–
  Screening Morocco : contemporary film in a changing society / Valérie K. Orlando.
    p. cm. — (Ohio University research in international studies, Africa series no. 89)
  Includes bibliographical references and index.
  Includes filmography.
  ISBN 978-0-89680-281-0 (soft cover : alk. paper) — ISBN 978-0-89680-478-4
(electronic)
  1. Motion pictures—Morocco—History—20th century. 2. Motion pictures—
Social aspects—Morocco. I. Title.
  PN1993.5.M8O86 2011
  791.4309646—dc22
                                                            2010051519

To Aunt Irene in loving memory

Contents

Illustrations

Fig. 0.1. Poster for the Berber film *De l'autre côté du fleuve*, Cinéma de Sidi Kacem, Morocco, 2009

Preface

Screening Morocco: Contemporary Film in a Changing Society focuses on Moroccan films produced and distributed from 1999 to 2010. Since 1999 and the death of King Hassan II, which ended *les années de plomb* (the Lead Years, 1963–99), Morocco has transformed, socioculturally and politically. Encouraged by the more openly democratic climate fostered by young king Mohammed VI (popularly known as "M6"), men and women filmmakers today explore the sociocultural and political debates of their country while also seeking to document the untold stories of a dark past. Male and female directors such as Nabyl Ayouch, Farida Benlyazid, Ahmed Boulane, Yasmine Kassari, Nabyl Lahlou, Hicham Lasri, Narjiss Nejjar, Zakia Tahiri, and Lahcen Zinoun, to name only a few, present the face of an engaged multiethnic and multilingual Morocco.

Their cinematography reveals a country that is dynamic and connected to the global sociocultural economy of the twenty-first century. At the same time, they seek to represent the closed, obscure past of a nation's history that has never before been told. Films such as Farida Benlyazid's *Casablanca* (2002); Kamal Kamal's *La symphonie marocaine* (The Moroccan symphony, 2005); Nabyl Lahlou's *Tabite or Not Tabite* (2006); Narjiss Nejjar's *Les yeux secs* (Dry eyes, 2002) and *Wake Up Morocco!* (2006); Lahcen Zinoun's *Faux pas* (False steps, 2003); and Ahmed Boulane's *Les anges de Satan* (Satan's angels, 2007) expose audiences to some of Morocco's most pressing questions and issues. These include human rights abuses, the former incarceration of thousands during the Lead Years, women's emancipation, poverty, and calls for social justice. Such issues make up the fabric of a country that has come to be known as "le Nouveau Maroc" (the New Morocco).

In general, films and documentaries made in the last decade are significantly more critical and candid about Moroccan sociocultural and political issues than in the past. During the Lead Years, films would metaphorically or symbolically criticize the social situation, but filmmakers learned never to be overtly critical. Filmmaker Mustapha Derkaoui notes in an interview conducted in the late 1990s: "We don't want to make subversive cinema. . . . It's more that we must make cinema an adequate means of denunciation, and not a force with the goal of blind and intolerable subversion. . . . [In the past,] cinema was constrained by the government's fears at the time. . . . Officials allowed much less experimentation and innovation in films" (Carter 2000, 68).[1]

Since 1999, films have probed the societal realities of contemporary Morocco, unfettered and uncensored—that is, as long as filmmakers do not overtly criticize the king and Islam and do not promote themes that are pornographic. This shift to embrace a more social-realist cinematic discourse—one that is critically analytical of contemporary society—reflects the societal and political transitions that have taken place in Morocco in the last decade. Increased political transparency has fostered meaningful debates in the public sphere and opened up Moroccan society since the end of the Lead Years. These debates have encouraged Moroccans to look at their role and place as a modern nation in an increasingly globalized world.[2]

This book discusses not only new thematic trends in Moroccan cinema, but also how the industry has developed since it was first founded during the French protectorate (1912–56). It analyzes issues of language and distribution that have influenced how films are made in the country. The Moroccan filmmaker, more often than not, has the choice of making his or her film in Arabic, Berber, or French; and this language choice becomes a defining hurdle in terms of marketing, distribution abroad, and audience reception.

Questions about cinematic language extend to whether or not Moroccan cinema can be considered francophone, as some scholars have claimed. France's role and the predominance of the French language in certain sectors of the Moroccan population must be taken into consideration when discussing cinematic production in the country. Yet, in reality, many of the films made in-country are destined for purely Arabic-speaking audiences (however, they are always screened with French subtitles). Often, funding dictates the language the filmmaker ultimately uses to make a film. For the most part, recent large-budget films such as *Marock* (Marrakchi, 2005), *J'ai vu tuer Ben Barka* (I saw Ben Barka get killed, Le Péron and Smihi, 2005), and *Le grand voyage* (The long journey, Ferroukhi, 2004), made primarily with foreign funding and destined for both Moroccan audiences and an international market, use French. *Les anges de Satan* (2007) and *Casanegra* (Noureddine Lakhmari, 2008), although considered successes, were filmed almost exclusively in Moroccan Arabic and were not distributed abroad. Certain, more "artistic" films, such as Nabyl Lahlou's *Tabite or Not Tabite* (2006) and the short film *Faux pas* (2003) by Lahcen Zinoun, use both Arabic and French and specifically target Moroccan audiences.

My work seeks to assess to what extent the language chosen for certain filmic dialogues is effective in conveying the filmmakers' desired messages. Additionally, do films destined for audiences primarily at home dictate what language is used in a film? In Lahlou's *Tabite*, French is the language in which the protagonists (who are all dissidents, exiled during the Lead Years) describe the despotic past of Morocco, the brutality of the police officer Tabite, and whether or not to go back to Morocco to make a film about their repressive experiences. Yet Arabic is the dominant language once the dissidents return home to confront their oppressors and challenge the status quo. The issue of language is an important one in a society that is refashioning itself in the global age. A central hypothesis of this book is that a filmmaker's decision of whether or not to use French depends on whom she or he wants to influence and what message is to be communicated through a particular film.

Thematically, films in both Arabic and French have become increasingly subversive in their content since the late 1990s. In the mid-1990s, Moroccan cinematic discourse began opening up and challenging sociocultural and political restrictions. At the dawn of the twenty-first century, now even politics are fair game for Moroccan filmmakers, as is evident in Nabyl Lahlou's *Tabite or Not Tabite*, Hicham Lasri's *L'os de fer* (The iron bone, 2007), and Ahmed Boulane's *Les anges de Satan*.

This book analyzes films in the context of the social-realist genre, which has been popular in African cinema since the beginning of postcolonial filmmaking. African film scholar Manthia Diawara points out that filmmakers working in the social-realist genre draw on contemporary experiences in order to "oppose tradition to modernity, oral to written, agrarian and customary communities to urban and industrialized systems, and subsistence economies to highly productive economies" (Diawara 1992, 141). As with other filmmakers on the continent, Moroccan cineastes scrutinize the polarities between certain forms of modernity (which tend, in reality, to be neocolonialist) and traditional practices that tend to hinder sociopolitical enfranchisement in African societies.

The social-realist context is useful in explaining how sociocultural and political transitions in today's Morocco are portrayed on the screen through very divergent scenarios. For example, the 2005 film *Marock* is about the sexuality and the coming-of-age of two teenagers, one a Jew, the other a Muslim. The larger messages of the film concern certain identity crises rooted in religion, which are currently being debated in the country. *La symphonie marocaine* (The Moroccan symphony, Kamal Kamal, 2005) portrays the story of street people in Casablanca, calling into question existing disparities in class, economic means, and education. *Où vas-tu Moshé?* (Where Are You Going, Moshé?, Hassan Benjelloun, 2007) retells the obscure story about the exodus of Jewish Moroccans to Israel in the early 1960s. These films urge audiences to think about the sociocultural, political, and historical realities of Morocco. In my view, contemporary Moroccan cinema accurately portrays the reality of the country, and filmmakers have succeeded in generating awareness and discussion within Moroccan society that impact and advance change as the country moves forward in the millennium.

Film scholar Sandra Carter aptly points out that "whether Moroccan filmmakers use melodrama, social realist cinema, *auteurist* abstract intellectualist style, comedy or action-adventure, their films [always] express something about the people and nation of Morocco" (Carter 2000, 74). Considering Moroccan cinema today, we can affirm that it is a medium that functions as a sounding board for a society that is remaking itself. Contemporary films are essential in the accurate documentation of past history and present realities. Through new cinema magazines such as *Cinémag* (founded in 2008), as well as cinema reviews written up in newspapers and newsmagazines such as *L'Opinion*, *Le Journal Hebdo*, and *TelQuel*, Moroccan filmmakers provide forums through which to analyze, reflect, and debate the contemporary issues important to the vitality of cinematography and the larger society of contemporary Morocco. The numerous Internet blogs founded by young Moroccans interested in film, such as *Blog Riad, Blog Rachid Naim, Bladi Net, Save Cinemas in Morocco,* and *Blog Nadif,* contribute to ongoing dialogues that are, and will be, important to the sustained popularity of Moroccan films at home.[3]

The films discussed in this book were chosen based on the questions and issues raised above. It must also be emphasized that, due to the weak distribution structure of the Moroccan film industry, most films are obtainable only directly from filmmakers or as pirated versions bought in the medinas of the large cities of Casablanca, Rabat, and Fez. Therefore, my discussion of Moroccan films in this book has been primarily dictated by what films I could find during several research trips to the country. Lack of adequate distribution is one of the principal reasons most Moroccan films are never screened or even heard about abroad. This book discusses at length the challenges faced by filmmakers and the film industry that have to do with funding, distribution, and audience attendance in Morocco. These hurdles and how they are overcome will ultimately determine the viability of the industry in Morocco in the new millennium.

The introduction to this book, "Moroccan National Cinema: The Making of an Industry," provides an overview of the history of Morocco's national cinema. Although the Centre cinématographique marocain (CCM) was established in 1944 by the French, at the time of independence King Mohammed V immediately recognized the value of a solid cinematographic industry in building a postcolonial nation. He therefore decided to invest heavily in it. In 1956, the monarchy viewed film as a medium through which not only to shape the cultural contours of the newly independent Morocco, but also to distribute its propaganda. In the throes of nation-building, the king considered the establishment of a state-controlled film industry as vital to uniting a population that had the potential to factionalize into tribal, regional, and nationalist fiefdoms.

Morocco, like all former French colonies, was influenced by France's conception of cinema as the "7ème Art," an art form that was essential to the cultural richness of the nation. Even before independence, many Moroccan filmmakers (as well as other filmmakers from the formerly French-colonized diaspora) traveled to Paris, France, to study at the prestigious Institut des hautes études cinématographiques (IDHEC, Institute for the Advanced Study of Film). In 1985 it was renamed La Fémis (l'Ecole nationale supérieure des métiers de l'image et du son, National School of Higher Education for Image and Sound Careers). From the 1950s, and subsequently long after decolonization, France has played a significant role in the training of filmmakers from its former colonies. Therefore, to this day, in terms of style, the influence of French filmmaking has left its mark on the industry and filmmakers in Morocco.

Chapter 1, "Theories and Polemics: Moroccan Films as Social-Realist Texts," discusses how Moroccan filmmakers, much like their colleagues across Africa, engage audiences through social-realist frameworks that, as Manthia Diawara suggests, "thematize . . . current sociocultural issues . . . [drawing] on contemporary experiences." Moroccan filmmakers who work in the social-realist style impart to audiences that "the real heroes of social transformations in their country are women, children, and other marginalized groups that have been pushed into the shadows by the elites of tradition and modernity" (Diawara 1992, 141). Films such as *La symphonie marocaine* (The Moroccan symphony, Kamal Kamal, 2005) and *Les yeux secs* (Dry eyes, Narjiss Nejjar, 2002) are exemplary, social-realist films that give voice to those who have never had one in Morocco's past. The plight of those who live in poverty and illiteracy with little hope of escape is brought into the spotlight in order to generate awareness among the more fortunate. Films such as those mentioned above demonstrate that through the camera's lens social change, cultural awareness, and community activism are founded.

Chapter 2, "Issues, Contexts, and 'Culture Wars': *Marocains Résidants à l'Etranger* (MREs) versus Filmmakers at Home," explores the questions on many Moroccans' minds: "Is Moroccan cinema francophone or arabophone? Are films made by *Marocains residents à l'étranger* (MREs, Moroccans living abroad) more apt to challenge the sociocultural mores of Morocco than those made by filmmakers who prefer to stay at home, facing intense scrutiny from government officials and traditional audiences? These questions have defined the issues associated with Moroccan filmmaking in the last decade.

In the last ten years, films made at home have been shot primarily in Moroccan Arabic and/or Berber. However, these films are always distributed in the country with French subtitles in order to reach audiences from predominantly French-speaking enclaves in the large cities of Casablanca, Rabat, and Fez. This sector of the population is often elite; its children attend French-speaking high schools and are sent to France to further their educations. French-language films appeal also to those primarily French-speaking Moroccans who live abroad but come home every summer to infuse much-needed money into Morocco's GDP. The language debate for Moroccan filmmakers is one that has dictated the parameters of funding and distribution both at home and internationally and is certainly at the heart of Morocco's culture wars as the country seeks to define and negotiate its identity in the new millennium.

Chapter 3, "Bad Boys, Drugs, and Rock 'n' Roll: The Urban Stories of Morocco," discusses the films *Casanegra* (2008), *Les anges de Satan* (2007), *L'os de fer* (2007), and *Casablanca* (2002) in the context of the symbolism inherent in Moroccan urban landscapes. Moroccan films made since 1999 have increasingly used a cityscape, viewed as hostile and violent, to study the sociopolitical ills of the country. Cities such as Casablanca, Tangier, and Agadir provide backdrops against which to expose the underbelly of Moroccan daily life replete with poverty, unemployment, exploitation, and the hopelessness of the dreams of Moroccan youth.

Chapter 4, "Prison, Torture, and Testimony: Retelling the Memories of the Lead Years," explores *la mémoire refoulée* (suppressed memory) of the Lead Years, during which random incarcerations and disappearances of thousands took place. In recent years, prisoners' testimonials have been the subject of many films. Cinematographic renditions of the stories of former prison detainees—victims of torture and state abuse—such as *Jawhara* (2003), *La chambre noire* (The black room, 2004), *Mémoire en détention* (Memory in detention, 2004) and *Faux pas* (2003), offer depictions of the past that reveal the most abject spaces of a secretive era. The fact that these films were widely distributed in theaters across Morocco and, subsequently, were shown on television without censorship, reflects today's more politically liberal climate.

Chapter 5, "Women's Voices: Documenting Morocco through Feminine Lenses," provides an overview of some of the most original and engaging films made in Morocco by women. Many of these films have never been distributed or screened outside the country. Since the late 1990s, women have increasingly taken up their cameras to film the transformations taking place with respect to sociocultural traditions that impede women's social and political enfranchisement in Morocco. Yasmine Kassari, Narjiss Nejjar, and Leïla Marrakchi, young cineastes making their marks on the industry, have been inspired by older, more experienced filmmakers such as Farida Benlyazid, Farida Bourquia, and Zakia Tahiri. These women are bold and brash, as attests Nejjar, who insists, "I do what I want, I write what I want like I want. . . . And I will continue to harass consciences

Fig. 0.2. Cinéma Rif, Tangier, Morocco, 2009

by making films ... films and films ... so that we women will never again be inarticulate puppets, wallflowers walking on eggshells, but rather full-fledged citizens."[4] Films such as Leïla Marrakchi's *Marock* (2005); Nejjar's *Les yeux secs* (2002) and *Wake Up Morocco!* (2006); Yasmine Kassari's *L'enfant endormi* (The sleeping child, 2004); Farida Bourquia's *Deux femmes sur la route* (Two women on the road, 2007); Zakia Tahiri's *Number One* (2008), as well as the earlier *Women's Wiles*

Fig. 0.3. Downtown cinema of Sidi Kacem, Morocco, 2009

(1999) by Farida Benlyazid, portray Moroccan women as dynamic and resourceful as they struggle to exist within the paradigms of a very patriarchal society where they are often disproportionately affected by illiteracy and poverty.

The conclusion, "The Future of Moroccan Cinema?," reveals some of the challenges that will continue to confront Moroccan filmmakers as they investigate the transitions taking place in their society. As film industries have shown in other developing nations such as Brazil and India, film in Morocco will persist as a valuable medium through which to scrutinize the sociocultural, historical, and political changes taking place in contemporary society. Additionally, Moroccan filmmakers, much like their Brazilian and Indian counterparts, have made significant contributions to international cinema. Although still somewhat limited, the increased visibility in recent years of Moroccan films abroad, at festivals and in art houses, renders evident the industry's commitment to film as both an art form and a medium to be used to generate awareness about Morocco as a modern nation. Moroccan filmmakers should be commended for seeking to develop and impart their own, unique concept of cinema with regard to themes, images portrayed, and messages conveyed in the larger context of world cinema. In the years to come, Moroccan filmmakers will continue to confront issues of language, audiences, and resources, all of which impact how the industry will develop and what goals are set for the future.

Finally, the aim of this work is to reveal to readers to what extent Morocco's national cinema has demonstrated impressive vitality, rigor, and sustainability over the last forty years despite the debilitating Lead Years, an era of fear and repression. It is obvious that the industry's longevity is due to filmmakers' dedication to finding the middle ground between producing works that are politically committed to changing mind-sets and pleasing audiences' tastes. Despite enduring hurdles stemming from issues that are primarily economic, Moroccan cinema in the new millennium rivals national cinemas in the developing world, particularly those in India, Brazil, and Mexico.

Acknowledgments

I wish to thank the following people and institutions for their support of this project: the American Institute of Maghrebi Studies (AIMS), for a generous grant in the summer of 2009 that allowed me to travel to Morocco and visit with filmmakers and people in the industry; and the University of Maryland's Office of International Travel, for a grant to fund travel to various cities and film festivals.

Special thanks to my University of Maryland colleagues and graduate students in the Department of French & Italian in the School of Languages, Literatures, and Cultures; and the Film Colloquia group, particularly Caroline Eades and Elizabeth Papazian, for their continuing support of my work on African cinema. Warmhearted thanks to filmmakers Hassan Benjelloun, Nabyl Lahlou, Hicham Lasri, and Lahcen Zinoun, as well as producers Rachida Saadi and Noufissa Sbaï for the interviews they granted me. Also, I would like to thank the employees of the Centre cinématographique marocain (CCM), especially General Counsel Kamal Mouline, for his candid assessment of the state of filmmaking in Morocco and valuable statistical information pertaining to the current industry.

I would also like to express many thanks to Margaret Braswell, who provided valuable information on women's filmmaking in Algeria; and to my friends and colleagues both in the United States and Morocco who helped me during the research for this project: Safoi Babana-Hampton, Ammara Bouchentouf, Soumia Boukhtil, Mitchell

Cohn, Samira Douider, Youssouf Elalamy, Mohammed Hirchi, Majid Kettaoui, Rida Lamrini, Mary McCullough, Abdellah M'dhari, Lucy Melbourne, Jonathan Smolin, Larbi Touaf, Joëlle Vitiello, and Mary Vogl. Many thanks to Tracy Sharpley-Whiting for her suggestions. Heartfelt recognition must go to Belinda Hopkinson for her valuable editorial suggestions, which greatly improved the manuscript. Last, but certainly not least, I would like to thank my family, and my husband, for their loving support during the writing of this book.

I am heavily indebted to theories worked out in my previous monograph, particularly chapter seven in *Facophone Voices of the 'New Morocco' in Film and Print: (Re)presenting a Society in transition* (Palgrave Macmillan, 2009).

I would like to thank *Cinergie* for permission to use in chapter 5 a photo of Yasmine Kassari from their website: www.cinergie.be.

All other photos were taken by me; and unless otherwise indicated, all translations from French are my own.

Introduction

Moroccan National Cinema

The Making of an Industry

> Nous n'avons pas le luxe de faire un cinéma de luxe.
> (We don't have the luxury of making luxury films.)
> —Hassan Benjelloun

In order to understand the development of Morocco's cinematographic industry, it is important to acknowledge how the country's history shaped it. Like many former colonized countries in the postcolonial era, Morocco seeks to revisit its past by reconstructing its history to reflect the voices that have been effaced by violence, human rights abuses, and oppressive regimes since the end of French occupation in 1956. Since 1999, the country has turned many pages of its dark past known as *les années de plomb*, "the Lead Years" of King Hassan II's reign (1963–99), in order to move forward to embrace the global age, all the while wrestling to keep its cultural uniqueness intact. Yet transition has created a schizophrenic state that is continuously contradicting itself on a variety of subjects, from matters of human rights and freedom of the press to economic reform. It is for this reason that at one moment the liberal, generally leftist intellectuals in media and the performing arts, producing in both Arabic and French on the page and on the screen, can openly criticize the government, and the next be sanctioned in the courts, obliged to pay heavy fines for having "offended" the powers that be.

Morocco's Complicated Past: Imagery, Identity, and Colonial Legacies

From 1912 to 1956, Morocco was a French protectorate. However, some scholars explain that to call it a protectorate would be a "myth" because, as Jacqueline Kaye and Abdelhamid Zoubir point out in *The Ambiguous Compromise: Language, Literature and National Identity in Algeria and Morocco*, "French policy in Morocco aimed to undermine both the secular and religious authority of the Sultan" in order to install complete French colonial domination (1990, 11). France implemented a "Berber policy" in order to weaken Arab-Islamic institutions in the country. Typical of Western colonial regimes, "divide and conquer" was the general modus operandi during French occupation of the Maghreb. If a comparison must be made between the varying degrees of French colonial imperialism in the region, then occupation should be studied at the level of indigenous policies. In Morocco, as in Algeria, Berbers and Arabs were pitted against each other in order to subdue indigenous revolt. However, as scholars note, French colonialism in Morocco was not as "genocidal in intention as in Algeria, for there was never the intention of making [the country] a 'colonie du peuplement'" (a settled colony) (Kaye and Zoubir 1990, 11).

In Algeria, land was confiscated and people were displaced. However, in Morocco, unlike in Algeria, "the French cultivated the traditions of the Moroccan people" (Kaye and Zoubir 1990,13). By no means should France's colonial policy in Morocco be viewed as positive. However, the colonizers' imprint on Morocco is vastly different from that on Algeria because France's colonial missions in both countries were quite different. In Morocco, France concentrated on encouraging a mythical realm, one immersed in Oriental imagery. It was hoped that this fascinating space would entice the French adventurer to come and *see* the country. Morocco "became a vast national park," wherein "the traditions of its people became subject to the interpretation of the French and were written down" by an array of Orientalists who commercialized and packaged what they saw or heard about in the country (13). It is for this reason that Morocco under the French, and certainly due to the work of General Hubert Lyautey (1854–1934),[1] who was responsible for "managing" the culture of the country, became the Oriental fantasy that Europeans craved (13).

This ideal led to a literary *imaginaire*, as Edward Saïd describes in *Orientalism*: "Orientalism expresses and represents that part culturally and even ideologically as a mode of discourse with supporting institutions, vocabulary, scholarship, imagery, doctrines, even colonial bureaucracies and colonial styles" (1979, 2). The literary *imaginaire* as cultivated by the great French authors of yore—Pierre Loti, André Gide, Eugène Fromentin—writing in the late nineteenth and early twentieth centuries, would later be transcribed into the fantastical images of Morocco promoted in films made by French directors. Colonial filmmakers contributed to the "tropes of empire," fueling the *Mission Civilsatrice* that would endure well into the twentieth century (Slavin 2001, 150). "The colonial film of the 1920s supported policy goals in Morocco, and those of the 1930s praised the Foreign Legion"; therefore, artistic imagery coupled with military power melded in the minds of viewers and sustained the desire for colonial lands (Slavin 2001, 4). Films such as *Le grand jeu* (The big game, 1934), *La bandera* (The brigade, 1935), *Pépé le Moko* (1937), and *La belle équipe* (The lovely team, 1938) drew on the *imaginaire*-inspired texts of earlier French authors to highlight the unfettered possibilities the white man could enjoy in the Maghreb (Slavin 2001, 166).

Particularly, Julien Duvivier's *La bandera*, starring heartthrob Jean Gabin as Pierre Gilieth, who murders a man in Paris and then loses himself in the colonies to escape his crime, offers a quintessential example of French colonial films of the era. On the lam, Gilieth flees to Barcelona, where he enlists in the Spanish Legion and sets sail for Morocco and the Spanish colony in the northern part of the country. There he meets the alluring Aicha, a Berber dancer and sometimes prostitute. In the meantime, he must elude Lucas, a fellow Frenchman and a mercenary detective, who has also enlisted in the brigade in order to pursue him. If Gilieth commits another crime, Lucas can extradite him. Gilieth knows he is being watched. Aicha promises to help him escape to the French zone of the country if he will marry her. Before they leave, rebels from the Rif (depicted as marauding "Moors" dressed in traditional garb) attack the Spanish fort. Gilieth performs his duty to ward off the intruders and is promoted to corporal by his wounded captain. Before he dies, the captain makes Lucas swear that he will not continue to pursue Gilieth. As they are besieged, Lucas and Gilieth, as well as their fellow countryman Mulot, try to hold the fort, but in the end Gilieth is shot and killed. Lucas must break the news about the fallen hero to Aicha.

Although its plot is simplistic, *La bandera* exemplifies the prominent themes of the day. Morocco is viewed as a country where escape is possible and where the white man can be a hero, a lover, and live by his own rules without the fetters and constraints of the society and culture of the *Métropole* (i.e., mainstream France with all its social conventions and limitations). The image of Morocco as a vast theme park for the colonizers' unfettered exploits was established earlier on through the literary narratives of French masterpieces by Gustave Flaubert, Eugène Fromentin, André Gide, Pierre Loti, and Emile Zola.[2] This exotic image was continuously reified on the screen well into the twentieth century (Slavin 2001, 164).

Colonial films of the World War II era were steeped in French patriotism as they defined the images of a vast empire so powerful it could conquer the Nazis. Filmed in Algeria, *S.O.S. Sahara* (1938), directed by Jacques de Baroncelli and starring Jean-Pierre Aumont, Charles Vanel, and Marta Labarr, reveals the "Sahara as an immense desert, beautiful and fascinating" but also treacherous for the "European who is, despite everything, in danger of dying" (Mcgherbi 1982, 110–11). *L'appel du bled* (The call of the village, 1942), by Maurice Gleize and starring Jean Marchat, Pierre Renoir, and Madeleine Sologne, also focuses on the colonial who is haunted by "le déséquilibre démographique des deux camps" (the demographic disequilibrium of two camps), that of the colonizer in a face-off with the colonized. These films clearly demonstrate the colonizer's mission as one that compels him to sacrifice his well-being for the good of France's empire (116–17).

The Cinematic Fragmented Text

Colonial films and literature in the early twentieth century drew upon France's reliance on the burgeoning field of ethnology to justify its thirst for empire. Ethnography succeeded in mythologizing an entirely *new* civilization in Morocco based on a set of "linguistic, ethnic [and] religious definitions of identity" (Kaye and Zoubir 1990, 13). Berber culture, viewed by the French as more mysterious because of certain pagan and animist rites, was encouraged as a means of subduing the influence of Arab Islam, considered too unified, rebellious, and generally hostile to the French civilizing mission. Berber *maraboutism*[3] and fraternities, important in Berber belief, were encouraged in order to undermine the importance of the Arab mosque in Moroccan culture. France hoped that by creating schisms between Muslims and Berber-animists, contradictions would appear within Moroccan society and thus make the people believe they were not unified by religious conviction (16). Morocco, therefore, would need the presence of the paternal colonizer to maintain order.

France became the author of Moroccan history and identity, creating an ideal that would render virtually impossible discrimination between Orientalized myth and reality, fiction and fact. At the time of decolonization, the mythical layers of a fragmented identity, created by the colonial machine, remained and were later used during King Hassan II's reign. A master of dissimulation, he maintained the status quo, manipulating and victimizing the population for years. At the same time, the sustained high illiteracy rate (50 percent) has continued to contribute to Morocco's impeded self-analysis, since many people do not have the analytical tools to question and scrutinize the difference between myth and reality and fact and fiction.

Today Moroccan literature and film still reflect the influences of the French cultural imprint and the enduring *imaginaire* cultivated in colonial times. Additionally, indigenous, primarily Berber oral tradition as represented in many parts of North Africa has influenced the manner in which narration, both on the screen and on the page, is construed in postcolonial society. Both the French and the Moroccan indigenous realms contributed to the contemporary, very unique, Moroccan multicultural identity. Even today, Moroccan authors and filmmakers, seeking to recapture the past through literature and film, waver between the mythical and the real in their efforts to depict the reality of their history. Constructing a world of images between the real and the surreal or unreal creates a fragmented narrative space, whether in text or film.

Well-known Moroccan poet and author Abdelkébir Khatibi explains in his work the nature of what he views as Moroccans' strained identity, divided between fact and fiction. For Khatibi, living in a *bilangue* (dual-language) legacy comprising an Arab-Berber identity, rich in mythical representations and cultivated in a centuries-old (primarily Berber-influenced) oral tradition, and, at the same time, experiencing the French rationalist model of education, has contributed to a duality inherent in all aspects of Moroccan society, including the arts, cinema, and literature.

The French model of *récit* is built from a body of knowledge that relies on the individualist's penchant for a controlled story line where reality, recounted in linear fashion, is rendered first and foremost (Khatibi 1983). In *La violence du texte* (The violence of the text), Marc Gontard notes that for the francophone Moroccan author, French has caused "la dérégulation du système narratif" (the disturbance of the narrative system), thus exposing the tensions the author faces when he seeks to narrate traditional oral and mythical tales. These are at the heart of the society's knowledge, in the written postmodern language of a foreign voice (Gontard 1981, 66). The disjointed or deformed text positively blends styles, rendering Moroccan cinema singular, both thematically and structurally. The "deregulation" of narrative systems, melding the imaginary and the real, has become a thematic staple of the Moroccan cinematic oeuvre. Benlyazid's *Women's Wiles* (1999), Nabyl Ayouch's *Ali Zaoua* (1999), Saâd Chraïbi's *Jawhara* (2003), and Kamal Kamal's *La symphonie marocaine* (2005) are but some of the films made in the last decade that draw on these two realms of *being* to construct their narratives.

The Development of the Moroccan Film Industry: Past and Present

France's conception of cinema as the "7ème Art" greatly influenced the cinematographic industries of its former colonies. Newly liberated nations continued to develop cinema according to the models left by the colonizers at the time of independence. Britain bequeathed very little in the way of a film industry because during its colonial era it preferred to invest more in television and radio. Hence, countries such as Nigeria, Kenya, and Zimbabwe did not cultivate national cinema models like those found in West and North Africa, which had been under French colonial rule.[4] "Films directed by Africans in former French colonies are superior, both in quantity and in quality, to those by directors in other sub-Saharan countries formerly colonized by the British" (Diawara 1992, 21). In the postcolonial era, France has continued to aid African cinema in its former colonies, thus, as scholar Manthia Diawara points out, making "it easier for French distributors to maintain their monopoly on the African market" (31). Very little investment of this type has come from Britain to African anglophone regions. This reality has its roots in the colonial past, as Nwachukwu Frank Ukadike notes in his work *Black African Cinema*:

> Different patterns of film production within francophone and Anglophone regions derive from the contrasting ideological pursuits of the colonial French and British governments. For example, while the French pursued the so-called assimilationist policy, British involvement with its colonies was pragmatic business. Similarly, observers point out that while the French "gave" feature film to its colonies, the British "gave" theirs documentary. This notion supports the argument that the cultural policy adopted by France encouraged film pro-

duction in the francophone region whereas in the anglophone region, where film production did not pass the economic priority test . . . the tradition of British documentary filmmaking [remained]. (1994, 109)

France's concept of film and what function it should perform in society continues to influence national cinemas in the former French colonies. The historic role of film in the shaping of national identity also created the futures of national cinemas in decolonized North and West Africa. The "7ème Art," first conceptualized by the French Lumière brothers, Louis and Auguste, was a defining component of the cultural contours of France at the end of the nineteenth century. From the 1890s to the mid-twentieth century, film played a critical role in determining colonial ideology both at home and abroad in the colonies. The Lumière brothers were known for the cameramen they sent out all over the world. Many traversed the well-established colonial empire and filmed the environments of exotic others across Africa, Asia, and the Middle East, sending the film stock back home to eager audiences. These early films fueled colonial desire and were a pivotal mechanism in sustaining the empire. In 1896, when the first Lumière productions were screened in Lyon, "les chasseurs d'image" (image hunters) were enlisted into Auguste and Louis Lumière's legions to document the wonders of the Maghrebian empire on camera (Megherbi 1982, 13).

The first decades of the twentieth century in North Africa and the Middle East primarily featured passive groups of the colonized who "served as subjects . . . for the film industries of Europe and the United States." Rarely were films produced by indigenous directors (Ghareeb 1997, 120). In 1922, however, Tunisian Albert Samama-Chikly made *Zohra*, followed by the first full-length Egyptian film, *Layla*, produced by a native Egyptian woman, Aziza Amir, who also starred in the leading role.[5] The film was released in November 1927 and is accredited with having launched the Egyptian film industry (Shafik 2007).

In Paris, La Fémis (l'École nationale supérieure des métiers de l'image et du son),[6] formerly known as the IDHEC (Institut des hautes études cinématographiques), is still world-renowned for training filmmakers and has schooled a host of African filmmakers from the former colonies. These include Sembène Ousmane, Safi Faye, Férid Boughedir, and Merzak Allouache, among many others from the 1950s to the present. From the initial days of the Lumière brothers' experimental films, France established the concept of a national cinema, which meant the state would always subsidize filmmakers' works. The subsidy model, known as *l'avance sur recettes*, was adopted by newly liberated African countries, which have since created their own national cinemas in Algeria, Morocco, Senegal, and Tunisia. In 1956, in the wake of independence, Morocco's national cinema was used by returning king Mohammed V to "contribute to national consciousness and national awareness [by offering a means] to construct a nation from a population accustomed to thinking only of tribal and regional loyalties" (Carter 2000, 66–67). From early on, King Mohammed V realized that film would play an integral role in spinning the sociopolitical messages of the state's and the monarch's propaganda in the newly independent kingdom. Cinema would be the key to developing the homogeneous, unified identity that state institutions relied on to support public social sectors and the arts (Carter 2000, 66–67).

Founded in 1944 while Morocco was still a French protectorate, the CCM (Centre cinématographique marocain), with studios in the Rabat suburb of Souissi, became more active as a state agency immediately after independence. In the beginning it timidly funded only short films and documentaries, but later took over distribution and funding projects for Moroccan films in the 1980s (Tebib 2000, 60).

Moroccan film history can be divided into three eras spanning the monarchies of King Mohammed V and his son, Hassan II: 1956–70, 1971–85, and 1986–99. These time periods reflect the development of cinematography in terms of technical advances, funding, and political influences in the country. This past laid the groundwork for the vibrant film industry of the new Moroccan cinematographic millennium on which this book focuses.

During the first era of Moroccan filmmaking (1956–70), the national industry employed filmmakers as government employees, primarily concentrating on making documentaries and newsreels as trailers for foreign films or to be shown in film caravans that toured the country (Carter 2000, 67). The CCM sent filmmakers abroad to France, Russia, and Italy to learn the trade. At the same time at home, the CCM established a studio, lab, film stock, and trained personnel. Filmmakers, however, concentrated only on regional and development issues that could be filmed as documentaries (Carter 2000, 67).

From 1971 to 1985, the second era of filmmaking, the industry sought to develop an auteur group of young filmmakers, thus fostering a more artistic style. Conversely, the market was increasingly influenced by audiences' desire for entertainment films. Under King

Hassan II, censure played a role in dictating subject matter. The influx of films from the United States, India, and Egypt cultivated a certain vision of the cinematic industry among audiences who more and more expected to go to theaters to be entertained. The auteur style, as in France and other parts of Europe, was viewed as too artistic and "intellectual" and, although subsidized by the state as a valuable tool "contributing to the national patrimony," drew only small audiences (Carter 2000, 67). Progressively, from the mid-1980s forward, middle-class cinemagoers, preferring entertainment over artistic style, became a significant force that shaped the parameters of filmmaking. Bollywood and Hindi films, certainly since the late 1980s, have cultivated Moroccan audiences' tastes for lighthearted, entertaining films that draw the masses to theaters.

By the 1980s, the "Third Cinema movement" of the 1960s and 1970s, a revolutionary artistic offspring of burgeoning independent nations, had begun to influence audiences across the globe as it increased the popularity of non-Western films internationally. Particularly, African films became more readily available in the United States and Europe, thus fostering cinematographic exchanges that were transatlantic and transnational. As elsewhere in Africa, social awareness, activism, and technology contributed to encouraging a new vision of cinema in Morocco that was more connected to an increasingly social-realist ideology. Moroccans began to experiment with themes, challenging the politics and conventions of their society as they sought answers to postcolonial problems such as poverty, illiteracy, and corruption.

Ciné-clubs sprang up, as did literary, cinema-focused magazines that discussed the film industry in the same manner as the French journal *Cahiers du cinéma.* Young people became educated about the power of film as a social-realist tool to encourage change in society. Of course, this meant the Third Cinema movement was viewed as dangerous by the monarchy, and filmmakers bore the brunt of censure (Carter 2000, 67). Film subjects, if political, were only metaphorically or symbolically rendered. Morocco's youthful population in the late 1980s, as well as the slow crumbling of the Lead Years beginning in the early 1990s, influenced changes in the themes depicted on Moroccan screens. Increasingly, filmmakers dared to make films that touched upon sensitive issues such as unemployment, sexuality (heterosexual and homosexual relations), and political corruption (70). Films such as Ahmed Kacem Akdi's *Ce que les vents ont emporté* (Talk is easy, 1984), Mohammed Abboulouakar's *Hadda* (1984), and Mustapha

Derkaoui's *Titre provisoire* (Provisionally titled, 1985), among others, demonstrate the Third Cinema movement's influence on themes and styles, despite the oppressive Lead Years.

By the mid-1990s the social-realist, politically committed films of West Africa, particularly those of Sembène Ousmane, Gaston Kaboré, and Med Hondo, were influencing Moroccan filmmakers. Films shot by cineastes in Moroccan Arabic destined for Moroccan audiences were successful box-office hits. Hakim Noury's *Voleur de rêves* (Thief of dreams, 1995) tells the story of a man who confronts life after prison; Fatima Jebli Ouazzani's *Dans la maison de mon père* (In my father's house, 1997) discusses the very sensitive subject of lost virginity before marriage; and Nabyl Ayouch's *Mektoub* (Destiny, 1997) depicts drug use and police corruption.

Contemporary Moroccan Cinema: Filming a Changing Society

Although the Lead Years were oppressive, the Moroccan film industry, unlike that of Tunisia, never "officially" succumbed to state censorship. Paradoxically, "Tunisia is regarded as the Arab state with the lightest film censorship. [But] films must be submitted to the Ministry of Culture and a department of censors for approval" (Ghareeb 1997, 123). Conversely, in Morocco there is no such oversight by the Ministry of Culture or the CCM. Yet, ever since the end of the Lead Years, filmmakers, like authors and journalists, have practiced self-censorship that denotes a fine "red line," which journalist Driss Ksikes, writing for the francophone newsmagazine *TelQuel,* claims is alive and well in contemporary Morocco.[7] Well-known director Mohammed Tazi also evokes the "red line" when explaining how censorship works in his country: "One can criticize many aspects of life in one's country as long as [the] red line is respected. The red line involves respecting the state, religion, relations between men and women and the classes. . . . However . . . this red line can be and is moved around" (123). In an interview, Kamal Mouline, adviser to the CCM's marketing department, explained that Morocco has never maintained a state censor. Filmmakers, he emphasized, "just know" not to tread heavily on "religion, the monarchy, or into the realm of pornography."[8]

In the last decade, Morocco has led the way in North African filmmaking, crafting a cinematic industry that reflects the shifts and transitions in its society as well as the larger Maghreb region. Although attendance is decreasing, Moroccan filmmakers have repeatedly produced two or three full-length features a year in Arabic, Berber, French, and/or a mixture of all three languages. Recently films made in Berber such as *Les yeux secs* (Dry eyes, Narjiss Nejjar, 2002), have been funded by the CCM and widely promoted. The Tenth Annual Festival of Cinema at Sidi Kacem (April 23–27, 2009) devoted its entire week to honoring Amazigh (Berber) films such as *Itto titrit* (Mohammed Oumouloud Abbazi, 2008), *Tamazight oufella* (Mohammed Mernich, 2008), and *Sellam et Dimitan* (Mohammed Amin Benamraoui, 2008). In the last twenty years, several homegrown films have bettered the attendance records of North American, European, and Egyptian imports. Notably *Un amour à Casablanca* (Love in Casablanca, Abdelkader Lagtaa, 1991), *A la recherche du mari de ma femme* (Searching for my wife's husband, Mohammed A. Tazi, 1993),[9] *Marock* (Leïla Marrakchi, 2005), and *Casanegra* (Noureddine Lakhmari, 2008), all of which set box-office records.[10] Despite the increasing popularity of films made at home, the CCM still must struggle with funding strategies to finance an industry that generates little income and is solely dependent on state subsidies.[11]

One of the enduring legacies of the structure of the cinematographic milieu, as modeled on France's subsidy-based national model, is that Moroccans have not figured out how to transform "the overall conception of the industry" (Carter 1999, 413). Inventive ideas have not fostered sustainable ways of transforming filmmaking "from being a beneficiary of State and tax monies into being a generator of income, an employer of masses of unemployed, a supporter of the State," rather than a burden (Carter 1999, 413). Although theater attendance is generally good, it has still decreased, falling from 33 percent in 1980 to 18 percent of capacity in 1995 (Carter 1999, 672). According to Kamal Mouline with the CCM, each decade since 1980 has presented specific setbacks to the film industry's theaters. In the 1980s, videotaping and rentals significantly reduced theater attendance. In the 1990s, the "invasion" of the satellite dish (*la parabole*) allowed families to stay at home and watch films from Europe and the Arab world on satellite TV. And last, in the 2000s, DVDs and downloads from the Internet, as well as theater owners' lack of foresight

Fig. I.1. 7ème Art Cinema, Rabat, Morocco, 2009

in changing single-screen movie houses to multiplexes, have contributed to lackluster theater attendance.[12]

Defunct theaters present a monumental obstacle for Moroccan filmmakers trying to assure that their films will be distributed. While cinema houses increased in number from independence to the early 1980s, throughout the 1990s the country witnessed a decline in the number of screens available. Between 1980 and 1993, 57 theaters were created, but 72 closed (Carter 1999, 671). From 2000 to 2009, the number of theater "salles" (cinemas) dropped from 149 to 40. The majority of these are in Casablanca, Rabat, and Fez, where closures have been routine (Bennani 2010, n.p.). There are, however, several notable cinema houses that have significantly contributed to the vitality of film as a stable cultural art form. The 7ème Art Cinéma in Rabat (see figs. I.1, I.2) and the Cinémathèque in Tangier, formerly known as Cinéma Rif (see fig. I.3), have become vibrant centers for promoting Moroccan films. They routinely host well-attended national film festivals (Tangier, Fez, and Marrakech), seminars on film, and have been responsible for generating national and international interest in filmmaking in Morocco.

Fig. I.2. 7ème Art Cinema, Rabat, Morocco, 2009

Today considered in the larger category of Arab cinema centers, Morocco is second only to Egypt for the most films made per year. In 2009, Morocco produced a total of fifteen feature-length films and four shorts (Bennani 2010, n.p.). In the Maghreb, when compared to Algeria and Tunisia, Morocco's industry enjoys the most autonomy and has had the least governmental interference since 1999. Whereas Tunisian cinematic production in the past was touted as the most avant-garde and, for better or worse, as the most "Europeanized" of the three Maghrebian countries, today Morocco has surpassed its Maghrebian neighbors in quality, themes, scope, and number of films produced each year.[13]

From the outset, Maghrebian filmmakers distanced themselves from Middle-Eastern, Arabic cinematic traditions. Unlike Egypt and the Mashriq region (Lebanon, Syria, Jordan), Maghrebian cineastes preferred to cultivate an original body of work that challenged what was considered as "un vieux cinéma arabe" (an old Arab cinema) (Tebib 2000, 60). Maghrebian cinema, therefore, has always viewed itself as particularly unique: "The role of Maghrebian cinemas is to represent a cinema profoundly innovative for the Arab World" (60). At the dawn of

Fig. I.3. Cinéma Rif, Tangiers, Morocco, 2009

the postcolonial era, Maghrebian cinema sought to combat the "cinéma d'évasion hors des réalités" (cinema of entertainment out of sync with realities) of the everyday, in order to evoke "un cinéma d'expression" (a cinema of expression) that reveals a social, political, and cultural authenticity. Morocco did succeed early on in creating both a "cinéma intellectuel" and a "cinéma populaire," thus pleasing a diverse array of spectators (62). The many festivals, ciné-clubs, cinema conferences, and blogs on the Internet generate a vibrant discourse about film across the country, from large cities like Casablanca to smaller towns such as Sidi Kacem. These forums have kept enthusiasm alive for an art form that often promotes very quintessential Moroccan themes.

Language:
Is There a Francophone Cinema in Morocco?

The question as to whether or not Moroccan film may be considered "francophone" depends on which Moroccan cinema is being discussed.

The debate is certainly at the heart of Morocco's culture wars, which reveal two very divergent realms pitted against each other. Language tends to dictate the paradigms of class, region, and social strata and how these are depicted in film. In a 2005 interview, well-known film critic Mustapha Mesnaoui reflects upon the split identity in the cinematographic industry and in the larger country. This duality is due to the industry's insistence on using two different languages to build a national cinema:

> Moroccan society is composed of two principal clans. The first is francophone, the second arabophone. I'm not talking just about the language used but also about the lifestyle and the mentality, which change according to these milieus. In effect, on the one hand we have people who use French in order to transmit their ideas and thoughts . . . on the other, the arabophones who have done the same thing. In the case of the first, they have more choice as far as newspapers and magazines; the others are condemned to lapping up theoretical books from the East or works with religious tendencies. Moreover, each regards the other as foreign and not as co-citizens unified by the same visions and goals. What is considered entertainment by one may be perceived by the other as depravity, even danger. (Ziane 2005, n.p.)

Mesnaoui alludes to much more at the core of the debate characterizing "the malaise of Moroccan culture." He faults Moroccan cinema for not really having enough "principles" to respond to the shifting sociocultural and political phenomena fueled by language occurring in the country today (Ziane 2005, n.p.). One of these phenomena, of course, is the rise of Islamic fundamentalism (*intégrisme islamique*) in Morocco. Islamic radicalism is associated with highly rhetorical and inflammatory classical Arabic shouted from the minarets of mosques by radicalized imams. Most Moroccans feel that this Arabic does not reflect the morals and values of their country or their religion. Cinema is a highly effective medium through which to analyze and isolate religious radicalism, while promoting the *Marocainité* (Moroccanness) of a population that sees its country and culture as Berber and Arab, multilingual, multicultural, Islamic, Jewish, and animist.

Questions surrounding language as it molds contemporary Moroccan identity also influence cinematic funding. Whether or not a film's dialogue is primarily shot in French or Arabic has created a two-tier system that hinders the development of original film styles. Films predominantly shot in French are usually funded, in part, by France, other European-francophone countries, and/or Canada. Domestic productions, particularly Berber-language films, rely on the CCM and the filmmakers' private resources (many filmmakers working at home have their own production companies). This does not, however, preclude the CCM from proudly listing all Moroccan films in its annual catalog, even those funded internationally and made by filmmakers living abroad. In its most recent report, "Cinéma marocain filmographie générale: Long métrages, 1958–2008" (Moroccan filmography: Feature-length films, 1958–2008), the CCM makes no distinction between films made and funded solely at home and those produced with monies primarily from foreign backers (France, Spain, Canada). In 2008, "50 Years of Filmmaking" was celebrated with special editions of the filmography report promoted in posters touting the CCM's success in maintaining a viable film industry for home and abroad (see fig. I.4).

The brochure for "Du fonds d'aide et l'avance sur recettes" (funding and subsidies), listing films made from June 2003 to November 2005, such as *Le grand voyage* (2004), *Marock* (2005), and *J'ai vu tuer Ben Barka* (2005), indicates that all these feature-length films received only minimal CCM funds.[14] These films made by MREs (*Marocains résidants à l'étranger*, Moroccans living abroad) incorporate a significant amount of dialogue in French, opened almost simultaneously in Morocco and France, and were screened immediately at international film festivals such as Cannes, Venice, Montreal, and Toronto. Conversely, films such as Nabyl Lahlou's *Tabite or Not Tabite* (2006), solely funded by CCM funds and not as of yet screened outside Morocco, use both French and Moroccan Arabic.[15] The dual-language screenplay, according to Lahlou, artistically fulfilled the goals of his film, but did not aid in facilitating distribution outside Morocco, even though subtitles were provided each time the dialogue switched languages.[16] The seemingly split Arab-French personality of Moroccan cinema does present difficulties in distribution, but ultimately contributes to its sustained vitality, as Rachid Chenchabi pointed out more than twenty years ago:

> French is the language that has been the most successful in profoundly penetrating the Maghreb. The result is that it is a daily instrument of communication for a significant part of the

50ᵉᵐᵉ anniversaire du film marocain

1958 - 2008

Le fils maudit 1958, Vaincre pour vivre 1968, Quand mûrissent les dattes 1968, Soleil de printemps 1969, Traces 1970, Mille et une main 1972, Silence sens interdit 1973, De quelques événements sans signification 1974, la guerre du pétrole n'aura pas lieu 1974, Feu vert 1974, Chergui ou le silence violent 1975, Noces de sang 1977, Les cendres du clos 1977, Brèche dans le mur 1978, Ô les jours 1978, Al kanfoudi 1978, Ou cachez-vous le soleil? 1979, Le mirage 1979, Le facteur 1980, Amina 1980, Le gouverneur de l'île shakerbakerben 1980, Transes/ Al hal 1981, Le grand voyage 1981, Poupées de roseau 1981, 44 ou les récits de la nuit 1981, Amok 1982, Pas dans le brouillard 1982, Les larmes de regret 1982, De l'autre côté du fleuve 1982, La braise 1982, Lalla Chafia 1982, Les beaux jours de Shéherazade 1982, Le coiffeur du quartier des pauvres 1982, Le drame des 40000 1982, Brahim Yach 1982, Batoru 1983, L'impasse 1984, Zeft 1984, Les copains

Taghounja 1984, Titre provisoire du jour 1984, Hadda 1984, Cauchemar 1984, Le jour du forrain 1984, L'âme qui brûl 1984, Ce que les vents ont emporté 1984, Shams 1985, L'ombre du

gardien 1985, La compro-Jouha n'est pas mort 1987, Caftan d'amour 1989, La terre du défi l'enclume 1990, La fête les chardons floriféres 1991, Un amour à Casablanca normale 1991, La dame du enfants perdus 1991, Fiction du crime 1992, Les cavaliers la recherche du mari de ma femme 1993, L'enfance voler 1993, Yarit 1993, Je (l)i au passé 1994, Les sept portes de la nuit 1994, La prière de l'absent 1995, Le résistant inconnu 1995, Moi l'artiste d'hier 1998, Les casablancais 1998, Rue le caire 1998.

mission 1986, Abbas ou 1986, Une porte sur le 1987, Badis 1988, Kenzany 1989, Le marteau et des autres 1990, Ymer ou 1991, La salle d'attente 1991, Chronique d'une vie Caire 1991, La plage des première 1992, La nuit de la gloire 1993, A

Ruses de femmes 1999, Mabrouk 1999, Ali zaoua 1999, Elle est diabétique hyper-tendue et refuse de crever 2000, Histoire d'une rose 2000, Tresses silencieuses 2000, Du paradis à l'enfer 2000, Yacout 2000, Ali Rabia Jugement d'une femme L'homme qui brodait lèvres du silence 2000, Mokhtar Soldi 2001, Au Amour sans visa 2001, Saber 2001, Cheval de vent 2002, Et après 2002, Le poête 2002, Une minute de soleil de mogador 2002, Casa-Le paradis des pauvres Casablanca by night 2003, 2003, Les voisines d'abou de l'âme 2003, Jawhara bandits 2003, A Casablan-2004, La chambre noire 2004, Tinja 2004, Mémoi-L'enfant endormi 2004, Le 2004, Marock 2005, Elle est et refuse toujours de crever 2005, Juanita de Tanger 2005, Islamour 2006, La Où vas-tu Moshé? 2006, velo 2006, Les anges de Samira 2006, Moroccan monstre 2006, Tissée de Titrit D wayour 2006, Amour voilées 2007, attendan Pasolini 2007, Ex-chamkar 2007, whatever lola wants 2007, Kherboucha 2007, Les cris de jeunes filles des hirondelles 2007, Number one 2007, Tamazirte ouffa 2007, Kandisha 2007, Tu te souviens d'Adil? 2007.

et les autres 2000, 2000, Soif 2000, des secrets 2000, Les Les amours de Hadj delà de Gibraltar 2001, Taif nizar 2001, Mouna 2001, Les années de l'exil 2002, Une histoire d'amour en moins 2002, Les amants blanca, Casablanca 2002, 2002, Les yeux secs 2002, Mille mois 2003, Face à face Moussa 2003, Les fibres 2003, Rahma 2003, Les ça les anges ne volent pas 2004, Casablanca day light res en détention 2004, grand voyage 2004, Tarfaya diabétique hyper-tendue 2005, J'ai vu tuer Ben Barka 2005, Symphonie marocaine beauté éparpillée 2006, Le jeu de l'amour 2006, Le satan 2006, Les jardins de dream 2006, Nancy et le mains et d'étoffe 2006, Adieu mères 2007, Casa negra 2007, En 2007, Entre parenthèses Française 2007, Itto titrit

المركز السينمائي المغربي
Centre Cinématographique Marocain

Fig. I.4. Poster for the CCM's fifty-year anniversary

population in the three countries, with regard to mass media: journalism, radio, television, and cinema. (1984, 231)[17]

Since the late 1980s, "cinéphiles maghrébins" (Maghrebian filmgoers) have acquired their cinematic knowledge through Moroccan cinema journals and reviews modeled after founding film texts such as *Cahiers du cinéma* in France. These journals are, for the most part, written in French or are bilingual, and have promoted increased international critique and analysis of Moroccan cinematography. In general, Moroccan cinema is discussed in the context of world cinema as the reviews in cinema journals seek to encourage readership from abroad.

Cinema magazines evolved in the late 1970s when most Moroccan newspapers also began dedicating pages to cinema news (Carter 1999, 331). *Lamalif* and *Kalima*, two outstanding newsmagazines, also habitually included cinema sections in their pages. Magazines devoted exclusively to film included *L'écran marocain* and *Cinéma 3*. Although *Cinéma 3* had a short run in the 1980s, producing only four issues under the supervision of Noureddine Sail (currently the director of the CCM), it did succeed in establishing a homegrown film critique forum that was later continued in Moroccan national papers such as *L'opinion* (Carter 1999, 331). The recently founded French-language *Ciné mag: Magazine du cinéma et de l'audiovisuel au Maroc* (first edition published in 2006) is the first magazine of the millennium dedicated solely to cinema that offers in-depth interviews with filmmakers, both at home and abroad, and critical analyses of current films.

Today, feature articles in francophone weekly newsmagazines such as *TelQuel* devote a significant amount of editorial space to culture and the arts. Journalist and director in chief of *Nichane* (now defunct), Driss Ksikes, who is also the nephew of filmmaker Nabyl Lahlou, often writes extensive film reviews of the latest films that are thought-provoking, critical, and informative. Overall, film criticism is primarily written in French. A cadre of critics has succeeded in founding a vibrant milieu of discussion that has departed from the more-subjective views of those unschooled in cinema. The open forums reflect the extended freedom of the press and the influence of capitalist consumption, which, for better or worse, increasingly drives the industry in the current era.

1

Theories and Polemics

Moroccan Films as Social-Realist Texts

Moroccan cinema, although conceived as a national cinema, developed quite differently from the cinemas of Algeria and Tunisia due to ideals about nationhood, visions of identity, and a divergent colonial experience. In order to contextualize the role and place of national cinema today in Morocco, it is important to understand its development in relation to the politics of the postindependence era. The three countries of the Maghreb colonized by France—Algeria, Morocco, and Tunisia—developed film industries based on the politics that evolved during independence struggles and immediately after in the burgeoning nations that resulted. Algeria and Tunisia organized independent states built on Marxist-socialist ideology, which, over the years, became single-party republics. Conversely, in 1956 Morocco reinstated its exiled monarchy, preferring to modernize the sultanate rather than adopt another, more Western form of government.[1]

All three countries boast film industries that are vibrant and, despite political conflict over the years, have continued to make thought-provoking films. Algeria and Morocco have based their national cinema industries loosely on the French notion of national cinema as a socialized institution, funded almost entirely by investments from the state. Tunisia, on the other hand, never officially established a national center for film production, although filmmakers do obtain financial backing from the Société anonyme tunisienne de production et d'expansion cinématographiques (SATPEC, Nonprofit Company for the Production and Expansion of Tunisian Cinematography), set up in 1957 to "manage import, distribution, and exhibition of films" (Armes 2005, 20).

Although Tunisian filmmakers are more *auteuriste*—that is, they succeed in developing their own individual styles—the state still plays an important role in the development and sustainment of the industry. In general, the concept of "national cinema," whether or not a center houses it, means that "cinema is both an industry and an art" and serves the function of articulating the particular sociocultural and political attributes of a nation. National cinema as a rule "does not just standardize. [It] also particularizes" (Hayward 1992, 13). In all three countries, from early on, cinema served to foster debate about sociocultural (if not overtly political) issues as the countries shifted from colonialism to being postcolonial nations.

Algerian, Moroccan, and Tunisian film industries were based on the French model, but due to differing political credos in each country, they developed very divergent philosophies, scopes, and visions. Of the three industries, Morocco's is the only one to have been founded by the French in 1944 and then almost seamlessly passed to the independent state in 1956. Morocco's film industry and the CCM itself have emerged from an interesting blend of colonial legacy and a unique view of nationalism (co-opted in 1956 by the monarchy of Mohammed V). The industry, as it contributed to the politics of nationalist movements at home, was also influenced by the Third World movements of the 1960s and 1970s (and the Third Cinema genre that was founded during this time). In the early days of postcolonial filmmaking, an artistic and singular Moroccan flair, gleaned from a rich multiethnic and multilingual heritage, set the country's industry apart from those of its neighbors to the east.

Colonial Legacies and Nationalist Movements

Moroccan film history has been shaped by the sociocultural and political climates of both pre- and postcolonial eras. Understanding the country's unique history during these periods allows us to delve more deeply into the decisions made that would ultimately form Morocco's film industry in the new millennium. In 1956, at the time of independence from France, Mohammed V, returning from exile in Madagascar, immediately understood the importance of film as a valuable tool for propaganda that could be used to encourage a sense of national identity, unity, and allegiance to his monarchy. Unity among tribes and ethnicities (Berbers, Arabs, Muslims, and Jews) became the most important aspect of his mandate and essential to promoting the Moroccan state and monarchy as a single entity that would ensure the prosperity of the postcolonial era. However, actualizing the goal of unification between these divergent sectors proved to be a daunting task in the early years of independence.

Although estimates vary, Berbers have always made up at least 40 percent of Morocco's population. During the colonial period, Berber tribes were typically used by the French to divide Moroccan loyalty. The colonizers encouraged the belief that because Berbers had been conquered by Arabs, they owed the Arabs no allegiance. The Berbers, caught among Arab, French, and Spanish colonizers, never felt they owed loyalty to any individual dominating force. At the time of independence, in addition to the significant Berber population, another prominent minority group comprised the approximately 300,000 Jews living in Morocco (by 2003 this number had fallen to 5,500).

In 1956, in addition to ethnic and religious divisions, Mohammed V faced growing unrest in the Rif mountains from Berber tribes led by Muhammad Ibn 'Abd El-Karim El-Khattabi. Since the time of colonial occupation, 'Abd El-Karim and his rebels had waged attacks against the French and Spanish occupiers in the northern part of the country. In the years 1956–57, Berber tribes in the Rif repeatedly revolted against Mohammed V and the central government. Primarily, these tribes rebelled against the king's preference for a nationalism that sought to homogenize and efface their Berber heritage. Contrary to Mohammed V's penchant for unity, "the main content of the Berber identity vision was based on the recognition of Berber particularism." As scholar Karim Mezran explains, the Berbers' "rural base caused the Berber elite to embrace a vision that contained a strong social component. The words 'Muslim Socialism' described precisely this mixed vision that the Berbers [sought] to bring forward" (Mezran 2007, 38). However, calls for ethnic rights and claims to cultural, ethnic, or religious specificity for Berbers and other groups living in Morocco were thwarted at independence in the name of promoting Moroccan unity.

In Morocco, as elsewhere across the Arab world, Istiqlal, the ultranationalist Arab movement that built its ideology on strong Arabization with ties to traditional Islamic organizations, influenced the poli-

tics of independence (Mezran 2007, 31). However, the main leaders
of Istiqlal's ideology in Morocco were not successful in unifying into
one party as had occurred in Algeria. Unlike Algeria, where the rebellion against the French was led by the Front de la libération nationale
(FLN, National Liberation Front), a military and ideological movement that later became the dominant party after 1962, Morocco's liberation movement from early on was factionalized. Istiqlal's ideology
was adopted by Sidi Mohammed (who later became King Mohammed
V), conservative sectors of the population, and leftists who, through
the Union national des forces populaires (UNFP), headed by Mehdi
Ben Barka, sought to found a "vision of Moroccan identity [that]
was Arabist, anti-Islamic, anti-monarchical and pro-democratic" (35).
Ben Barka strongly believed that democracy in Morocco could be
achieved through "the action of a single Party . . . [and he] identified
the Istiqlal as the prototype of the 'party-nation'" (35). Neither fac-
tion, however, would recognize Berber enfranchisement, socially, politically, or culturally. Although Mohammed V sought to sustain unity
and rule in tandem with a state-government parliamentarian system,
he realized early on that Istiqlal and a socialist-modeled nationalist
party would be "his main rival for power and . . . a major obstacle for
the unity of Morocco" (41).

In keeping with the indigenous precolonial system, the monarch
of Morocco is also the "Leader of the Faithful," and his dynasty is directly descended from the prophet Mohammed. The king represents
the state and the national religion and rules by divine right. At the
time of independence, Mohammed V refused to reduce his function to
that of an elected official and, although some say he did seek to negotiate the omnipotence of his role in the building of the state, his word
remained the ultimate word of law as prescribed by God and Islamic
decree. Under his son, Hassan II, the dual role of king and religious
leader took on Machiavellian proportions. Mohammed V died in 1963.
From 1966 until his death in 1999, Hassan II ruled Morocco with an
iron fist, cloaking the country in the dark, secretive era of *les années de
plomb*, during which thousands of Moroccan citizens were victimized.
At the dawn of the Lead Years, journalist Zakya Douad, with her husband, founded the leftist journal *Lamalif* (1958–88), which provided
a resounding voice of opposition in Morocco. Capturing the climate
of the 1960s in her work *Les années Lamalif: 1958–1988 trente ans de
journalism au Maroc*, Daoud describes the iron curtain that fell on the

country in 1966 and definitively ended any possibility of dissent from opposition parties:

> In 1966 Morocco was living political and ethical problems that seemed insurmountable, the first deceptions of independence. What we didn't know then was that it was the end of the national movement, the eve of the first riots in Casablanca, the kidnapping of Mehdi Ben Barka. The regime was already all-powerful and had begun to be rigid; the opposition fractured and began to lose ground. We felt society falling back into archaisms, the weight of the past coming up again, the opportunists coming out, hearts and spirits drying up. This gestating political drama would wall us in an ideology, still hardy, on the left: Be cunning with adversity. To write was to resist. (2007, 427)

The 1960s' Revolutionary Philosophies and Literary Influences on Cinemas in the Maghreb

In many respects, Morocco's nascent nation faced the same challenges as other formerly colonized regions. National film industries in the Maghreb shared some similar paths as they plotted political courses in the postcolonial era. These industries in many ways revealed the same metamorphoses witnessed in national literatures. In the 1950s and early 1960s, the nationalist goals of authors active in anticolonial struggles in Algeria, Morocco, and Tunisia thematically focused on conceptualizing strong nation-states that would rebuild colonized societies left in shambles once independence had been achieved. The rhetoric of nationalism prescribed strong, collective unity as the basis for these new nations.

Nationalist agendas were inscribed in the literature (overwhelmingly written in French) of the times by some of the most notable authors and poets of the era of decolonization. These included Algerians Kateb Yacine (*Nedjma*, 1956) and Mohammed Dib (*L'incendie*, The fire, 1954); Tunisian Albert Memmi (*Portrait du colonisé précédé de portrait du colonisateur*, Portrait of the colonized and colonizer, 1955); Moroccan Driss Chraïbi (*Le passé simple*, The simple past, 1954); and Martinicans Aimé Césaire (*Discours sur le colonialism*, Discourse on colonialism,

1950) and Frantz Fanon (*Peau noire, masques blancs,* Black skin, white masks, 1951; and *Les damnés de la terre,* The wretched of the earth, 1961). Frantz Fanon's *Les Damnés de la terre* compels the *literati* of colonized nations to write "une littérature de combat" (combat literature), emphasizing that the duty of the author is "to call on an entire people to struggle for national existence." Combat literature "informs the national consciousness" and provides the impetus for the formation of the collective will necessary for liberation (Fanon 1961, 228).

The spirit of revolutionary literature supporting decolonization was transcribed later into the burgeoning national cinemas of newly independent countries. Frantz Fanon's "On National Culture," a monumental chapter in *The Wretched of the Earth,* maintained that a liberated country was only as strong as the culture it cultivated. This culture had to be freed of colonial influences, afford citizens a sense of attachment to their origins before colonialism, and define new parameters that would found original sociopolitical and cultural ideologies in the postcolonial era: "The crystallization of the national consciousness will both disrupt literary styles and themes, and also create a completely new public" (Fanon 1961, 239–40). The contours of a nation's independence therefore would be very much influenced by the writings of socially and politically committed authors. Their voices would be responsible for unifying the cultural pride necessary for the new, liberated nation. The nationalist author is an "évolué" (evolved), a writer of the elite who holds the responsibility of working as an outsider, on the peripheries of a culture in the making. She or he must influence the consciousness of the people, encouraging the shift from a colonized state of mind to one that is liberated. The author's independent consciousness, however, is not born overnight. According to Fanon, a colonized writer's sense of nationhood and national consciousness is molded through three stages, or phases. These both influence and mirror a people's evolution to independence:

> In the first phase, the native intellectual gives proof that he has assimilated the culture of the occupying power. . . . His inspiration is European. . . . In the second phase, we find the native is disturbed; he decides to remember what he is. . . . But since the native [author] is not part of his people, since he only has exterior relations with his people, he is content to recall their life only. . . . Finally, in the third phase, which is called the fighting phase, the native, after having tried to lose

himself in the people and with the people, will on the contrary shake the people. . . . He turns himself into an awakener of the people; hence comes a fighting literature, a revolutionary literature, and a national literature. . . . [Authors] feel the need to speak to their nation, to compose the sentence which expresses the heart of the people and to become the mouthpiece of a new reality in action. (Fanon, 2002, 222–23).

The importance of this passage is reified in later treatises written by film theorists from the postcolonial, developing world. In 1989, Teshome H. Gabriel, contributing a chapter to *Questions of Third Cinema*, notes that Fanon's theory on the importance of nationalist writing for decolonization could be applied to filmmakers working in newly independent countries across Africa. National cinemas were grounded by the belief that "culture is an act of insemination" and would help develop the socioeconomic and political ideologies of burgeoning postcolonial nations (Gabriel 1991, 30). Gabriel explains that, like Fanon's "phases," Third World filmmakers would move from a first stage wherein "foreign images" were "impressed in an alienating fashion on . . . audience[s]," to second and third stages "in which recognition of 'consciousness of oneself' serves as the essential antecedent for national and, more significantly, international consciousness" (31).

These phases/stages were conceived of within the parameters of an industry that evolved from one founded by the colonial occupiers in order to document the empire for France, to one that, after independence, became a social institution necessary for the cultural health of the independent nation. National cinema became more than an art form; it was "a public service institution" run by "mass participation enacted by members of communities speaking indigenous language[s]" but who were invested in unifying the new nation (Gabriel 1991, 33).

Three Maghrebian Cinemas

The Centre cinématographique marocain (CCM), founded in 1944 while Morocco was still under colonial rule, provided a very different vehicle for the dissemination of state-building ideology during and post French occupation than its sister countries, Algeria and Tunisia. In Algeria, for example, "film was seen to form a vital part of the liberation struggle by the FLN, the army and the Algerian provisional government (GPRA)" (Armes 2005, 15). It was an industry to be "ripped" from the hands of the colonizers who, according to historian Abdelghani Megherbi, had used cinema up to 1946 to promote "their own colonial image" to and among themselves, while at the same time spreading propaganda to aid in colonial domination of indigenous Algerians (1982, 39). Stealing the industry from the colonizers in order to use it against them became the modus operandi of the *maquis*.

Defiantly, even before the Algerian revolution had been won, films such as *Algérie en flames* (Algeria burning, 1959) promoted a free Algeria as a "site of solidarity" between the *maquis*, fighting for liberation, and French intellectuals in the *Métropole* who were sympathetic to the idea of Algeria as an independent nation (Armes 2005, 15). The Centre national du cinéma algérien (CNCA, Center for Algerian National Cinema), which produced three feature-length films between 1965 and 1966, and the privately run company Casbah Films, headed by Yacef Saadi, former FLN leader and whose own story inspired the infamous film *The Battle of Algiers* (1965) by Gillo Pontecorvo, proved to be important contributors to the Third Cinema movement in North Africa. From early on, independent Algeria coproduced a number of sociopolitically motivated films with acclaimed directors such as Greek-born Constantin Costa-Gavras. Certainly the most notable of these coproductions is Costa-Gavras's 1969 film *Z*, the story of a judge who, as an investigator, tries to uncover the facts surrounding the murder of a leftist politician in an unnamed country (Armes 2005, 16).

From the outset, shortly after independence, Tunisia's SATPEC dedicated itself to importing, distributing, and exhibiting films. In the early years following independence, Tunisia "had a vibrant film culture, with a ciné-club movement which dated back to 1950" and worked to internationally produce coproductions (Armes 2005, 21). Tunisia's film industry was a cultural art form well integrated into colonial society from the 1930s forward. In the 1950s, ciné-clubs were well established and concentrated their activities on documenting every aspect of the cinematic milieus of the country. Although it never founded an institution such as the CCM in Morocco or the CNCA in Algeria, from its inception, the Tunisian film industry encouraged an amateur filmmaking movement supported by the organization Association des jeunes cinéastes tunisiens (AJCT, Young Tunisian Filmmakers), founded in 1961. Similar organizations were not present in

Algeria and Morocco until much later. Tunisia was one of the first liberated colonial countries to host its own film festival: Kélibia in 1964 and Tunis in 1966. These festivals continue to be held today and are internationally recognized for the prizes they give to world cinema filmmakers (21). With regard to its development, Moroccan cinema differed significantly from Algeria and Tunisia. It was insular and ill-equipped to envision the production of feature-length films at the time of independence. Where socialist-Marxist ideologues (FLN in Algeria; Bourguiba in Tunisia) used film as a vehicle in defining the parameters of new Arab-Islamic postcolonial cultures within socialist republics, the Moroccan monarchy changed a colonial industry into an informational state-run tool, focusing primarily on economic development documentaries. At the time of independence, "the CCM [concentrated] . . . on the production of short films dealing with the sectors deemed to be state priorities, such as information, education, agriculture, and health. . . . The films made responded to the demands of the different ministries which also commissioned newsreels designed for state propaganda" (Armes 2005, 20). The first feature-length films produced by the CCM were not released until twelve years after independence.

Moroccan films such as *Le fils maudit* (The damned son, 1958) were highly moralistic, transmitting messages to audiences about the duty of family, the necessity of faith in God, and the importance of a code of ethics and allegiance to the nation/monarchy. In particular, this film tells the story of a young adolescent who becomes a delinquent because of negligent parenting. *Vaincre pour vivre* (Conquer to live, 1968), made ten years later, tells the story of Karim and unmasks the challenges of emigrating from a small village in the Rif mountains to the huge urban sprawl of Casablanca. The rags-to-riches tale follows Karim from poor country bumpkin to a popular singer making his fortune in the big city. The film also condemns that same urban landscape for corrupting those who come from the countryside. *Quand murissent les dates* (When the dates ripen, 1968) tells the story of two tribes divided by conflict until a new generation of young people, inspired by a collective and pragmatic spirit, is able to help negotiate their tribal differences.

The rhythm of production of these homegrown films was slow, and the filming techniques rudimentary. The poor quality of feature-length filmmaking at this time was due to, as one critic points out, the CCM's failure to train its employees, who were primarily used to producing short documentaries "intended to extend [a] 'folklore' tendency which was appropriate [only for] the commercial tourist short" (Armes 2005, 20). In the 1970s, the CCM funded only fifteen films, and the majority of these productions were made by three filmmakers: Mohammed Abderrahmane Tazi, Souheil Ben Barka, and Abdellah Mesbahi (29).

Narrative styles were influenced by Egyptian films of the era, which were inclined to be highly melodramatic, focusing on the daily struggles of traditional people against the challenges of the modern world. For the most part, Moroccan films in the 1970s were nostalgic and free of political commentary unless it was aimed at the past colonial occupation. The limited themes were primarily due to an industry that did not view itself as a mover and shaker of culture as in Algeria and Tunisia and because, as A. Tazi remarks, filmmakers believed their duty was to "craft" stories rather than invest in an "industry."[2] Much of this belief was due to the watchful eye of the monarchy, which closely monitored filmmakers' themes. As Tazi remarks, the "red line," which one could never cross, always meant that one had to respect "the state, religion, relations between men and women and the classes" (Ghareeb 1997, 123).

The CCM's insistence that filmmaking should be either to instruct in documentary form or confectioned as a work of art, devoid of any political underpinnings, hindered the industry's development and the making of any substantive films. The CCM as an institution remained on the peripheries of culture, rather than as an integral part of its production, at least until the end of the 1990s. Much of this had to do with the Lead Years and the rule of Hassan II, which defined the parameters of Moroccan filmmakers' expression. This is not to say, however, that Algerian and Tunisian filmmaking were without censure. But because these countries were defined by socialist movements supported by a commitment to Marxist ideology, filmmaking was recognized as a vital tool for newly minted governments striving to create strong national identities. Film was a medium that would rally the people and convince them to forge into unknown territory. Conversely, since Morocco reverted back to a politically traditional system similar to the era of precolonial occupation, film remained relegated to a peripheral domain, viewed as Western and foreign to the conservative will of the monarchy. Cinema was an art form perhaps, but not needed or necessary in the traditional daily life of the King-dom of Morocco.

As a pure art form, Moroccan cinema was later described by Tu-nisian filmmaker and critic Férid Boughedir as an example par excel-lence of a "cinema of extremes": one able to draw upon the glitz of Egyptian musicals and the intellectualism of the French cinemato-graphic tradition (Dwyer 2004, 116). However, the CCM's view of film as first and foremost an art form persisted in hampering their commercialization. This view, in my opinion, endures today, thus lim-iting the commercialization and distribution of films.

Third World Movements and the Politics of Opposition: Was There a Third Cinema in Morocco?

Morocco's path to independence, which in the end resulted in the reinstallation of the monarchy, differed immensely from Algeria's, which favored a republic founded and ruled by the dominant FLN Marxist, military, and political party. Also in contrast to Morocco, in the 1960s Tunisia's omnipotent Habib Bourghiba culled the country's seemingly Marxist-prototype government to found some of the most progressive ideologies in the Arab world. Both countries were heavily influenced by Third World movements, which tended to be social-ist and populist, promoting independence from persistent Western neocolonialism. The inherent values of these movements lay in their platforms for equality and the effacement of class divisions.

In the Morocco of the late 1950s and early 1960s, the UNFP (Union nationale des forces populaires, National Union of Popular Forces) party and movement for social justice were very much present and fostered political ideology favoring a socialist multiparty system. However, from early on the party's efforts to defy the political will of the monarchy were stymied. Mehdi Ben Barka is perhaps the most fa-mous oppositional political figure of this time. As leader of the UNFP, Ben Barka was a symbol for the Moroccan populist Third World movement, as well as a promoter of socioeconomic liberation across Africa, Asia, and Latin America. He succeeded in rallying factions into one cohesive party in order to oppose what he viewed as the conserva-tive domination of Mohammed V. For Ben Barka, Istiqlal had to be a "prototype of the party-nation" that would foster a multiparty system in the country (Mezran 2007, 35). However, Ben Barka's version of an Istiqlal multiparty system was "entwined with Arab nationalism and the supremacy of Arab symbols" and therefore, as mentioned previously, fostered little unity among Berbers, Jews, and Arabs (36).

In the early 1960s Ben Barka lived in exile, threatened by Hassan II, who had decimated all political opposition to the monarchy. Traveling the world as a proponent of Third World movements, Ben Barka's contribution to international politics is most significantly noted in his participation in the Tricontinental Revolution, which was dedicated to opposing Western hegemony in South Asia (specifically Vietnam), Latin America, and Africa. As an international opposition leader striving to combat Western hegemony, Ben Barka's legacy is entwined with those of Frantz Fanon, Che Guevara, and Ho Chi Minh. Still today, the socialist opposition leader is an enigma. The French-Moroccan film *J'ai vu tuer Ben Barka* (I saw Ben Barka get killed, 2005), by Serge Le Péron and Saïd Smihi, documents Ben Barka's dedication to the social movements of the 1960s and his subsequent assassination. As the film suggests, these movements fueled an entirely alternative view of the world's economic and social reality as never before seen. They were also considered a threat to Western capitalist systems and to totalitarian governments in postcolonial countries.[3]

Third World movements, specifically the Tricontinental movement, not only challenged Western socioeconomic and political systems, they also promoted the rethinking of artistic production conceived through Western models that had automatically been adopted by postcolonial nations. Film became the perfect artistic medium through which to experiment with new forms of artistic production, intermingled with politically didactic messages. Notably, Third Cinema proposed "the destruction of the old modes of conceiving cinema and . . . old image[s] shaped by colonialism and neocolonialism" in order to found "a new cinema [that depicted the] construction of a throbbing, living reality which recaptures truth in any of its expressions" (Armes 1987, 99).[4]

The Third Cinema genre questions power structures (colonial and postcolonial), aims at liberation for the oppressed, whether socioeconomically or politically construed, and proposes racial equality. Third Cinema addresses questions of identity and community within the nation about which it speaks and, most important, seeks to reveal the hidden struggles of women, impoverished classes, minority groups, and others who generally cannot speak for themselves or are not given a voice by dominant power structures. It is a cinematic genre based on an ideology of hope that new nations would articulate their structures and institutions in a new manner, freeing themselves of the former colonizers' yoke and inefficient models.[5] The founding of a Third Cinema was viewed as an integral component of the emergence of "popular struggle and a growing awareness of a distinctive Third World identity [bringing] . . . intellectuals . . . into a new relationship with the mass of their fellow countrymen" (Armes 1987, 83). Films of this era sought to reveal the unjust power structures of the colonial past as well as to uncover new neocolonial paradigms that, it was feared, would continue to oppress long into the future.

Works made by filmmakers in Brazil, Cuba, and parts of Asia and Africa exposed the power of film as a tool not only to educate but also to give a voice to the masses. Early films that chronicled this belief are numerous and include works by Sembène Ousmane (Senegal), Mohammed Lakdar-Hamina (Algeria), and Med Hondo (Mauritania). However, these filmmakers realized from the beginning of the postcolonial era that state-run socialist industries were hypocritical, promoting at first the "desire to change the lives of [their] people," but then subjecting their filmmakers to "censorship, imprisonment, exile and enforced silence" (Armes 1987, 92). Filmmakers in Morocco also were aware of just how dangerous the Third Cinema movement would be viewed by the monarchy. Certainly during the Lead Years, they bore the brunt of censure. If political themes were evoked, they were only metaphorically or symbolically rendered until the end of the 1990s (Carter 2000, 67).

In an interview during the Naples Festival I corti dal Mondo, held in 2008, Abdelhatif Laassadi, member and spokesperson for the CCM, stated that while under the French protectorate and until the mid-1970s there was a censorship body, the main function of which was controlling the distribution of foreign films in the country because domestic productions were still rare at the time. Since the mid-1990s, however, censorship—whether of foreign or domestic films—has been almost nonexistent. For example, in 1997, during the Tetouan Film Festival, CCM officials opted to screen *Al-Massir* (Destiny, 1997), by Egyptian cineaste Youssef Chahine, a film that had been banned in most countries in the Arab world due to its worldly theme that suggested there had been peace and harmony between Christians and Muslims during the twelfth century.

Moroccan films of the 1990s tended to focus on love, life's hardships, and man's incapacity to change his destiny. *La plage des enfants perdus* (The beach of lost children, 1991), *Fiction première* (First fiction, 1992), *La nuit du crime* (The night of the crime, 1992), and *L'enfance volée* (Stolen childhood, 1993), among others, offer glimpses into the lives of average Moroccans struggling to find their paths in the complexity of everyday life. Yet the paths taken by protagonists are never politically motivated or openly critical of the monarchy and the Moroccan state.

Successful Third Cinema movements were notable certainly in Latin America, where the genre was used as a vehicle to promote grassroots socialist ideals for its promising democracies.[6] Conversely, in Morocco the genre never got off the ground, primarily because filmmaking was hampered by societal views that considered film a Western art form and commodity. The monarchy preferred film to serve its cause rather than contribute to cultural development. It was not until the end of the 1990s that filmmakers embraced an auteur independent style and began to challenge their audiences with sociopolitical themes, encouraging them to view film as an important medium for the expression of Moroccan culture, society, and politics.

Two films contributed dramatically to changing the scope of the industry: Abdelkader Lagtaa's *A Love Affair in Casablanca* (1991) and *Looking for My Wife's Husband* (1993) by Mohammed Abderrahmane Tazi (Dwyer 2002, 118). Both films enjoyed the approval of audiences, which assured significant box-office success. Despite the seemingly socially taboo themes of sex outside marriage (*A Love Affair*), and the underlying message that women should be emancipated from traditionalist practices of polygamy and repudiation (*Looking for My Wife's Husband*), both films heralded a new era of filmmaking in Morocco. From now on screenplays would provide new socially committed messages documenting the transformations taking place in the country, while also providing Moroccans a form and forum in which to raise social consciousness as the Lead Years waned.

Social Realism and Moroccan Cinema: *Le Cinéma Engagé* of the New Millennium

The Third Cinema movement of the 1960s can be credited with launching a new era in filmmaking. Perhaps the most prominent aspect of this era was the "challenge [to] official versions of history" and the genre's ability to offer "an alternative to Western classical norms" (Gabriel 1991, 57). New films were born in that era and through the genre reflected the social-realist views of filmmakers across the continent of Africa. Films such as Sembène Ousmane's *La noire de* . . . (Black girl, 1966) and *Le mandat* (The money order, 1968), followed by *Xala* (The curse, 1973), opened up the world of didactic filmmaking destined to sway the primarily illiterate masses who had been disenfranchised by postcolonial governments. Less than fifteen years after independence, postcolonial nations across Africa had already become ineffectual and corrupt. Films of the 1980s, such as *La vie est belle* (Life is beautiful, 1986) by Ngangura Mweze; *Nyamanton* (1986) by Cheick Oumar Sissoko; and *Zan boko* (1986) by Gaston Kaboré, were critically acclaimed for the social activism they promoted (Diawara 1992, 142).

Africans began to recount their narratives according to their own value systems while openly criticizing the constraints of Western modernity and African traditionalism. On the heels of groundbreakers such as Senegalese Sembène Ousmane; Tunisians Férid Boughedir and Moufida Tlatli; and Moroccan M. A. Tazi, young Moroccan filmmakers were inspired by the end of the 1990s to write screenplays that were pertinent to the daily lives of their fellow citizens. As the Lead Years waned, filmmakers making films at home took the credo of the social-realist style to heart. Through didactic dialogues, they portrayed the realities of Moroccan society and culture, debating current social issues in the country as well as in the Maghreb, on the continent of Africa, and in the larger Arab world. Film scholar Manthia Diawara defines social-realist films as those that

> thematiz[e] . . . current sociocultural issues. The films in this category draw on contemporary experiences, and they oppose tradition to modernity, oral to written, agrarian and customary communities to urban and industrialized systems, and subsistence economies to highly productive economies. The filmmakers often use a traditional position to criticize and link certain forms of modernity to neocolonialism and cultural imperialism. From a modernist point of view, they also debunk the attempt to romanticize traditional values as pure and original. The heroes are women, children, and other marginalized groups that are pushed into the shadows by the elites of tradition and modernity. (1992, 141)

Although warming to the idea of social-cultural and political-activist filmmaking later than their colleagues in sister Maghrebian countries, Moroccan filmmakers in the new millennium are making some of the most thought-provoking films today in the Maghreb and, indeed, in the Arab world. They have become *engagés* (committed), adhering to the prescriptions of Fanonian logic for sociopolitical change. The socioculturally and politically committed Moroccan filmmaker confronts issues that represent the collective consciousness both in and outside his or her country. They are critical of themselves as well as of how they are perceived by others, notably Westerners. Contemporary Moroccan films represent an activism that extends beyond the cinematographic realm to promote sociopolitical and cultural dialogues that force audiences to think about their environments, while also introspectively reviewing the past.

Increasingly films reflect a humanist response to the challenges of our era, which means, as Jean Bessière notes, the "individual is implicated actively in the development of the world, admits responsibility for what happens, [and/or] opens a future of action." The filmmaker's engagement "designates an act by which the individual links himself with his future being" (Bessière 1977, 13). Sociopolitically engaged filmmakers invest in the pure ideal of committed activism; that is, their works reflect the notion that they, as intellectuals, take a position that is "willed" and determined by their dedication to becoming "involved in the response to events" occurring in their society (Schalk 1979, 5). There are overarching assumptions that we can make about socially committed filmmakers. They are politically active, outspoken, possibly embittered because of "insupportable alienation" from mainstream society (23). They are, in the true sense of the historically French term *engagé*, committed to the "conscience of humanity" (27). Moroccan films such as *J'ai vu tuer Ben Barka* (2005), *Les yeux secs* (2002), and *Marock* (2005), as well as many others made since 1999, are some of the finest examples of contemporary works of sociopolitically committed filmmakers who seek to explore society as ready and willing to look critically at its past, present, and future.

Filmmakers since the end of the Lead Years adhere to new credos that include the pursuit of truth and accuracy in historical and modern-day depictions of their society. They act as "position takers," functioning in "the field of positions" possible in an open and tolerant society (Bourdieu 1993, 35). These positions concern the rights of women (Hassan Benjelloun's *Jugement d'une femme*, A woman's trial,

2002); homosexuals and children (Nabyl Ayouch's *Ali Zaoua*, 1999; *Whatever Lola Wants*, 2008); human rights abuses and torture (Jillali Ferhati's *Mémoire en détention*, Memory in detention, 2004) in the past; and poverty in the present (Kamal Kamal's *La symphonie marocaine*, The Moroccan symphony, 2005). Moroccan filmmakers today operate as free agents in a society of equal exchange that is not limited or determined by cultural mores or political prerequisites.

As Morocco has become more economically competitive due to IMF structural readjustment, strong trade agreements with Europe and the United States, and infrastructure-building within the country, the Kingdom of Morocco can most definitely be considered a developing country with GDP development on par with that of nations such as Brazil. With "economic capital" comes "large social capital," which, according to Pierre Bourdieu's theories on cultural production, means that as a society grows materially richer "in economic, cultural and social capital," it then "moves into . . . new positions" that comply with the "expectations of the cultivated audience" (1993, 68). Moroccan filmmakers thus are able to define a *habitus*, a "system of dispositions" that "empha[sizes] milieu over characters, the determining context over the determined text." In the habitus, the filmmaker is "sole master" of a new "complete universe" (71). She or he is free to make a personal interpretation of culture and to "utter 'in public' the true nature of the field and . . . its mechanisms" (73).

Thus, it can be surmised that Morocco's more open and unfettered socially committed cultural production is linked to the prosperity it has seen since its regime change and the conscious effort since 1999 by state authorities to commit to social change. Cultural production and the functioning of society—made up of its politics and institutions—are mirror images in the Bourdieuian sense. One reflects the other and, in today's context, one cannot exist without the other. Consequently, film is both a product and a contributor to the sociocultural and political realms of today's Morocco.

Some of the best examples of the symbiosis between film and society-culture-politics are found in films that delve into past infractions of human rights abuses committed during the Lead Years. Since Mohammed VI's coronation, and the formation of the IER (Instance d'equité et reconciliation, Committee for Human Rights and Retributions) and the CCDH (Conseil consultative des droits de l'homme, Consultative Council on Human Rights) in 2004 and 2007 respectively, the documentation of infractions has not only become a way of establishing official public records of abuse, it also has provided artistic inspiration. Films such as *Jawhara* (2003); *Mémoire en détention* (Memory in detention, 2004); *La chambre noire*, The black room, 2004); *J'ai vu tuer Ben Barka* (I saw Ben Barka get killed, 2005), and *Faux pas* (False steps, 2003) (see chapter 4) flush out the *mémoire refoulée* (stifled memory) of the past in order to make audiences aware of a history never before told, while also marking a point from which to depart in order to assure that abuse never takes place again. Each testimonial film on human rights abuses committed during the Lead Years becomes a "travail de mémoire" (a work of remembering) for the Moroccan people. The cinematic oeuvre made from/about the past for present audiences serves to both appropriate and negotiate the past so that each viewer will "progress in his own future individuality" (Zekri 2006, 200). Similarly, each film made about the past becomes a "lieu de mémoire" (a place and space of remembrance) for the collective consciousness of the people, preserving the narratives of Morocco in the new millennium.

2

Issues, Contexts, and "Culture Wars"

Marocains Résidants à l'Etranger (MRE) versus Filmmakers at Home

Is Moroccan cinema francophone or arabophone? Are films made by *Marocains résidents à l'étranger* (MREs, Moroccans living abroad) more apt to challenge the sociocultural mores of Morocco than those made by filmmakers who have stayed at home? These are two of the focal questions associated with Moroccan filmmaking and the discourse emanating from it in the last decade.

Over the past ten years, domestic films have been shot primarily in Moroccan Arabic and/or Berber. However, these films are always distributed in the country with French subtitles in order to draw audiences from predominantly French-speaking enclaves in the large cities of Casablanca, Rabat, and Fez. This sector of the population is often elite; its children attend French-speaking high schools and are sent to France or other francophone European countries to further their educations. Films in which the French language is privileged appeal to those Moroccans living abroad—immigrants and their children—who are primarily French speaking and come home to Morocco every summer. The language debate for Moroccan filmmakers is one that has dictated the parameters of funding and distribution both at home and internationally. The debate is certainly at the heart of Morocco's culture wars, which reveal two very divergent camps pitted against each other: one arabophone, the other francophone.

Films such as *Marock* (2005) by filmmaker Leïla Marrakchi, who is an MRE, challenge the sociocultural and religious traditions of the homeland. Marrakchi's depiction of the shifting sexual mores among young people living in Casablanca, as well as the influence of Western hip-hop culture, resonated with younger generations at home and abroad. In general, MRE films describe the strains of immigration and assimilation, and the alienation experienced by families in Europe, as well as when they come home. Another example of a successful MRE film is Ismaïl Ferroukhi's *Le grand voyage* (The long journey, 2004), which focuses on the generational divide between a father and his son in France. It also reflects the larger message that, regardless of religion or ethnicity, there are universal values we all share that are rooted in our common humanity.

Whatever Lola Wants, Lola Gets (2008) by Nabyl Ayouch, a third example, offers an interesting twist to East-West relations through belly dancing. Ayouch is a multifaceted filmmaker who has one foot in Morocco and the other in France due to his dual heritage—his father is Moroccan, and his mother, French. Where *Ali Zaoua* was made at home, exclusively in Moroccan Arabic and designated for primarily audiences in Morocco (although the film was later screened to critical acclaim at several international film festivals), his most recent film, *Whatever Lola Wants*, was shot in the United States, Morocco, and Egypt in English, French, and Arabic. Filmmaker Yasmine Kassari's *L'enfant endormi* (The sleeping child, discussed in chapter 5) is set in Morocco and focuses on a traditional folktale and milieu, yet is funded heavily by the Belgians. Kassari, for the most part, resides full-time in Europe. These filmmakers, as well as others, live a dual life—split between the East and the West, the religious and the secular, and the French and the Arabic languages. They view the world as global citizens and are dedicated to democratization and humanist values in their homeland as well as abroad.

Without a doubt, although MRE films are often significantly funded by France, Belgium, Canada, and to some extent Spain, Morocco's CCM also invests in order to prove that Moroccan-funded productions can please international audiences. The CCM strives to demonstrate its commitment to internationalizing its contemporary cinema by offering moviegoers at home and abroad a meaningful experience in film. Because the majority of films encourage universal humanist messages, they appeal thematically to all regardless of nationality, race, religion, or ethnicity. Perusing the CCM's website (http://www.ccm.ma/), film aficionados notice that the center does not distinguish between MRE directors and those residing and working exclusively at home. For example, Nabyl Ayouch, Yasmine Kassari, and Leïla Marrakchi, among others, who primarily live in France, Belgium, and elsewhere in Europe, are listed with directors who work in Morocco. The funding debate reveals interesting polemics that are constantly surfacing. Films made by Moroccans living abroad enjoy a certain status in the Moroccan cinematic oeuvre that is interesting on many levels. Today, Moroccan "résidants à l'étranger" draw a significant amount of foreign investment that is injected directly into the Moroccan economy. In fact, film production is one area where international development and investment by MREs are most evident. Since 2000, a film's success on the international market has been increasingly determined by how much funding and press it receives from coproducers abroad. Thematically, it would be simplistic to say that international funding dictates the subjects of films, as West African filmmakers have claimed in the past.[1] It must be noted, though, that films made with international monies overwhelmingly tend to reflect the ideologies and issues of the Moroccan diaspora rather than the specific, narrow subjects of current interest at home.[2]

It is also true that Moroccan and, in general, Maghrebian filmmakers "run the risk of having to change [their] scenario[s]" when financed abroad mainly because "the Western viewer becomes a major factor in the filmic equation" (Rosen 1989, 36). In short, certain stereotypes are constantly portrayed about the home country because Europeans equate the picturesque and the desert sands with North Africa, and MREs know that in order to screen their films in Europe, certain leitmotifs must remain (the exotic is evident certainly in Ferroukhi's *Le grand voyage* [2004]). Nevertheless, foreign-funded films also reflect the more open sociopolitical climate of the New Morocco. Since 1999, foreign-funded films have been regularly screened in Moroccan cinemas, despite controversy (*Marock* in 2005), thus defying more conservative, traditional Islamic sectors of the society. Young audiences have emphatically supported international MRE productions because they associate them with what they think is most important: connection, not only to their own country, but to the outside world. Filmmakers and audiences realize that "international production implies international distribution, international audiences, [and] international thinking as well" (36).

Several successful films made in the last five years stand as excellent examples of the increased global awareness of the Moroccan film industry since the end of the Lead Years. All exemplify current so-ciopolitical and cultural discussions and debates that are relevant and important on both sides of the Mediterranean. The shifting sexual mores and the influences of pop culture on young people as explored in Leïla Marrakchi's *Marock* and Nabyl Ayouch's *Whatever Lola Wants* resonated not only with Moroccan youth, but also with the immigrant second and third generations in France's major metropolitan *banlieues* (large, urban suburbs that are ghettoized primarily by mainstream French culture). For example, topics such as the strains of immigra-tion, assimilation, and alienation in Europe, as well as the more inti-mate, generational divide between father and son as depicted in Ismaïl Ferroukhi's *Le Grand Voyage*, allow audiences of disparate backgrounds, ethnicities, and values to come together in the harmonious milieu of the "worldliness" of the Moroccan cinematic text. This worldliness has added to the appeal of Moroccan cinema at home and abroad.

In the last four years, ticket sales in Morocco for the top-selling films made by both MRE filmmakers and those solely residing at home are as follows: *Casanegra* (Noureddine Lakhmari, 214,473); *Abdou chez les Almohades* (Abdou at the Almohades' house, Saïd Naciri, 190,000); *Amours voilées* (Veiled loves, Aziz Salmi, 179,341); *Ma-rock* (Leïla Marrakchi, 150,000); *La symphonie marocaine* (The Moroc-can symphony, Kamal Kamal, 120,000); *Whatever Lola Wants* (Nabyl Ayouch, 110,000); and *Ex Chamkar* (Mahmoud Frites, 106,696).[3]

This chapter offers a sampling of MRE films in contrast to films made at home in order to explore to what extent issues such as fund-ing, technical advances, and access to equipment for filming and mon-tage influence how films are made. Are foreign-funded films more successful at the box office? Do they benefit technically from foreign funds? And do filmmakers who receive backing from abroad feel com-pelled to make films whose themes extend beyond Morocco to appeal to audiences on universal levels?

MRE Films: 1999–2008

Nabyl Ayouch's Whatever Lola Wants *(2008):*
Belly Dancing Instead of Bin Laden

During the Dubai International Film festival in 2008, Nabyl Ay-ouch emphasized that his most recent film was made with the goal of attacking unfavorable stereotypes promoted in the West that are associated with Arab peoples: "It's so much better to give the image of the Arab world through belly dancing than Osama bin Laden. . . . It's all a question of misunderstanding and it's not because we are different, that we can't talk or understand each other."[4]

Whatever Lola Wants is Nabyl Ayouch's third feature-length film. The film's international appeal stems from its international settings and cast, as the film crisscrosses the globe from New York City to Cairo (however, many of the Cairo scenes were shot in Morocco). The cast includes American (Laura Ramsey as Lola), Lebanese (Carmen Lebbos as Ismahan), and Moroccan actors (Assaad Bouab playing Zakaria, an Egyptian). The film was primarily shot in English and Arabic, but all English dialogues were dubbed in French for distribution in Europe, Morocco, and on DVD. At the time of this writing, the film has yet to be released in English in the United States. *Whatever Lola Wants* was produced with French-Canadian backing and additional funds from the CCM.

Lola is an aspiring modern dancer who lives in Brooklyn and works part-time at a post office in downtown New York City. In the evenings, she moonlights as a waitress in an upscale restaurant where she sometimes breaks into a song-and-dance routine, habitually singing her favorite song, "Whatever Lola Wants." The meanings behind the choice of this quintessentially American musical classic, written by Jerry Ross and Richard Adler, are not lost in translation. The number was the title song of and was sung by Gwen Verdon in the popular 1955 musical *Damn Yankees*, which ran on Broadway for years and was revived numerous times. The play and the song denote nostalgia for an era viewed as simpler, more peaceful, and hopeful. Ayouch's America is one of big lights, big shows, and big dreams, and touts a particular brand of American naïveté that is from a former era.

Lola's exposure to the Arab world, like that of most Americans, is limited. In the wake of 9/11, and as we are caught in the throes of wars in Afghanistan and Iraq, Ayouch's views on American ignorance about the world are not subtle. His protagonist is the "typical and average American from Wisconsin" (which Ramsey, in an interview, admits she is). Her fascination with Egypt and belly dancing comes by way of her gay Egyptian friend and coworker at the restaurant, Youssouf, who left Egypt when he was young and doesn't plan on going back because of his sexual orientation. The two spend evenings in Youssouf's apartment watching his videos of the famous Egyptian belly dancer Ismahan, who was forced to go into hiding after a public "incident" that was considered indecent. In the meantime, Lola meets Zakaria (Zak), a young, rich Egyptian living in New York (working in an undisclosed profession), to whom she delivers mail every day. Just after they finally do fall in love, Zak decides to leave to go back to Egypt, stating that Lola's desire to dance instead of having children and "being a woman" is behavior he cannot accept: "You don't want a woman's life," he tells her. Despite this affront, Lola decides she will leave for Egypt to learn belly dancing from a real master and also look for Zak. Youssef is shocked by her decision, telling her, "What do you know about Egypt? . . . The only country you know is Wisconsin." Headstrong and sure of herself, she sells everything in her apartment, quits her postal job, and hops onto a plane. When she arrives in Cairo and finds Zak, he takes her to a hotel in a questionable neighborhood where hotel managers can be bought off to overlook the usual mandated "marriage certificates" needed for a couple to rent a room. Zak, although enjoying the sexual interlude, tells Lola she needs to go home and that Egypt is "no place for her." He also makes it clear that the kind of dancing she wants to do is for whores. Her insistence that she doesn't care about the cultural caveats associated with belly dancing leads him to refuse her, claiming her lack of cultural sensitivity is "typically American. . . . You come here and you think you already know our customs." He gives her money to return home, and she throws it out the window as he drives off.

Lola decides to hunt for the famous dancer Ismahan to see if she will give her belly-dancing lessons. After finding the elusive matriarch of the illicit dance form in a house obscured from view by a high wall, Ismahan rebuffs Lola's request to study belly dancing with her, stating that Lola will never be able to learn to do the moves the right way. As the film progresses, we learn that Ismahan is a broken woman with a past who has resigned herself never to dance again. It is only after Lola befriends Ismahan's young daughter and wins over the head manservant of the house that Ismahan finally agrees to lessons. In order to earn money, Lola decides to see what dancing gigs she can get in the local café-clubs in the neighborhood of the hotel she is staying in. In the club adjacent to her hotel (where she has convinced the owner to let her stay, even though she is alone), she becomes a hit and, after several frustrating days, makes friends with the regular dancers.

All her exploits are accomplished with her minimal knowledge of Arabic and an American "can-do" attitude. While dancing in the café-club, Nacer, a local celebrity and well-known impresario search-ing for dancing talent to hire out to weddings and other high-class functions, offers her a job. Lola's big break comes when she is invited to dance at a wedding for a rich bride and groom. Ismahan tells her to be wary, suggesting that "it's only because you are blond that you are exotic." A dancer's fame has a short shelf life, she emphasizes. Lola ends up being a success the night of the wedding, much to the chagrin of the other dancers, one of whom states, "I didn't know we were hir-ing from the States now."

As the film comes to a close, Lola the Outsider is finally accepted, forcing her rivals to admit that she's "not bad for a foreigner." While dancing at the wedding, she is also noticed by Madame Aïda, owner of the famous Nile Tower, the crème de la crème of belly dancing, cabaret-like shows. It is also the establishment where Ismahan danced regularly at the peak of her career. At the Nile Tower, Lola becomes the lead attraction, bringing in international crowds. Her routines mix East and West, belly dancing and Broadway show dances that are reminiscent of both Hollywood and Egyptian classic films. In one scene, Lola comes out onstage in a top hat and spats, singing her eponymous song. Following this act, she does a number in a tradi-tional belly-dancing costume.

A resounding theme of the film is the universal values that exist in our globalized world. As Carmen Lebbos explains in an interview, the film is really about two women from opposite cultures who find common ground. Ismahan is the classical Arab woman, whom Lebbos describes as "closed" due to the societal norms to which women are expected to adhere. Although from the more relaxed Lebanon, Leb-bos maintains that her character is an Egyptian woman living alone in Cairo, an excessively patriarchal society that is unforgiving and judgmental. Lola becomes Ismahan's confidante and only link to the outside world. She slowly reveals to the young woman that because of a prying photographer who took a picture of her as she shielded an admirer, her husband had to divorce her. The admirer, who we later learn is the impresario Nacer, has never stopped longing for her and leaves notes by her door every morning. These are left unanswered because Ismahan feels too ashamed over her divorce and broken home. For her public indiscretion, she is treated as a "whore" and harassed every time she ventures outside.

Ayouch's film dwells on certain preconceived notions about men and women, both Western and Arab. The contrast between what is viewed as "free" and open in the West, juxtaposed to the enclosed, hermetically sealed Arab East, dictates much of the dialogue and the context of the film. Arab men are often manipulators of women and operate with machismo in order to seduce them. In one scene, impresario Nacer tells Lola to forget her Egyptian beau because he will never be able to be true to her due to the power his family has over him and the stifling traditions of his culture: "When a Western man falls in love, he marries who he wants; when an Arab man falls in love, he marries someone else." Women are free only onstage, in the belly-dancing milieus of the seedy café where Lola works and finally befriends her coworkers, and as stars in Nile Tower.

Ayouch's choice of theme, which automatically precludes setting the film in Egypt, demonstrates to Moroccan audiences that there are "other" Arab countries that are much more hostile to women in public space. Contrasting the two worlds of the United States and Egypt on the Moroccan screen begs audiences to ask the question: Where do Moroccan women position themselves between these poles of feminine (dis)enfranchisement? Ismahan is also caught in the middle of extremes and universalities about Arab women. Her slow emancipation from the fetters of Egyptian traditionalism and the weight of her society's judgment of her personal life are read as standard texts in the gender-divided societies of the Arab world.

It is only after an outside influence, Lola, penetrates her dark, foreboding world that Ismahan can be liberated from the shackles of her past. This liberation is physically portrayed in the slow changes in her style of dress. In the initial stages of her rapport with Lola, she continues to cover her head with a scarf and wear a dark, hijab-like dress that covers her from head to foot. She explains to Lola how to do certain belly-dancing moves from her chair, thus refusing to engage physically with her past. It is only after being influenced by Lola's light American "go for it" naïveté and energetic will that Ismahan finally comes out of her shell. The colors of her dresses become brighter, her veil is shed, and her hair is let down, tied only with bright ribbons. Her home, too, breaks the chains of the past. The dark vines and trees that have grown up around the house are cut back to let light in through the windows. Ismahan begins working in her garden, weeding and cultivating her roses, which had succumbed to years of neglect.

When Lola finally does decide to go back to America after her successful run as leading belly dancer at Nile Tower, she is a woman transformed. In a speech she makes to her adoring audience at Nile Tower at the end of her show, she acknowledges that Americans in general are naive about Arab cultures and that she must go home to "bring Egyptian culture to the US" and to tell her fellow citizens that Egyptians are "welcoming." Yet before she goes, she publicly attributes her success as a belly dancer to Ismahan, much to the shock of the crowd, who is well aware of the fallen star's past. Nacer, sitting in the audience, realizes that he must convince Ismahan that he loves her still and wants to be with her no matter the social stigma that is attached. Ayouch's message that individual happiness should take precedence over sociocultural traditions and mores is blatant.

Nabyl Ayouch's film, although lighthearted and glitzy, is more about extracting and then studying human reactions to stereotypes than about pitting East against West. His film is no more Arab than it is American, as he focuses on the human connections that are possible and that extend beyond barriers of race, ethnicity, nationality, and religious conviction.

Leïla Marrakchi's Marock *(2005):* *Being Jewish in Contemporary Morocco*

Thirty-two-year-old Leïla Marrakchi's first feature-length film, *Marock* (2005), reflects the current debates and sociocultural dilemmas faced by a society in transition. Her depiction of the teenage love between a Muslim girl and a Jewish boy in the upscale neighborhoods of Casablanca's richest enclaves succeeded in opening up a nasty debate, revealing Morocco's own brand of "culture wars." The film attacked not only sexual taboos but also the larger questions of religious tolerance, archaic class structures, and the economic disparity between rich and poor in contemporary Moroccan society. The film was criticized on the right by Morocco's conservative Islamic party, the PJD (Parti de la justice et du développement, Party of Justice and Development), as "attacking the sacred values of Islam and good morals,"[5] and hailed on the left by the more globally connected, urban youth of the country's most recent generations for having challenged, as one critic notes, "the fundamental myths (religious and other) of the legendary social hypocrisy of Morocco." Needless to say, the film can be read as a metaphor for a schizophrenic society that seeks to locate its contemporary identity somewhere between the vestiges of the past and the possibilities of the future.[6]

This analysis explores *Marock* as a societal metaphor that captures the sociocultural climate of a country today striving to be tolerant and inclusive as it seeks to vanquish the negative remnants of its past. In the history of Moroccan cinema, few films made by either men or women have generated as much controversy as Leïla Marrakchi's *Marock*. Upon its release, the film's publicity posters alluded to its basic content, which promised a tantalizing story of "youth . . . its quest for liberty . . . its thirst for all that's forbidden." The filmmaker tested her society's increased openness as she compelled audiences to think about the clashes inherent in her society along the lines of identity, nationality, religion, gender, and tradition.[7] Although the script is somewhat weak on story line—a basic boy-meets-girl love story in which the boy, who drinks and drives too fast, dies in a car wreck in the end—it is bold in the statements it makes about contemporary Moroccan culture. Marrakchi's film, with a budget of 1.8 million euros, was a box-office success both at home and abroad. In 2005 in France, the film enjoyed an audience of 150,000 viewers and won the prestigious "Un certain regard" prize at the Cannes Film Festival (Boukhari 2006, n.p.).

Rita, a seventeen-year-old Muslim girl, and Youri, a seventeen-year-old Jewish boy, are living life in the fast lane in the rich, bourgeois areas of Casablanca as the Lead Years are waning (toward the end of the 1990s). The time frame of the film is significant in that it denotes the *jeunesse* of Morocco as situated on the cutting edge of the new, more liberal reforms about to take place a few years later in the post–Hassan II era. Their nightclubbing, drinking, and illicit sexual exploits debunk the usual, picturesque views of rural and poor Morocco that are the general backdrops for the majority of Moroccan films. Marrakchi reveals that, yes, there are very rich, elite people in Morocco who live in Western comfort, drive BMWs and Mercedes, occupy villas rivaling those found in Beverly Hills, and who are essentially removed from the realities of 99 percent of the population. These elite echelons of Casablanca are constrained by no barriers, as revealed through the character of Rita's brother, Mao, who killed a street kid as he drove too fast through Casablanca's poor neighborhoods. To avoid jail time, Mao's father paid off the poor family for the loss of their child and sent his son to London.

Rita and Youri, high school students at Lycée Lyautay, a well-known Casablanca French-speaking high school for the rich and famous (modeled on the French public secular school), fall in love right before the baccalaureate exams that will subsequently ensure them access to the prestigious universities of Europe and elsewhere abroad. Their education is in French and, even among themselves, the language is predominantly French, provoking one critic to denounce the film as the product of "the maneuvers of new lobbies that hide behind coproduction. . . . [It is] a film [that] uses images to transmit an ideology that defaces the values of Morocco and Moroccans. It's a means to hide acculturation and the new francophonie."[8] The criticism was aimed primarily not at the sexually explicit scenes— which a few years ago would never have made it past censorship— but rather at what was perceived as the promotion of "a Zionist message" against Islam.

One of the most provocative scenes for Islamic conservatives occurs halfway through the film when Rita makes love to Youri, who wears the Star of David around his neck. Rita can't take her eyes off the emblem, so Youri takes it off and hangs it around her neck, stating, "I'll give it to you, so that you won't look at it anymore and will think of other things." This act was viewed primarily by the PJD Islamist party as a metaphorical conquest of Islam by Zionist operators. Marrakchi (who is married to a French Jewish film producer and director) states that it was the scene that "a mis le feux aux poudres" (literally translated: lit the fire under the powder keg).[9]

Scenes that seem more for shock value rather than screenplay development are repeated throughout the film. Yet the filmmaker's ultimate message (stated by Youri) that "we are all Moroccans first and Muslims or Jews second" is monumental and resonates profoundly in a country that, only a year before the film's release, suffered deadly terrorist bombings by Islamic fundamentalists in several Casablancan Jewish neighborhoods. Sitting in Youri's BMW before going to celebrate the successful outcome of their exams, the young couple discuss the future of their relationship and how to reconcile religious differences:

> YOURI: You Muslims want everyone to convert, but you don't make any effort [to convert] yourselves.
> RITA: I don't give a damn about their stupid religion. . . . All I want to do is to kiss you when I want to, and where I want to. . . .

Further criticism was directed at Marrakchi for choosing to time the events of the film during Ramadan, the holiest month of the year.

Her characters show irreverence for the prescriptions of the sacred month—Rita refuses to fast, claiming she has her period (which allows her to avoid the ritual), and her father, who is seen and heard very little in the film, states in a one-liner: "If I had to fast one more day, I would have ended up killing someone." These comments are coupled with many derisive remarks about traditional rituals in Islam, including the most provocative scene in the film, where Rita barges in on her praying brother, Mao, as he lies prostrate on the floor. In skimpy hot-pink shorts and tight-fitting, spaghetti-strapped tank top, Rita ridicules her brother's newfound devotion to prayer:

> RITA: Mao, where's the blue jeans that you . . .
> *She stops. Before her, Mao, prostrate on the floor, is praying.*
> RITA: What's going on with you? Did you fall on your head? Have you gone crazy? Do you think you are in Algeria or what? Are you going to become a "barbu" (an Islamic fanatic), is that it?
> *Mao ignores her and continues praying without paying any attention.*
> RITA: Dad ! Mom ! Your son has gone crazy! . . . Okay, where is that fucking pair of jeans. . . . Okay, I found them, thanks. . . . Hey, you're pointing in the wrong direction, Mecca is over there!

One of the most critical debates surrounding the film was whether or not it should be censored. Should a film, viewed by many as attacking the values of Islam and promoting a more Zionist message as some critics stated, be censured in a country whose official religion is Islam, and whose leader of the state is also the leader of the faithful? In an in-depth article published by *Le journal hebdomadaire* in June 2006, the debate is scrutinized from the two opposing sides. The article, "Marock: Le vrai débat" (Marock: The true debate), presents views from the left and the right of the censorship argument. Pundits from PJD supporters, who condemned the film, and secular intellectuals on the left of Moroccan politics, who supported it, are interviewed. In a country professing to support democratic reform and foster an open society, the debate certainly encompassed many questions about identity, freedom of speech, and religious tolerance. Abdellah Zaâzaâ, president of the Association RESAQ, which gives aid to young people in poor areas, states that the criticism and call for censorship of the film by the PJD party was a direct attack on those who struggle for "the construction of a Just State" that is all-inclusive, regardless of religious affiliation or ethnicity. He positively viewed the film, stating that it captured the universality of the problems that all Moroccans face:

> Notably, I discovered that the young of the bourgeoisie confront the same problems as those in poor areas: sexual frustration, the problem of virginity, the place of Jewish Moroccans in this country. And this last point is the most important: Morocco lost 300,000 of its Jewish citizens between 1950 and 1960. And now, when we speak of MREs, we only evoke those who are Muslim and not Jewish.[10]

Exodus and immigration are also subjects of commentary in *Marock*, as is the case in *Où vas-tu Moshé?* (Where are you going, Moshé?, Hassan Benjelloun, 2007). Not only does the filmmaker refer to the Jews who left in the 1950s and 1960s following Morocco's independence, she also alludes to the massive brain drain of young people of all faiths who leave their country in search of a better, more lucrative life in Europe, Canada, and the United States: "Tout le monde veut se casser d'ici" (Everyone wants to get the hell outta here), notes one of Youri's friends. As Jews, Youri's parents are contemplating leaving Morocco for the United States because, as he tells Rita, "they've been scared since the beginning of the Gulf War" (the first one, that is). Perceived religious persecution, however, is not the only reason Rita ultimately leaves for Paris to continue her studies after Youri dies and her friend Sophia flees to Canada to get married. Rather, Marrakchi points out that one of the tragedies of contemporary Morocco is the unwillingness of those who have money and intellectual capital, no matter their religion, to stay and invest in their homeland to positively change the infrastructure, educational levels, and financial opportunities for everyone.

Marrakchi's film obliges all Moroccans—Muslims, Jews, rich, and middle class—to ask themselves some tough questions that will continue to expose one of the defining challenges that plague the New Morocco: how to convince the population that these troubling societal issues, as the journalists writing the article "Marock: Le vrai debat" point out, are "real problems linked to our society."[11] *Marock* offers a telling commentary on the undebated and not yet confronted realities of the past and the present. It clearly reveals that there are still many skeletons in Morocco's closet clamoring to get out.

Ismaïl Ferroukhi's Le Grand Voyage *(2004): The Humanist Road Movie*

Ismaïl Ferroukhi's *Le grand voyage* (2004) is a sociorealist film text reflective of our globalized era. Ferroukhi's film is unique for the universal humanist messages it reveals. These include the internationalism of Islam as a religion of peace and how important it is for people of all faiths, growing up in the new millennium, to be tolerant. Ferroukhi has been one of the few filmmakers allowed into Mecca to film the hajj. This singular experience aids the filmmaker's goal of promoting Islam as a religion that brings together millions of diverse people from all corners of the world. *Le grand voyage* leaves a lasting impression on audiences that effectively counters today's stereotyping of Islam and Arab peoples in our post-9/11 world. Moreover, *Le grand voyage* is a film that counters the West's general view of Islam as hostile and unforgiving and as a religion that promotes only bombs and terrorism.

This analysis explores Ferroukhi's film as one that offers a social-realist commentary within a humanist perspective on the larger, international topics of our era. It is a film that scrutinizes the contemporary challenges of our time and seeks to rectify the miscomprehension we have about others (perceived disparities not only between Westerners and Muslims, but also between Muslims and Muslims), all the while dispelling the notion that we are incapable of living with one another in peace. Ferroukhi's film can be considered, as Edward Saïd remarks, as offering a new "discourse [on] humanism" that challenges the "canonical" in order to propose "unwelcome interventions" of the status quo that defines the world in which we live (Saïd 2004, 23).

Analyzing the film through its religious spirituality encourages us to challenge the perceived notion that humanism can only be grounded in terms of secularism as Saïd notes: "The core of humanism is the secular notion that the historical world is made by men and women, and not by God, and that it can be understood rationally. . . . That we can really know only what we make or, to put it differently, we can know things according to the way they are made" (Saïd 2004, 11). Ferroukhi works against the notion that secularism is incongruous with trust in God, spirituality, and divine intervention. Rather, his film demonstrates what Saïd terms as a "worldliness" that offers both a secular humanist and a spiritually determined hermeneutic system of understanding. In short, Ferroukhi demonstrates that the secular can be integrated into the spiritual to create a space for hybrid humanism. The film suggests that secularism should not have the monopoly on the "promise of universality and reasonableness," as Janet Jakobsen and Ann Pellegrini point out in their volume titled *Secularisms*. Secularism, because it is inherently moralistic, as the scholars note, can connect "a number of elements—most notably, modernity, reason, and universalism—into a network that has strong moral as well as descriptive implications. The broad historical narrative generally associated with secularization develops these moral implications by describing change over time" (2008, 4). Ferroukhi's film offers an excellent example of the increased global foresight of the Moroccan film industry to engage in humanist questions since the end of the Lead Years. It equally exemplifies current sociopolitical and cultural discussions, debates, and revelations that are important on both sides of the Mediterranean.

What is most profound about the themes of many contemporary MRE productions is that they describe an international universality that allows audiences all over the world to enter a realm that, while portraying Moroccans, also renders their "being in the world" in the context of a universal humanism that is identifiable for all audiences regardless of nationality, race, religion, ethnicity, or secular beliefs.

Le grand voyage is Ismaïl Ferroukhi's first feature-length film. When it was first screened at international film festivals in 2004, it was described as a "gentle, culturally loaded road movie."[12] It is the story of a French-Moroccan teenager, Réda (who has lived all his life in Marseille, France), who is forced by his very traditional father to accompany him on a pilgrimage to Mecca. The defining difficulty for Réda is that his father insists on making the trip by car. Midway through the film, Réda obliges his father to tell him why he did not want to go by plane. The father replies: "God says . . . to go by foot, and if not by foot, by mule, and if not by mule, by car." In short, it is better to choose the most laborious path in order to retain the purity of the hajj.

Réda also follows an arduous path. His involves assimilation into secular French society as a young, second-generation Maghrebian who shares little with his traditional parents' homeland or their former life in Morocco. Obtaining his baccalaureate, an obligatory hurdle for all French high-school-age youth but one that will ensure his entry more easily into mainstream France, is hindered by his father's insistence that he accompany him on the religious pilgrimage. The baccalaureate exam is only two weeks away, and for Réda it will be the second and last opportunity to evade the immigrant life of the *banlieues*. The young man's love for a non-Muslim white French girl, whose picture he longingly looks at throughout the film, is also another aspect of life in France that his father finds difficult to accept.

Although Ferroukhi's film often panders to clichés about immigrant life in France and, more generally, about father-son relationships, such as the old not understanding the young or, as one Moroccan film critic states, "a road movie that operates under the contrived notion that old people are smart and young people are big dumb animals," the story does redeem itself both by the beauty of the camerawork and by the more global, humanist messages that it reveals (Gonzales 2005, n.p.). In the throngs of people, scenes capture an amazing event that takes place with "two million extras," as Peter Bradshaw of the *Guardian* notes.[13] Islam, viewed as a religion that brings together millions of diverse people from all corners of the world, leaves a lasting impression on audiences that effectively counters today's stereotyping in the West.

Metaphorically, the unity of Islam is depicted with wide-panning shots of young Réda being absorbed into the throngs of people as he searches for his father, who does not return from the last leg of his pilgrimage, the walk to the Kaaba. Réda's absorption into the mass of humanity present in Mecca is crafted with deft camerawork and wide-angle aerial shots, showing the young boy in a yellow T-shirt and jeans, very Westernized in his demeanor, being engulfed by thousands of serene pilgrims in white robes and headscarves. Although standing out in his Western attire, Réda is surrounded by a multiculturalism that is also unified, metaphorically evoking the idea that faith allows believers from all parts of the globe to come together in peaceful harmony.

Human compassion and forgiveness also play central roles in the development of Ferroukhi's screenplay. Both father and son are confronted with the choice of whether or not to forgive each other, as well as others they encounter along the road, after several adverse incidents. As they cross the continents of Europe and Asia, making their way to Saudi Arabia, their love and respect for each other are repeatedly tested. In Turkey they meet Mustapha, who helps them negotiate with the Turkish immigration authorities who stop them on the border. When Mustapha expresses a desire to come with them on the hajj, Réda's father categorically refuses, acting on a premonition. His son perseveres in convincing him to change his mind, and the Turk accompanies them but then is accused by the father of stealing their money. Jettisoned from the car, the Turk is left behind, but later Réda discovers that his father had forgotten (intentionally? we are not sure) the money was hidden in an old sock. The son, who never suspected Mustapha would steal, chastises his father for not trusting a fellow Muslim as the father has always preached. Subsequently, Réda's drinking and clubbing compel his father at one point to try to leave him behind and embark on the rest of the journey by foot. After both these incidents have tested their love for each other, Réda asks his father: "On ne pardonne pas dans ta religion?" (Don't people pardon in your religion?). In the end, father and son are finally able to find middle ground in their differences, recognizing that they will always be separated by religious ideals, experiences, cultural references, and generational divides.

A characteristic of many Moroccan films, Ferroukhi makes a point of blending the surreal, the spiritual, and the real in order to depict, as scholar Farid Al-Zahi notes, "a space for mystery and expectation," wherein the characters have "an opportunity for liberation from the self and other." This space becomes a milieu of negotiation for both father and son because they are caught "between loss of sense and meaning, and between the present and the future" (Al-Zahi 1995, 268). Both are confronted with the surreal possibilities in life when an elderly Bulgarian woman stops them in the middle of nowhere, gets into the backseat of their car, and then motions them to continue straight ahead. The few words she speaks are incomprehensible to the father and son. They finally leave her in a hotel because, as Réda states, "cette vieille me fait peur" (that old lady gives me the creeps).

Long after they abandon her, he is haunted in his dreams and daydreams by her presence. When they are stuck in Sofia, Bulgaria, while his father is hospitalized after having almost frozen to death in their stalled car as they tried to cross the mountains, Réda swears he sees her through a bus window standing on a street corner. Dressed in black and the traditional attire of a past that is still present in Central Europe, she is for Réda a harbinger of ill fortune, symbolically representing the fragility of his father's quest and his own misgivings about their journey.

Réda's nightmares are also intermingled with the reality he is living on the journey with his father. The gulf between father and son is metaphorically rendered in the vast plains of desert sands that increasingly separate them. Moving further and further away from the secular, European culture he knows, Réda is hurled closer and closer to the metaphysical and spiritual East of his father's origins. The desert is a surreal place of dreams and realities. At one point, Réda wakes up in the sands of the Sahara to see his father, dressed in the traditional clothes of the nomads who live in southern Morocco, walk by with a herd of sheep. When he calls out to him, the young man begins sinking into the sand.

In reality, where the desert is a place of purgatory for Réda, it is a haven for his father, offering a sense of renewal and open space in which to breathe. As they approach Mecca, they meet other pilgrims from all over the Muslim world with whom the father converses in Arabic. His son remains on the peripheries of the pilgrims' space, unable to communicate in his father's tongue.

Language barriers also heighten the misunderstandings between father and son. Réda's knowledge of Moroccan Arabic is limited to a few phrases he can use to respond to his father. His father's insistence on speaking only Arabic to him, even though he knows French, alludes, on a larger scale, to the divide between immigrant parents and their children born in France—a resounding theme in the works of many MRE filmmakers. The first generation seeks to hold on to the country of origin's roots; the second wants only to assimilate into Europe. Réda has more facility with English than his parents' mother tongue, which he uses to negotiate with passport agents, hotel owners, and those he asks for directions. Ferroukhi's subtext is that in today's global society, Réda's generation understands the interconnectedness that a lingua franca brings rather than the hermetically sealed language of the parents.

Le grand voyage ends at the final destination of the father's pilgrimage. When the old man goes to pray one morning at the Kaaba, he doesn't come back. His son later finds him in the morgue. His body is washed and buried by Réda and the pilgrims they met on their journey to the holy site. Réda takes back with him to France not only the memory of his father's last journey, but also a newly found comprehension of his own being in the world with respect to his religion, homeland, and heritage.

Ferroukhi does not preach for the supremacy of Islam over other religions, but rather emphasizes the diverse connections between men and women from many countries and ethnicities that can be made in peaceful harmony when they come together to practice their faith. The film's themes suggest that people are compassionate and that, often in our contemporary world, we ignore this singular human trait. Ferroukhi's film text is both a secular and a spiritual humanist project that, as Saïd notes, "constructs fields of coexistence rather than fields of battle" (2004, 141). Such a work must promote the idea that, again according to Saïd, "peace cannot exist without equality; this is an intellectual value desperately in need of reiteration, demonstration, and reinforcement" (142).

Films at Home: Taboos, Controversies, Conflicts,
and Revisiting the Past in the Present

While MRE films have been shown at film festivals and on theater screens in the United States and Europe in increasing numbers in the last few years, so-called Moroccan cinema at home, the films not distributed outside the country's borders, must confront its own set of unique hurdles. Film critic Mustapha Mesnaoui claims in a 2005 interview in the newspaper *Le matin* that Moroccan film lacks vision, and this is one of the reasons for waning audience attendance. He created quite a scandal in cinema circles when he dismissed the entire industry by stating, "Nous n'avons pas de cinéma marocain" (We don't have a Moroccan cinema) (Ziane 2005, n.p.). Mesnaoui accuses Moroccan filmmakers of avoiding their sociocultural responsibilities. Additionally he claims that cinema plays no role in shaping policy in civic society. Contrary to his views, Moroccan cinema is very sociopolitically engaged and reflects the transitions the country is making and enduring in contemporary times.

Since 1999 filmmakers, both male and female, working solely in the country have tackled a host of topics that ten years ago would never have been put on the screen. While there are many films that offer engaging commentary on transitions taking place in Morocco, the following films most aptly capture the polemics of the sociocultural and political shifts in society since the end of the Lead Years. These films also prove Mesnaoui's criticism is ill-placed. Indeed, Moroccan cinema is sociopolitically committed and filmmakers do work as social activists, seeking to educate their audiences about their own history, politics, and religion in the present as well as in the past.

The screenplays of the films presented in the second half of this chapter were shot primarily in Moroccan dialectical Arabic, filmed entirely in Morocco, and date from 1999 to the present. They offer audiences didactic, social-realist screenplays depicting life in contemporary times or provide revisions of stories that need to be retold to favor the voices of the unheard: the poor female victims of corrupt policemen in *Tabite or Not Tabite*; the Jewish exodus from Morocco immediately after independence in the early 1960s in *Où vas-tu Moshé?*; and the poverty and despair conquered by the power of friendship as portrayed in *La symphonie marocaine*. These films do not propose any prescriptions for solutions to the host of socioeconomic disparities they explore or rectification for the errors and abuses of the past. Rather, they expose issues that filmmakers believe are crucial for society to address if progress is to be made. They equally challenge certain models adopted in the name of modernity and cast a critical eye on contemporary culture.

The events, for example, on which Nabyl Lahlou's *Tabite or Not Tabite* are based have been referenced in film magazines as comprising a historical moment that gripped the entire population in a "grave tourbillon [qui] pollua l'atmosphère du Maroc" (a grave whirlwind that polluted the atmosphere of Morocco) (Tizourgni and Guennouni 2005, n.p.). "L'affaire Tabite," although focusing on a past event, reveals important questions about power and the abuse of it that still haunt Morocco in the present. The film reminds audiences of the hurdles persistently facing those striving to build a democratic society that is just and free of corruption.

Kamal Kamal's La Symphonie Marocaine *(2005):* ### *Only Music Can Save the World*

Kamal Kamal has become internationally known for his very atypical films. Director and producer of two feature-length productions, *Tayf Nizar* (Nizar's Ghost, 2001) and *La symphonie marocaine* (2005), Kamal Kamal focuses on the lost, the marginalized, and the dark specters that continue to haunt Moroccan society. In 2007, as organizer of a colloquium on Moroccan film, the filmmaker emphasized that "film can't change the world, but can change ideas."[14] *Tayf Nizar*, made in 2001 and distributed across Morocco in 2002, revisits atrocities committed during the Lead Years. "Nizar" refers to Nizar Kabani, the Syrian poet and statesman who fought for freedom throughout his life (1923–98). Paralleling the reference to Nizar, Khalid, a doctor in Casablanca, is engulfed in an investigation in the city that eventually uncovers mass graves of political dissidents killed during the Lead Years. Interestingly, *tayf* means "he who has completed the procession ritual around the Kaaba," . . . or, in the figurative sense, "he who has turned" or "he who one has made turn like a dumb animal."[15] This secondary meaning is significant, since the film's entire dialogue was shot in classical Arabic, which surprised Moroccan audiences as well as those across the Arab world. Although not very well received in Morocco, the language choice was perceived across the Arab world as an attempt to make a universally Arabic language film that would rival the box-office sales of Western movies.

La symphonie marocaine, screened in theaters four years later, was very different in scope from Kamal Kamal's first work and proved to be a success among audiences at home (if not among critics) primarily because of its theme: The film championed the plight of "les petites gens" (the little people)—the poor and destitute—of contemporary Moroccan society. The work also reflects the filmmaker's own first love, music. Born in 1961, Kamal Kamal studied the traditional musical forms of Morocco such as *musique gharnati* and the pedagogical *solfège* technique, which relies on teaching pupils how to sight-sing. Each note of a musical score is assigned a solfège syllable (or "sol-fa syllable"). The filmmaker integrates his experience at the Conservatory of Oujda throughout the film into characters who know only instinctively how to play their instruments, and then learn to sight-read in order to play the musical score of an orchestra. In 1986, Kamal Kamal organized the Festival des arts populaires (Traditional Arts Festival) in Saïdia and, two years later, the Festival of Rai Music in Oujda. In 1993, he moved to Paris to study screenwriting, which he completed in 1996. Since the late 1990s, he has worked in Morocco on video clips for television and his own film screenplays.

Kamal Kamal's international work, as well as his goal of blending East with West musically and thematically, influenced the themes of his second feature-length film. *La symphonie marocaine* appeals to international audiences because it draws on universal human emotions and themes such as: There is no honor in war; in poverty there is beauty; and music is a human source of inspiration that can transcend divisions between classes, ethnicities, and nations. Kamal Kamal's plot is basic and, as he notes, is meant to show that "only those who give with their heart remain in people's memories."[16] The film unfolds around the story of Hamid, who in 1982 deserts the Moroccan army to go and fight in Lebanon against the Israeli invasion. Although a military man, he is also an accomplished accordion player and composer. Hamid, played by the famous Moroccan musician and actor Younes Migri, comes home maimed (he lost an arm) and mentally tormented from the war after having fought against the Israelis for several years. Embittered, handicapped, and destitute, he reflects on his past life and the futility of war. At one moment he states: "Arabs and Israelis are all the same in death. . . . When their bodies were carbonized, lying there on the ground, I couldn't tell the difference, no nationality marked them."

Hamid lives with his demons, "his monsters," and with other has-beens and destitute former musicians in train boxcars parked next to a municipal dump in the port area of Casablanca. Following the death of Balahcen, an old inhabitant of the dump who plays the traditional Moroccan lute, Hamid and Kafi (also a composer and music teacher who has fallen on hard times) rally their fellow musically gifted misfits around a dream. The composers will form an orchestra to play in a competition at Albert Hall in London. Both men believe that their symphony will honor Balahcen's memory while also winning the competition for best musical score. The prize will be an invitation to London to perform their music. The hard part is convincing Kafi's former students to come to the scrapyard to practice, since the real Philharmonic Orchestra of Morocco is "too expensive."

In Kafi and Hamid's orchestral score there is one defining solo for accordion, which Hamid wrote when he could play the instrument with two hands. This is no longer possible until one day Kafi introduces him to Ahlam, a young woman whose mother died of a heart attack, leaving her an orphan. Kafi explains to Hamid that since she has nowhere to go, he must look after her. We later learn that inadvertently Hamid caused Ahlam's mother's death when he rushed by on his motor scooter and ripped her purse from her arm, knocking the elderly woman down in the street. Because the purse contained her heart medicine, she was unable to recover. Ahlam "sings like an angel" and also can play the accordion. She will be the voice and the hands of Hamid when the time comes to perform his solo piece for accordion in the symphony.

The film, although weak on plot, encourages reflection on the human condition of our times replete with wars, injustices, and abuses of human rights: "Misery can push us to madness," notes one of the musicians as he comments on not only his life in the margins, but the state of human societies that cannot rid themselves of violence. The orchestra is made up of young men and women who are talented, yet alienated by a society that makes no place for them. In a larger context, Kamal Kamal's principal themes are focused on entreating us to invest in young talent, disavowing the need to make war and forgiving those who have committed heinous acts. Indeed, forgiveness and inclusion are two themes that underlie the film.

Kafi entreats Rebeba, a young Moroccan French-speaking Jewish woman (who is also a former student and magnificent cellist), to renounce packing her bags to immigrate to Canada. He convinces her to stay, to be a part of the orchestra, to forgive her country for its racism against its Jewish population, and to honor her father, who chose to stay in Morocco as a Jew. His plea, "You can still achieve your dreams here," echoes the general sentiment promoted since 1999 by Mohammed VI that Morocco must make peace with its past and the thousands of Jews who were more or less forced to leave in the 1960s. Rebeba asks for Hamid's pardon after having accused him of clandestinely joining the Lebanese army specifically to kill Jews in Lebanon. Ahlam eventually pardons Hamid for the death of her mother in the closing scenes, telling him: "If ever I meet the man who ran my mother down, I will forgive him."

Forgiveness is a virtue that the characters easily embrace. Improving their overall state of well-being, however, proves to be more complicated. The filmmaker's poignant criticism of the rampant poverty and the waste of human talent that result from bureaucratic elitism and corruption in Moroccan society are themes not lost on audiences. "You get a diploma from the conservatory and you still find yourself living in a scrapyard," one of the musicians points out, thus indicating the futility of striving to better one's life in a country that is ruled by an autocratic, powerful elite.

The characters, however, continue to struggle against misfortune, planning to go forward with their musical goals. When they are not accepted to compete in London for the British prize, they decide to build their orchestra's stage in the scrapyard in order to perform Kafi and Hamid's composition. The overwhelming socioeconomic hurdles of the characters, complicated by physical impairments (Hamid's lost arm, the orchestra saxophonist's incapacity to speak and his slight retardation) and lack of resources (water, electricity), make succeeding elusive, but also represent the driving thematic force of the film. When Ahlam falls, injuring herself and smashing Hamid's accordion, which she was holding, the symphony's solo is almost lost. Hamid must resort to stealing an instrument from a shop, only to have an accident on his moped on the way back that gravely injures him. Although he arrives with the accordion in time for the orchestra's opening and Ahlam promises to play his solo to honor his work, he knows that he will die from his injuries. He asks to be moved closer to the stage so that he can hear the solo when the time comes. However, when Ahlam is supposed to play, the stolen accordion will not work. She then resorts to standing and singing the music as Hamid slowly dies, confronting a masked demon for the last time.

The melodrama of the film detracts somewhat from Kamal's universal messages against war in the Arab world and, more particularly, outcries against poverty and inequality at home. Critics found fault also with the presence of the royal princess, who is invited to attend the scrapyard performance. Although the filmmaker's insertion of the princess in the film symbolically pays homage to Mohammed VI's dedication to the poor (he is known as the King of the Poor), this "graft onto the screenplay is noxious," notes Karim Boukhari, writing for *TelQuel*, a leading Francophone weekly newsmagazine. The princess, dressed in a traditional caftan, arrives in her limousine to fanfare and pomp, which detracts from Kamal's social criticism and gives in to "sticking political correctness into the film, which, in the beginning, was not at all the filmmaker's intentions" (Boukhari 2006, n.p.).

Though the film falls short in making resonant social commentaries, it is unique in its appreciation of music, particularly certain styles that are indigenous to Morocco. The film's musical repertoire includes pop music inspired by the tunes of well-known 1970s Moroccan groups such as Jil Jilala and singer Lemchaheb, as well as the traditional music of Dart bina doura and Khlili, recognizable to all Moroccans. These pop and traditional groups are juxtaposed to "la grande musique"—the classical compositions—played by the Conservatory of Music in Casablanca. "By rearranging these songs, I wanted to first pay my respects to the wonderful groups that have rocked many generations for thirty years and also to pay homage to traditional Moroccan music," explains Kamal Kamal.[17] Music has the

Fig. 2.1. Nabyl Lahlou, Rabat, Morocco, 2007

ability to heal and to transgress social barriers of class and, as the filmmaker points out, "musique peut sauver le monde" (music can save the world).

Nabyl Lahlou's Tabite or Not Tabite *(2006):* Straight Up in Morocco

Nabyl Lahlou's film about "l'affaire Tabite," a well-known historical event that still looms large in the national psyche of Morocco, premiered in February 2007. Lahlou, known as the "Woody Allen" of Moroccan cinema, has a history of pushing limits in his surrealist cinematic representations of topical issues. A man of the stage first and foremost, Lahlou pays particular attention to detail as far as lighting and the diction of his actors are concerned. Although he has made eight feature-length films, he was barred from the screen for ten years in the 1990s because of several films in which he proposed controversial subjects that often criticized the status quo of Moroccan politics and societal norms and customs. Lahlou has enjoyed a long career that began in 1978 with the film *Ali Kanfoudi*, and continued through the 1980s with *Le gouverneur de l'île de Chakerbakerben* (The governer of Chakerbakerben Island, 1980), *Brahim yach?* (1982), *La nuit du crime* (The night of the crime, 1982), *L'homme qui brait* (The man who brays, 1984), *Komany* (1990), *Les années de l'exil* (The years of exile, 2001), and the most recent, *Tabite or Not Tabite*.

Nabyl Lahlou continues his exploration of the surreal within the real in his eighth feature-length film, *Tabite or Not Tabite*. This latest production is in keeping with the filmmaker's avant-garde style evident in previous films such as *L'homme qui brait*, *Komany*, and *Les années d'exil*. Lahlou's title, a play on words, depicts Tabite, a corrupt police officer, for who he really is and was—a sexual predator. It also draws on the ironic humor of three languages: *Tabite* in Arabic means "straight up, inflexible and solid," reflecting, of course, sexual innuendo. In rather vulgar slang, *ta bite* in French means "your dick" (penis), and, of course, "to be or not to be" implies the stage of Shakespeare and classical Western theater. Indeed, many scenes are shot in theatrical settings, thus revealing Lahlou's talent as a man of the theater. His blending of the surreal with the reality of Morocco's oppressive political history is a unique quality of the film.

Tabite or Not Tabite, formulated within the framework of the crime-spy genre, explores the real-life story of police commissioner Tabite, who in the 1980s filmed himself as he committed a series of rapes. Tabite's crimes also serve as a platform to scrutinize the many years of dirty politics, torture, and abuse of human rights in Morocco during the Lead Years. For years, Tabite was able to cover up his crimes with bribes and power wielding because most of his victims were poor and defenseless. The perpetrator, like so many other abusers of power, was able to avoid punishment until the early 1990s—that is, until two of his victims, who happened also to be the daughters of rich and influential men, decided to press charges. Lahlou makes no concessions in exposing the fact that when the elite are threatened, action is taken. In 1992, the story was exposed in the press, and Tabite was tried and hanged.

Tabite's story reflects a time in Morocco during which police violence, torture, and abuse were inflicted upon the innocent or those from the political opposition who questioned the system and promoted transparency and free elections. Retaliation from the monarchy and the powerful forced thousands into political exile. One of the lead characters, Ali Brahma (played by Mourad Abderrahim), is an MRE who lives in France but returns to his homeland in 1992 for his father's funeral. Despite the fact that he left when he was fifteen, "can't read Arabic and only speaks a smattering of the local dialect," and doesn't observe the traditions of Ramadan (much to the chagrin of his brother, who accuses him of not being a "true Muslim"), he is enraptured by the politics of his country and the possibility that things might be changing. Ali becomes so intrigued by the Tabite story due to the journal articles and media hype he discovers in the press while in Morocco, he decides to write about it.

During the plane trip home to France, he meets Zakia Malik (played by Sophia Hadi, who is Nabyl Lahlou's wife), with whom he decides to write first a theater production based on the Tabite affair, and then a screenplay. It is at this point that the real and the surreal merge as Lahlou's film becomes a play within a film, connoting and contextualizing Moroccan history within the present. Zakia Malik is complex, becoming multiple persons and victims. She is first victimized by Tabite, who puts out her eye on the stick shift of his car (a phallic symbol alluding to his sexual crimes). As the representative and avenger of many women, she haunts him in his dreams, finally bringing him to justice. Zakia's role melds into a second as the wife of Zakaria Malik, a political dissident living in exile in Paris, who eventually decides to return to Morocco and become prime minister. Lahlou himself is "multiple," playing the roles of Tabite and Zakaria Malik throughout the film.

The film's intricacy metaphorically reflects the reality of Moroccan politics, particularly its warring factions and the nebulous power of a system—the *Makhzen*—whose omnipotence is impossible to combat.[18] Those who profited from the system, as the film denotes, were responsible for the torture and death of hundreds. The lucky few who were able to escape into exile wonder if the country will ever change. Indeed, much of the film's plot is narrated in French by exiled dissidents living in Paris. Like one of the lead characters, Amal Ayouch, they, too, fled to escape death but now seek assurance, at the end of the 1990s, that things have changed enough to go back. Encouraged by the ascension to the throne of King Mohammed VI in 1999, the change in power seems to bode well for a more favorable and just political climate.

Fig. 2.2. Sophia Hadi, actress and lead female role in *Tabite*, Casablanca, Morocco, 2007

However, when Zakia and Ali return to Morocco to promote their film, they are sadly dismayed by the fact that, although some things have changed, others continue to remain the same, and new hurdles abound. For example, "Les barbes qui poussent comme des champignons" (beards that spring up like mushrooms), as Ali remarks speaking in French, reveal the filmmakers' (Ali's et Lahlou's) concern for the increasing evidence of Islamic "intégrisme" (fundamentalism) in Morocco. The returnees' hesitancy to feel completely comfortable in their homeland is reflected at one point when Ali observes upon completion of his film, "Si on arrive à mettre en scène ce film ça veut dire que le Maroc a vraiment changé" (If we succeed in showing this film, it will mean that Morocco really has changed).

Tabite or Not Tabite captures a period of time, 1990–2005, that is mired by its precariousness on both social and political levels. Lahlou's goal is to paint metaphorically the reality of Morocco, past and present, through the horrors committed by Tabite, as he points out in an interview published in *Le journal hebdomadaire*:

> This event . . . is a platform for retracing many years of political life in Morocco, viewed by people who live in France

Fig. 2.3. Hassan Benjelloun, Casablanca, Morocco, 2009

and who want to come back. I evoked their impression that nothing has changed, that Morocco is still a police system, the testimonials of oppression, their hope. . . . I made this film . . . in order to express sadness but also the hope that our country can change. It is a positive film. (Sefrioui 2006, n.p.)

Although positive in some respects with regard to the changing political tides in Morocco, *Tabite or Not Tabite* concludes by drawing audiences' attention to the repetition of human rights abuse on a universal scale in our contemporary times. Although Morocco might be remaking itself and improving its record, Iraq, Abu Ghraib prison, and Afghanistan, for example, loom large as places of torture and abjection. These are the new playgrounds for other perpetrators of violence, notably, as Lahlou points out, George W. Bush, who is condemned for war crimes at the end of the film. The filmmaker's message is clear: The torturers have changed faces and nationalities, but they are still among us. The film denounces the torturers of not only the past but also the present. In 2006, Lahlou's references to the war in Iraq and the American occupation there promoted a universal plea for justice. In 2009, Tabite's very Moroccan story still resonates internationally as we are reminded that the abuse of human rights and the total disregard for human dignity are ever present in the twenty-first century.

Hassan Benjelloun's Où Vas-Tu Moshé? *(2007):* My Brother the Jew

In a 2009 interview, Hassan Benjelloun emphasized that he has always thought film should be used as a tool through which to influence audiences, candidly stating that "Moroccans do not have the luxury of making luxurious films [purely for entertainment value]."[19] In keeping with this credo, Benjelloun has become one of the tour de force in Moroccan cinema production since 2000, making films that encourage audiences to think about a variety of subjects. *Jugement d'une femme* (2000) tells the tale of a woman who is incarcerated for having killed her husband in self-defense as he tried to strangle her when she asked for a divorce. *La chambre noire* (2004) (analyzed in detail in chapter 4) revisits the random imprisonment of political activists in the 1970s during the most repressive period of the Lead Years. Benjalloun's most recent film, *Où vas-tu Moshé?* (2007), recaptures for the first time on-screen a history that is seldom discussed, that is, the mass exodus of Moroccan Jews to Israel and elsewhere in the early 1960s.

Although the film was critically praised, received some financial backing from Canada, and was widely shown in Canadian film festivals, the CCM, bowing to Moroccan authorities, mandated that Benjelloun not give the film the title he preferred: "My Brother the Jew." The memory of the 1960s exodus and the complicity of the Moroccan monarchy in facilitating the departure of thousands is still raw and ill-defined in the post–Lead Years era.[20] For Benjelloun the exodus is also personal, since as a boy he experienced the loss of Jewish friends from his town overnight. The filmmaker recalls that he went out in the street one day and all the doors and windows were boarded up. "I ran to my mother and asked, 'Why are all the doors shut?' She told me, 'They have all gone to Palestine.' It was the first time I had ever heard of Palestine."[21]

At the time of Moroccan independence in 1956, the Jewish population numbered almost 300,000. Mohammed V, known for having protected Jews first during WWII against the Vichy government's Nazi laws, and later during the throes of independence from the ultra-Islamic nationalists, was revered by the Jewish community. Yet, where

Mohammed V was considered a hero among them, his son, Hassan II, was their traitor. Seeking to build a strong Islamic state with deep ties to the Arab world, Hassan II encouraged the Zionists' call to populate the newly created Israel by fomenting rumors that Jews were no longer welcome in Morocco. By the late 1960s, particularly after the Six-Day War of 1967, thousands of Moroccan Jews had left the country for the United States, Canada, and France. In the twenty-first century, Mohammed VI's policy of openly inviting Jews back to Morocco, in an effort to revisit and rectify this open wound of the past, has had little success. Museums honoring Moroccan Jews have been opened in Agadir and Casablanca, but it remains to be seen if Jews will come home.

Although the largest Jewish populations were concentrated in Fez, Meknes, and Marrakech, Benjelloun chooses to set his film in Bejjad, a small village in the Atlas Mountains. Moshé is the barber who eventually leaves but who becomes a symbol for the brain drain and know-how that left with the Jewish population of Morocco, as captured in one scene between several village men drinking together in the local bar:

> FIRST MAN TO HIS FRIENDS: I don't understand why you're glad the Jews are leaving . . . Don't forget that among them is the doctor, the engineer, the accountant . . .
> SECOND: All the better. More work for Moroccans.
> THIRD: Sorry, but they're also Moroccans.

Although Moshé, the barber of the village, becomes a symbol for a persecuted community, the story focuses on Shlomo Bensoussan (Simon Elbaz), who is the local clock repairman and a musician who plays the traditional *oud* in a musical group made up of Jews and Muslims. Their most popular venue is Mustapha's bar, which every night hosts villagers of all faiths who drink and play chess together. The bar is the focal point where debates about religion, nationalism, and the changing political tides of the country are discussed. Through the information passed between clients in the bar, Benjelloun crafts a film that often is didactic and docurealist in scope as he seeks to inform audiences about what happened in the past. His goal is not to take sides, but to blame the forces of power that manipulated and coerced average Moroccans into making choices they did not want to make. Shlomo's religion is secondary to the affinity he feels for his identity as a Moroccan who loves his country and his village, and whose ancestors, he notes, are all buried in the village cemetery: "Can an old man like me leave his country? My life is here in Bejjad. All my friends, Jews, Muslims, Christians . . . I have everything I need."

Although all the Jews of the village, including his wife and daughter, board the bus to take them to Casablanca and then to a boat for Israel, Shlomo refuses to go. He ends up being the last Jew in the village of Bejjad and a person of importance to Mustapha (played by the well-known Moroccan actor Abdelkader Lofti), the bar's owner, who can keep his business open only if "non-Muslims frequent the establishment." Much to the chagrin of the local Imam and Islamic officials who are hoping to rid the village of alcohol and foreign vices, the bar can remain open according to "Article 138, paragraph B of the Penal Code," as long as "there are non-Muslims in the bar drinking." Mustapha buys the bar from its French owner, "one of the last Frenchmen in independent Morocco," who is dying after having lived for years in the village.

As more and more Jews leave, Mustapha realizes that he must do all he can to keep Shlomo coming to the bar. Recalling 1961 and the deaths of hundreds of Jews on the boat *Ergos*, which sank off the coast of Morocco as they were trying to make their way to Europe, Mustapha urges Shlomo to rethink his decision to leave with his family: "Lots of Jews died. . . . They crammed them in so tightly, the boat sank. . . . Don't follow those Zionists. . . . And in Palestine, the barmen are all Polish. . . . Do you speak Polish? How will you order beer without foam? . . . What the hell would you do there? Think it over." Shlomo becomes a pawn, passed back and forth between the Zionists and Mustapha like a chess piece on the boards of the games played in the bar.

Mustapha's fear of losing the bar if Shlomo leaves is so great it forces him to drastic measures. He intercepts the Jew's letters from his daughter, Rachel (who finally arrives in Israel), and forces his son, Hassan, to translate her French into an Arabic that Shlomo can understand. Hassan, obeying his father but against his own will, leaves out many of the details of Rachel's unhappy experiences as an émigré in Israel. Benjelloun's point about language in Morocco as an important unifier in the country is a resounding theme in the film. Shlomo can speak and understand only Moroccan Arabic. Like his fellow Muslim villagers, he does not understand French and certainly has never had the need to learn Hebrew. His daughter writes in French because Moroccan Arabic is a dialect and, therefore, not a written language.

The *Marocainité*—Moroccanness—that unites Moroccans is a concept that has been a focal point in Mohammed VI's post–Lead Years' agenda for healing and combating "outside forces" that seek to make Morocco into a radical Islamic state. This leitmotif in the film is essential in bridging Benjelloun's narrative of the 1960s with issues to which contemporary audiences can relate. Rachel's tale of the promised land is ironically full of broken promises made by the Zionists and Israel. Upon her and her mother's arrival, there are no jobs, and racism against Sephardic Jews from North Africa is rampant. Rachel explains that "the Jews here are not like us. . . . They don't eat kosher. The peaceful life of Morocco seems far away. We often speak about it together. They put us in a camp to learn Hebrew. For jobs, they prefer Jews from Europe. North Africans stay unemployed." Rachel and her mother attend demonstrations fomented by Moroccan Jews who "want to go back to Morocco" as they wave Moroccan flags while chanting, "Morocco is our home."

Finally, out of guilt Hassan reveals to Shlomo that his father forced him to lie to him to keep him in the bar so it wouldn't have to close. The young man also divulges to the Jew that actually Rachel has left Israel and is married and living in Paris. Shlomo promptly decides to leave, asking, "Why did you lie to me? What did I do to you?" This poignant question echoes large in the context of Morocco's history. In the end, Shlomo does leave but not clandestinely at night, like so many other Jews. He tells his friends in the bar that he will "leave in the daylight, not like a thief in the middle of the night." His story's ending will be clear and well understood, as a good-bye that is heard by all, noted down, and retold.

When he finally reaches Casablanca to take the plane (not the boat) to Paris to join his daughter, he happens upon Berbkha, a mentally retarded older Jew of the village who, because of his mental illness, has been rejected by the Israeli authorities as unworthy of immigration to Israel. Left on the streets of Casablanca, he is destitute and hungry. Shlomo sends him back to the village and, in the final scenes in Mustapha's bar, which is now reopened, he is revered and celebrated as the last non-Muslim not to have left his village and his homeland.

Discussing his film, Hassan Benjelloun revealed in an interview that, although other Moroccan filmmakers still practice a certain amount of self-censure, avoiding the sensitive subjects of religion, the monarchy, and sex, his films have succeeded and received accolades for their sociopolitical themes. One of the reasons he has been able to address even these issues is because he makes his audiences responsible for thinking about them. Perhaps more subtle than his MRE counterparts such as Leïla Marrakchi, Benjelloun believes that even if sensitive, these subjects have to be addressed. Social engagement is not only a right, it is a privilege in a democratic society. For Benjelloun, it is the filmmaker who must build bridges between audiences and their history.[22]

Relying on the climate of the post-1999 era, during which Moroccan unity has been a key component of Mohammed VI's mandate, Benjelloun admits that his film is a sign of the times and the opening up of the closed doors of Morocco's past. The history that he portrays on the screen, whether in this most recent film or as in *La chambre noire*, is one that seeks to reveal all sides of the past: "Le sociale . . . les soucis de la société marocaine, la mémoire, les problèmes de la société, les tabous au Maroc, sont mes sujets de préférence" (The social . . . the worries of Moroccan society, memory, social problems, taboos in Morocco, these are my preferred subjects).[23]

In *Où vas-tu Moshé?* at no time is Israel idolized as a place that is a haven for Jews. Nor is Morocco made into a country where Jews feel they can live in peace and security, as depicted in the exchange between two of Shlomo's friends who try to convince him to leave the village and go to Marseille, France. Benjelloun's camera angle is interesting as it focuses on the two friends' faces while they directly look at the audience/Shlomo, entreating it/him to reflect on not only the Jews', but Morocco's turbulent past: "Israel is a trap, come live with us in Marseille. . . . Nothing is stable here with Ben Barka and Allal Al-Fassi's leftists. Life here is unsure. You know what we have lived through; our lives have never been easy. We've had to keep low profiles and hide. It's impossible to reason with him."

Benjelloun's raison d'être is to implore that reason champion over rash decisions and power plays between elitist authorities and religious officials who have free license to manipulate the little people caught between them. The futility of nationalist or religious doctrines and their inability to found any lasting positive changes for the Moroccan people are themes that resonate in a country that is still questioning its past in order to refashion a present that embraces its multicultural diversity, which has always been and will continue to be there.

3

Bad Boys, Drugs, and Rock 'n' Roll

The Urban Stories of Morocco

The modern city has been a favorite backdrop to some of the most compelling cinematic works of the twentieth and twenty-first centuries. In the West, the excesses and limits of cities have provided fodder for filmmakers' scenarios since the first Lumière brothers' films of the late nineteenth century (Shiel 2001,1). On-screen, the city in the twentieth and twenty-first centuries has represented "the ominous glamour of postmodernity, individualism, consumption, and electronic reproduction" (1). Western filmmakers have repeatedly cast the city as a dystopia, hostile and violent, afflicting man with the worst brutality. Certainly, futurist films such as *Blade Runner* (1982), *Mad Max* (1985), and *Demolition Man* (1993) have most effectively evoked the city as a dystopia for audiences in recent years. The cityscapes in these films are paradigms used to conceptualize a form of chaos that awaits humankind (at least in the West), which has failed to rectify the ills and corruption, greed and evil, within it. On a philosophical level, the dystopia is the result of society's refusal to heed "changing social norms and environmental conditions" that eventually negatively impact its human development (Edmonds 2003, 22).

Cinema has become the perfect medium through which to study the city as a source of inspiration and despair for the society found within its limits. Mark Shiel and Tony Fitzmaurice note in *Cinema and the City: Film and Urban Societies in Context* that the "nexus *cinema-city*,"[1] which inspires filmmakers to depict on the screen the city as either dystopia or the shining summit of man's architectural prowess, provides "a rich avenue for investigation and discussion of key issues which ought to be of common interest in the study of society and . . . culture" (2001, 2). Depicting the modern city on-screen allows "the relationship between culture and society [to be fully explored], particularly in what is now commonly referred to as the current global postmodern social and cultural context" (2). The city is a window onto power relationships and societal transformations and how these express "'modernity,' 'industrialism' and, in the case of the twenty-first century, globalized 'postmodernity'" (2).

The Moroccan films analyzed in this chapter use their cityscapes to interrogate the "geo-ecopolitical" debates that have arisen in formerly colonized countries (Bose 2008, 38). Globalization and localized, fast-paced urbanization of the cities of developing countries such as Morocco have forced urban dwellers to "confront [their] own modernities [as] analogous with transgressive [behavior]" that is unique to the times of our age and the cityspace in which it transpires (38). The modern urbanscape of Casablanca, in particular, offers filmmakers a sociocultural microcosm, or a place of convergence—a time-space *chronotope*—in which to develop their theories about and on the sociocultural and political transitions taking place currently in the country. Mikhail Bakhtin's "literary artistic chronotope" can be used as a cinematographic model, offering the perfect medium through which to fuse "spatial and temporal indicators" in present Moroccan life as well as past, historical memory. These indicators "are fused into one carefully thought-out, concrete whole. Time, as it were, thickens, takes on flesh, becomes artistically visible; likewise, space becomes charged and responsive to the movements of time, plot and history" (Bakhtin 1981, 84).

The films *Casanegra* (2008), *L'os de fer* (The iron bone, 2007), *Les anges de Satan* (Satan's angels, 2007), and *Casablanca* (2002) reveal that in the era of intense globalization, urban spaces in Morocco have become progressively more "fragmented, imploding, imaginative, subjective, unknowable and fantastic . . . linked with power and difference" (Watson and Gibson 1995, 293).[2] The modern city is for these filmmakers a corrupted human space that rejects the laws of traditional life, dislocates the individual from his or her clan, and leads to the dissolution of the social contract between man and his community. In the films analyzed in this chapter, the urban space is one that fosters reflection on the price of modernity, technology, and the hypothetical Western advances of the globalized age.

Many Moroccan films made since 1999 draw on the ills of urban milieus to study the unraveling of the sociopolitical fabric of the country. City images in films such as *Casablanca* (Benlyazid, 2002), *Les anges de Satan* (Boulane, 2007), *L'os de fer* (Lasri, 2007), and *Casanegra* (Lakhmari, 2008) posit urban spaces as "public emblems of fear and desire" (Haynes 2007, 133). The hostile streets and urban tensions encourage audiences to think about how the contemporary Moroccan city influences the individual and what she or he believes "constitutes life and what it means to be human" (Edmonds 2003, 22).

Casablanca, as an overwhelming urban space of gigantesque proportions depicted in almost all these films (except Lasri's, which takes place in Agadir), allows the filmmaker to posit social-realist images that expose the underbelly of Moroccan daily life, replete with poverty, unemployment, exploitation, and the hopeless dreams of Moroccan youth. On many levels, Casablanca is typical of most contemporary African cities, which are rife with contradictions that arise when modernity clashes with traditionalism, and the colonial past is melded to the globalized present. Throughout Africa, these clashes have been exacerbated by population shifts since independence that have brought thousands of rural people into overcrowded, urban slums located on the outskirts of large cities such as Casablanca, Nairobi, Dakar, and Lagos, to name just a few. Therefore, filmmakers find that inherent "social conditions of crime, violence, and overcrowding," as found in the modern African city, "provide useful material" for didactic, thought-provoking films (Oha 2001, 197).

The modern, contemporary tensions that arise from demographic dislocation influence sociocultural values and politics in Morocco, as elsewhere across Africa and the developing world. Social activist Noureddine Affaya and Driss Guerraoui affirm that "the Moroccan city is a true theater of social upheavals that affect Moroccan society" (2006, 41). Slums have sprung up around major cities because of the exodus of country people from rural areas. These slums are now working-class ghettos that have trapped their inhabitants in vicious circles of poverty (41). The erosion of traditional values as huge numbers of rural residents migrate to the cities seeking employment has encouraged filmmakers to look closely at how film can contextualize for audiences the urban spaces that often surround and close them inside a world that is unfamiliar and foreboding.

The films studied here depict Moroccans' concerns with how urban environments influence the human condition, family structures, and an individual's identity. Like their counterparts elsewhere on the continent, Moroccan filmmakers more often than not depict "urban environments [as] sites of frustration and disillusionment." Their films also scrutinize urban ills in an African context that expose the fact that "African cities invariably articulate relations of power" (Pfaff 2004, 104). Power is disclosed in many forms as associated with the neocolonialism of Western capitalist interests or the controlling, manipulative, and exploitive status quo maintained by the elite class. For Moroccan filmmakers, power struggles between rich and poor and haves and have-nots translate into reflexive paradigms that repeat themselves, remaining unchanged with time, since they are viewed as unalterable. Ironically, at the same time, Casablanca is looked upon with admiration because it represents a megatropolis at the crossroads of the past and the present, the traditional and the modern, the West and the East. With a population of four million, it is the largest city in the Maghreb and has become "a melting pot for the Moroccan nation. It is where the Morocco of tomorrow is being made, and where old territorial, tribal, cultural, and ethnic affiliations dissolve" (Vermeren 2007, 59).

Moroccan films depicting dystopic cityscapes are overwhelmingly masculine. The power, corruption, and violence of the streets are the sole purviews of men. Women are caught in the webs the city of Casablanca weaves for them. In Noureddine Lakhmari's *Casanegra*, Adil's mother is repeatedly severely beaten by her husband; and in Farida Benlyazid's *Casablanca*, poor women are victimized or sequestered by men who bind them by violence and economic dependency. Although certain stereotypes are challenged, such as the stigma placed on women living alone raising a child (Ghali in *Casanegra*) or working outside the home, contributing as an equal partner to the family's well-being (Amine's wife in *Casablanca* and the women of the modern, middle-class families in *Les anges de Satan*), for the most part these women's roles are unremarkable, still overshadowed by tradition and stereotypes associated with being Moroccan and female.

Casablanca is cast overwhelmingly as phallic. Its tall skyscrapers—particularly the Twin Towers (La Grande Casa), two twenty-eight-story concrete office buildings completed in 1998, in the heart of the city—sit squarely erect, continually reminding dwellers of the omnipotent masculine prowess associated with modernity. At the opposite end of the city, another quintessential masculine edifice is the Hassan II Mosque, which lies between the old medina and the

Fig. 3.1. La Grande Casa (also known as the "Twin Towers"), Casablanca

Atlantic Ocean. Built by King Hassan II between 1986 and 1993 as a tribute to himself at colossal financial expense (and to the detriment of his people who were bled dry by incessant taxes to pay for it), the mosque is the largest in the Arab world and remains today a testament to the power of the past and the continuing dominance of patriarchy rooted in Islam, the monarchy, and the traditional religious structures that will forever dictate the parameters of Moroccan culture. La Grande Mosquée, as it is known throughout the Arab world, was built to evoke the omnipotence of God and king.

Although Hassan II's reign represents an epoch most Moroccans strive to forget, they are constantly reminded of his legacy, which is captured in the mosque's minaret (the tallest in the world) and its

Fig. 3.2. La Grande Mosquée, Casablanca

huge, foreboding doors cast in bronze, copper, mosaic, and marble. Repeatedly visible as imposing landmarks in the backdrops of numerous Moroccan films—*Ali Zaoua* (1999), *Marock* (2005), *Casablanca* (2002), and *Casanegra* (2008), to name just a few—the Twin Towers and La Grande Mosquée are the two monumental symbols that most effectively represent contemporary Morocco as a country caught between two opposing poles: one representing the modernist, capitalist, secular future; the other the religious, archaic, obscure past.

Noureddine Lakhmari's *Casanegra* (2008): Mean Streets

Casanegra, by Moroccan Noureddine Lakhmari, opened in early 2008 and drew wide audience attendance. Technically one of the most refined films to be released in the 2000s, Noureddine Lakhmari's style appeals to the urban and globalized youth of today's Morocco. Lakhmari, in his forties, recently returned to Morocco after spending many years in the Netherlands and Norway, where he studied film and made several shorts: *Trapped by Night* (1999), *The Last Show* (1998), *Paper Boy* (1997), *Born without Skis* (1996), *Short Notes* (1995), and *The Silent Struggle* (1993). The characters depicted in these films are migrants, street people, and low-income workers; the lonely and forgotten in the unseen neighborhoods of European cities. In 2005 *Le regard* (The gaze), Lakhmari's first feature-length film, shot in Morocco, won accolades at several international film festivals. Thematically, *The Gaze* breaks with the filmmaker's earlier films to delve into the past of a Frenchman, Albert Tueis. In an earlier era, Tueis worked as an army photographer during the Moroccan rebellion for independence. Although taking many pictures during the time, he never published them. Years later, he returns to Morocco to find the negatives he buried there and is confronted with the painful memories of his past.

Much like the lead character in *The Gaze*, Noureddine Lakhmari's return to his country after years abroad affords him an unusual perspective as both insider and outsider of a society in transition. His fame at home was particularly established when he was asked by 2M, the principal state-run TV network of Morocco, to do nine episodes of a crime series called *El Kadia*. Influenced by American graphic crime-scene TV series such as *CSI, Hill Street Blues, Bones, Cold Case,* and *Without a Trace,* Lakhmari brought filming techniques and themes to Moroccan TV that had never been seen before. *El Kadia* features Zineb Hajjami, a female forensic police officer who, much like her American female counterparts, profiles murderers through the latest technical innovations and scientific inquiry in order to solve heinous crimes. Beautiful, feminine, analytical, and intellectual, Hajjami represents a new generation of police enforcement professionals who aspire to found a more just and transparent system of law and order in Morocco.

Although the plots are simplistic, Lakhmari touches upon a host of social messages, including that women can be police officers, differences between classes can be overcome, the sociocultural divide between urban and rural regions does not mean justice cannot be served, and, most important, that Morocco can aspire to cultivate a police culture that is dedicated to protecting human rights. Most specifically, the series expresses to audiences that times are changing and Morocco can be wiped clean of corruption.

All the episodes of *El Kadia* were shot with a handheld camera that follows the characters' every move. Glitzy scenes of Zineb in her lab

Fig. 3.3. Poster for the *El Kadia* crime series by Noureddine Lakhmari

scrutinizing gory cadavers after she cuts them open in order to find motives for murders dominate the fast-paced plots. Lakhmari's successful series, ironically shown during the month of Ramadan supposedly designated for religious reflection, demonstrated that Moroccan television was now globalized. Series revolving around violent crime were no longer the purview of Western imports; they could now be made easily at home. In a country whose murder rate is exceedingly low, pop-culture pundits commenting in newspapers and magazines now worry if fiction will influence reality.

Casanegra, which opened in 2008, brought Moroccan filmmaking into the techno-globalized age. Again, the influences of American pop-culture TV series and violence are integrated into Lakhmari's unique view of Casablanca. Shot primarily at night with untrained actors in some of the seediest neighborhoods of the city, the film opens with two young men running from the police. Through a flashback, the audience learns that the men are in their midtwenties and are searching to find their way in a society that offers them few opportunities. Although they survive by committing petty crimes, their jovial personalities and street banter endear them to viewers. Adil and Karim, played by Omar Lotfi and Anas Elbaz, two untrained actors, live by their street smarts, running small-time credit card fraud schemes (Adil) and by employing street kids to sell contraband cigarettes (Karim). Adil's one aspiration is to find $6,000 so that he can leave Morocco and join his uncle in Malmo, Sweden; while Karim, who is perpetually dressed in a black suit with tie and white shirt, dreams of climbing the social ladder to get a girl, acquire fortune, and live an easy life.

By way of these principal characters, Lakhmari touches upon a host of social issues that have plagued Morocco's youth for the last twenty years: increasing demographic numbers and high rates of unemployment among the young (23 percent of Morocco's population is under the age of fifteen). In an interview, Lakhmari claims that by using unknown and untrained actors, he was better able to "unleash the strength and violence that I expected from the characters."[3] It is Moroccan youth who are the most affected by disparities of class, the poverty of the streets, domestic violence, and drugs. Casablanca is, in fact, "Casanegra," according to Adil, who, comparing it to the pristine postcard of Malmo, Sweden, that he constantly carries in his pocket, remarks that the city is bleak and dark—a place to run from. In a soliloquy, Adil explains to Karim that escaping the crass city streets means no more traffic noise, no more aristocrats who run red lights because they drive fancy cars, no more drunks in the neighborhoods, no more beggars on the sidewalks who use kids who aren't their own to beg, no more Islamic fundamentalists who want to force us into Paradise, no more perverted Saudis and Kuwaitis who dirty this country, no more of my stepfather's mug which I have to see each morning, no more Casanegra. I want Malmo, a little house with a chimney and from where I can watch the snow fall.

Pirated copies of *Casanegra*, readily found in the medinas of Morocco's large cities, boldly sport DVD covers of African American author Blair Underwood's novel of the same title that was published in 2007. One wonders if Lakhmari read Underwood's novel, since several of his scenes resemble the hard-boiled plot hammered out by Tennyson Hardwick, leading protagonist. Guns, violence, rap music, and the *hood* feeling of the film are visual realities of urban culture, a culture embraced by street gangs not only in L.A. but in Casablanca. Lakhmari's style is definitely influenced by the American films of Tarantino, the Cohen brothers, Scorsese, and Lynch. Thematically, the East-West divide in *Casanegra* is nonexistent, thus rendering plot lines predictable and cliché, even though the dialogue is delivered in Moroccan dialectical Arabic.

When Adil and Karim see that their delinquent ways of making money are not producing the sums they had hoped for, they turn to petty criminal Zrirek (Mohammed Benbrahim), who stalks the dark Casablancan streets in his Mercedes with his little terrier, Nico, in tow. As a small-time thug, Zrirek extorts money from his "clients," who are restaurant and convenience store owners, by threatening them with a handheld drill. When he's not prowling the streets, Zrirek hangs out in his favorite nightclub with his girlfriend (played by famous Moroccan star Raluca), who tends the bar. Zrirek provides comic relief when needed, while also playing the role of tutor and mentor to the young men as they seek to fulfill their aspirations through a life of crime. At one moment, he is almost likable in a paternal manner as he comments on the fact that even though there are "more and more beggars in the streets these days," Adil should think twice about leaving his country for Malmo to become just another "immigré clandestin":

> Don't tell me you're going to go play the illegal game . . . like all that other human waste that the sea coughs up every

day. . . . Forget Europe; there's nothing better than your country. Over there you'll only be one more immigrant. . . . Here, even if it's superficial, at least they say hi to you in the streets.

In order to determine if they are up to the challenge of larger jobs, Zrirek decides to test Adil's and Karim's resolve to embark on a life of crime. He sends them to collect money from a cross-dresser who owes the thug. Lakhmari's commentary on class and particular characteristics linked with class privilege are meted out as the plot transpires. Interestingly, the rich transvestite speaks only French (Lakhmari blatantly sends audiences the message that sexual deviance is still the realm of people who are Westernized and French-speaking), accusing the young men, as he parades around in his silk bathrobe with a handheld camera, of being "fuckers who don't have anything better to do." After beating and leaving the cross-dressing aristocrat bloodied on the floor, Adil and Karim do a walk-through of the house, looking for the money they are supposed to collect. "I don't know where they find all this dough," Adil remarks. Scanning the palatial mansion Karim quips, "Here is Casa-Blanca."

As they peruse the villa, Karim finds a new Armani suit in a closet, while Adil, looking for the money owed Zrirek, finds huge packets of cash stowed away under a bathroom sink. The young men note that power and goods are the privilege of the rich who are French-speaking and fill their houses with Western comforts and inventions. Adil hides the fat packets of bills in his pants from Karim, convinced that the money will buy his mother her freedom from his abusive stepfather and his ticket to Malmo. When the boys report back to Zrirek, the young men's mentor then reveals a new, more challenging job for them: rig a horse race by doping the favored horse. Karim gets cold feet, convinced that he can go straight and win over his girl, Nabila (Ghita Tazi), a single mother who works as an antique dealer for rich, French-speaking clients. She is convinced that Karim is a respectable, well-to-do gentleman with whom she can found a relationship. Indeed, sexual mores are pushed to the limit as Lakhmari films a steamy love scene between the two, which was accepted by audiences (and the authorities' censure) without hesitation.

Women objectified by men, as objects of love or violence, are a recurrent theme in the filmmaker's scenario. Karim and Nabila's lovemaking is contrasted by the domestic violence ruling Adil's household. In one scene, Adil's mother is so severely beaten by his stepfather that the young man decides to use some of the stolen money to save her life. He puts her on a bus and sends her back to her dead first husband's family. "How will they be able to accept me again?" she asks, noting that she has no other options but to be dependent on her in-laws.

Aspiring to live up to his lover's expectations, Karim is convinced by his mother to call his father's former employer to get a "respectable" job. His father is now a handicapped man with cerebral palsy, presumably afflicted from having stood for years in the cold fish cannery where he scaled fish for 50 dirhams a day (less than US$5). Karim is hired, but lasts only one shift, after enduring the backbreaking labor and exploitation of El Hajji, whom he berates as an exploiter of the underclass. Again, poverty and lack of education keep Karim from earning the place he deems is rightfully his. "How did you stand it for thirty years?" he asks his silenced father. "The odor, the exploitation, standing on your feet eight hours a day? All that . . . why? Just to end like this?"

Pushed by his desire to change his fate, Karim finally agrees to help Adil dope the horse for the payoff from Zrirek. Of course, things go wrong. The horse escapes with the young men running quickly behind. The incongruous image of the wild, beautiful black racehorse running in the streets of Casablanca is ephemerally surreal. The animal's desire for freedom from the closed-in miles of concrete, glass, and decaying infrastructure mirror Adil's and Karim's desires for another life that will never be attained. In their car, they continue to search for the horse but end up crashing into Zrirek, totaling his car, killing his small dog, and badly hurting the thug. The money, lots of dirhams destined for the payoff, stays in Zrirek's trunk, since they must run to escape the police arriving on the scene. Escaping into the night, returning to where their journey began, presumably to face a fate that is unchanged, cinches the flashback. The audience finds itself back where it started, in the beginning, where nothing has changed to alter the fate of two young men caught in the abjection of contemporary modernity.

Hicham Lasri's *L'Os de Fer* (2007): The Outcries of Morocco's Disaffected Youth

"Even if you study, you'll be an unemployed broke ass just like us," says one "Haïtiste" (literally a "wall prop") to another as he stands against a

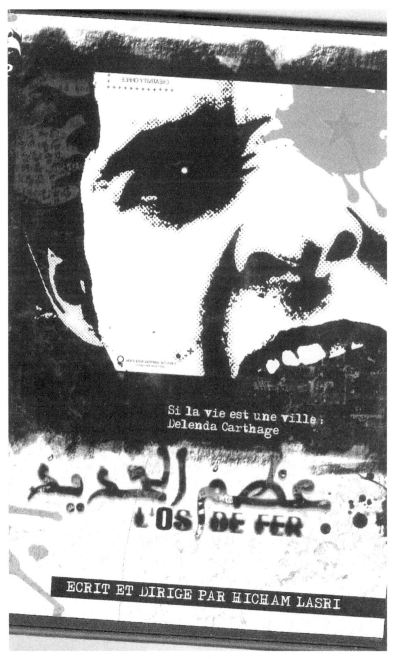

Fig. 3.4. Poster for Hicham Lasri's *L'os de fer*

graffitied wall in a disaffected "derb" (neighborhood) of the coastal town of Agadir. A scene from Hicham Lasri's feature film *L'os de fer* (The iron bone) is echoed in the opening note in his play *(K)rêve!* (2006):

> "Haïtiste" est un dérivé du mot arabe "Haït" qui signifie mur. Dans le jargon de la rue, un Haïtiste est une sorte de grade dans l'échelle de la régression humaine . . . un jeune homme qui ne fait rien de sa journée et qui passe son temps adossé à un mur. . . . Homme battu sur le terrain de la survie et qui échoue dans la décharge mondiale des laissés pour compte (2006, 11).

> (*Haïtiste* is derived from the Arabic word *Haït*, which means "wall." In street slang, a *Haïtiste* is a sort of rung in the ladder of human regression . . . a young man who doesn't do anything during the day and who spends his time leaning up against a wall. . . . A man conquered in the field of survival and who fails in the worldwide dump of those left to fend for themselves.)

Many of the themes thirty-three-year-old filmmaker Hicham Lasri explores in his written work recur in the screenplays for his films. Lasri's play's title, *(K)rêve!*, is multilayered, alluding to the principal character, K, or "(K)amal le haïtiste," who is a young man, inert, passing his time by leaning up against a wall. He is without resources or ambition, and watches the actions of others as he "dreams" (*rêver*) of a better life. "(K)rêve" also reads in French as "crêve," conjugated in the command form from the verb *crêver*, a slangish term that means "to die." K can dream or he can die and, as for many, these are the only two choices facing multitudes of Moroccan youth today.

K is reminiscent of the character K in Franz Kafka's famous novel *The Castle.* Instead of the ominous corridors faced by Kafka's protagonist, Lasri's K is caught in a labyrinth of possible dreams that he is kept from dreaming because he is trapped in a "no-man's-land of aborted dreams" (2006, 22). Mohammed Bigbrother is K's jailer, "the executioner for the World-Without, which is condemned to failure." As executioner, Bigbrother "cuts off the heads of people who give bad answers to his questions on the usefulness of sleep" (9). K is a prisoner with his Conscience, his "alter ego, which stutters and suffers from his handicap, feeling guilty because he cannot function properly to help

K" (9). Microbsoft is the visitor spirited down to the cell by what he claims is K's call for help. "My presence here is justified by the need for something: it's the common language of a Problem. . . . My mission is to repair the breach, to put an end to the perturbation that is causing the problem" (38). But K is incapable of defining his problem. What is it, really, other than to have had the misfortune of being born into no prospects and no future? "The only illusion that I have loved . . . is dead . . . and I'm the one who killed it," K states at the end of the play (138).

Hicham Lasri is one of the most politically committed young social-activist filmmakers currently working in Morocco. His novel *Stati: Roman à facettes* (2009) and his plays *Larmes de joie un jour de Zamzam et crissement de dents de cafard dans un champ de bataille passé à l'eau de javel ou La légende du 11ème doigt de Ash* (2007)[4] and *(K)rêve!* (2006) all reveal a dedication to bringing the plight of the disaffected young and poor of Morocco to the forefront. Like his writing, his films also dwell on the hopelessness of today's Moroccan youth, who are plagued by high rates of unemployment (about 62 percent), lack of work skills, and dismal futures with no financial security. Lasri studied film in France and Morocco and, in 2002, won first prize in the Maghreb-wide competition "Unnoticed Artists of the Maghreb." His short films, *Jardin des rides* (Garden of wrinkles, 2006) and *Ali J'nah Freestyle* (2004), as well as his three feature-length films, *Le peuple de l'horloge* (People of the clock, 2009), *Tiphinar* (2008), and *L'os de fer* (2007), explore the themes most pertinent to the youth of Morocco: how to be an individual in a society dominated by overbearing cultural mores and traditions (*Le peuple de l'horloge*); the lack of understanding between urban dwellers and Morocco's Berber peoples living in rural areas (*Tiphinar*); and the disaffection and hopelessness in the lives of young men (*L'os de fer*).

Lasri founded Ali n' Productions under the tutelage of well-known filmmaker Nabyl Ayouch, whom Lasri credits with having mentored him in launching his career. The independent-minded Lasri receives no funding from the CCM, and, therefore, the themes and messages of his films demonstrate a more edgy street savvy and critical scrutiny of the sociopolitical realms of Morocco. Ali n' Productions has been instrumental in funding Lasri's films and supporting his very independent ideals about how the medium can best be used to express the culture of Morocco's youth.

L'os de fer is an example of Lasri's desire to "paint a picture of Moroccan society that is founded on satire and the symbolic. It is a cry of distress about the indifference and stereotypes that society uses to describe young people" (El Mazouari 2007, n.p.). The film is the story of youth told exclusively by and for them. It is also a celebration of Morocco's hip-hop generation that owes its musical allegiance to Gnawa bands, past and present, whose music is unique to the Maghreb where it was founded. Well-known traditional music of bands such as De Nass El Ghiwane, Jil Jilala à Hoba Hoba Spirit, Amarg Fusion, and Abs is mixed with the tunes of contemporary Moroccan rappers. As Lasri demonstrates, the contemporary owes its unique hip-hop styles to its forefathers. Rappers Fnaïre, Bigg, H-Kayne, Koman, Rass Derb, Casa Crew, Fes City Clan, Hel-LMkane, Stylsouss, Awah, Ahmed Sultan, Negus4never, and Outcry are some of the featured artists whose songs are constantly present as a backdrop to Lasri's film. The messages of rappers are gleaned from the universal ones of the genre: calling on youth to defy authority, rise up and take what should be theirs.

The title *L'os de fer* is derived from the expression "the iron bone," an imaginary bone of exhausted energy that poor and homeless (primarily young) people gnaw on in order to keep going on and on and on. Metaphorically, the bone is a point of degraded energy that translates into a state of chaos and disorder, never ceasing to augment in size, squalor, and instability. As Lasri explains in an interview, the heart of *The Iron Bone* is reached "quand les rêves crèvent l'homme [et il] s'arrête sur place comme un automate sans ressources" (when dreams kill a man and he stops in his tracks like an automat without resources) (Najeb 2008, n.p.). Lasri's characters, three young Moroccan men—Ash (Mohammed Aouragh), Mikhi (Mustapha Houari), and Moulay (Tarik Boukhari)—"are members of a huge armada of people who find themselves in a train station looking at trains leaving for uncertain futures." In contrast to the majority who are beaten down and humiliated by poverty and despair, and who generally resign themselves to accepting their fate (or train to nowhere), the young men in Lasri's film seize their condemned futures in order to change them (n.p.). Their decision results in psychological damage, total despair, and eventual suicide.

Hicham Lasri's film seeks to capture the essence of contemporary times in Morocco. He equally searches to avoid clichés and stereotypes often associated with those communities afflicted with misfortune, street violence, and marginalization from mainstream society. As a universal message, the filmmaker incites his audiences to interrogate the ills of today's modern societies in which class and wealth disparity are predominant. His "haïtistes" live in Agadir, Morocco, but could easily be found in the mean streets of L.A., Chicago, Paris, or Berlin. They meld in with the dusty, hot decrepit *derbs* (neighborhoods) in which they live.

Agadir, far from the bustling streets of Casablanca, is known for its beaches, which are favorite resort spots for European (particularly French) tourists. Like other urban centers condemned by haphazard urban planning and overwhelming numbers of poor and destitute people migrating from rural areas, Agadir suffers its own modern social ills. This large city, the Berber capital of the south, is particularly interesting because it is the one urban center in Morocco that has been hailed as "modern" and completely representative of twentieth-century Moroccan architecture. The earthquake that flattened it in 1960 lasted only fifteen seconds but left little standing, and approximately fifteen thousand people dead. The destruction required that the city be completely rebuilt a few kilometers from its original location. *Agadir* in Berber means "wall," or an enclosed, fortressed city. Thus, the city's meaning as construed in the context of Lasri's film becomes interesting on many levels. Where once Agadir was fortified, after the earthquake the city became wall-less. However, Lasri's three young protagonists constantly must struggle against a multitude of barriers—either perceived or real—that both the city and society construe for them as marginalized victims. Agadir itself is often cast as a victim in contemporary Morocco: the farthest city in the south, more Berber than Arab, cut off from the more dynamic regions of the country, which leaves little opportunity for those who seek employment and a means of eking out a living.

In *L'os de fer*, the protagonists' stories are told as a series of flashbacks by all participants who are interrogated by a filmmaker sitting in a director's chair on the platform of a dimly lit studio. The language is that of the streets: Darija (colloquial Moroccan Arabic), mixed with the particular linguistic features of young people who live on the edge in *les quartiers populaires*. With lights, cameras, and crew surrounding the one big armchair from which each character delivers his or her narrative to the director, Lasri's story unfolds. The visual images of characters' faces on TV screens as they are filmed by the crew are often distorted, breaking up into static. The takes are fast-forwarded or replayed, creating overlaps and repetitions in the stories of not only the three men but those who knew them, saw them, or witnessed their recklessness. Even the protagonists, older and dressed as successful, accomplished men, comment on their own stories as they, too, sit in the armchair to answer the director's questions.

Bouncing handheld camera shots move between the present, the past, and the surreal of the young men's consciousnesses. One moment they are on the bus they have hijacked, the next by the sea, sitting on the sand with only an old wrecked boat behind them. The boat, a recurring image throughout the film, is stuck in the sand, much like the three young men's lives are stuck in inertia. Their lives keep repeating, like a broken record that plays the same story over and over again. Yet, being stuck is not simply the purview of the young and powerless. Inspector Daoud, sent to take Ash and Mikhi in, also repeats the refrain: "We are all caught in a scratched record that keeps repeating."

The mechanical aspects of the film evoke a technologically saturated milieu that definitely sets Lasri's generation apart from older filmmakers. His is a generation that depends on the technological functions of the modern age—iPods, digital cameras, cell phones, and television. Technology—its access and its inaccessibility—dictates the success or failure of each character's survival in society, as the film reveals. Ash can get by day to day only by being plugged into his Walkman, and Moulay counts on texting to "speak" for him, since he is mute. Like a machine, the lives of these young men are manipulated by the mechanical routines of the global age. To ensure the comprehension of this idea, Lasri constantly flashes the phrase "Insert Coin(s)" on the screen, and Fast-Forward and Rewind buttons meld into the images and decors of his cinematographic palette. Like in *(K) rêve!*, the filmmaker asks whether some technological Big Brother is directing our stories. Do we really have control over our lives and our futures?

L'os de fer opens with the three leading protagonists leaning up against a wall, their silhouettes traced around them in red spray paint in graffiti-like fashion. Outlined on the wall, like the body tracings of a crime scene, their cut-out beings are left behind them; the only mark on society they will ever make. The young men are fixed in indelible spray paint in the world as *haïtistes* living in one small corner of the *quartier populaire*. Their silhouettes on the wall also serve as a foreshadowing of the events to come. As is revealed slowly to the audience, they are dead men walking.

Ash lives in a dream world filled with the hip-hop, rap, and raï music to which he listens constantly on his outdated Walkman (too poor to buy a more advanced iPod), trying not to think about anything else. His whole world is his mother and his two friends, Mikhi and Moulay. Mikhi is enraged and unemployed and states that he has nothing to lose because he's "going to die anyway." He therefore dedicates his time to finding "causes" that can bring him meaning. Moulay is mute and communicates by texting messages on his cell phone. He is the only one of the three to have succeeded in obtaining his baccalaureate (high school diploma) and desires to attend university but cannot come up with the 120 dirhams (about US$15) for the bus pass that will get him there.

Mikhi and Ash invest all their energy in trying to help Moulay attain his goal, which ultimately leads them into an abyss of failure. They beat up small-time dealers and street sellers to no avail; 120 dirhams might as well be a thousand. They visit Lady Steel Toe (Siham Afoiz), named for the steel-toed boots she wears ("No jerk can ever stamp on my toes"). Interestingly, unlike *Casanegra* and *Les anges de Satan*, in which women are simply backdrops, cast as objects of sexual desire with very little dialogue, in *L'os de fer* Lady Steel Toe offers a rarely seen depiction of young women in Morocco. Although playing a minor role, Lasri makes sure that audiences understand she is sure of herself, stands her ground with men, and, certainly, is not going to be anyone's doormat. She knows what men probably think about her, but she doesn't care:

> Whores, chics, babes, tarts, birds, skanks, hos, sluts, cunts, twats, dames, all 'n all, it's just a hormone thing. It's just "Virility" as my grandpa used to say. . . . Guys need tenderness. They need a girl who can spice up their lives. They all come from ordinary families where women take care of everything; women feed them, women give them something to drink, women make them sleep. . . .

Lady Steel Toe is a young woman from the hood who, after telling the three young men that "pussies like them are always getting into trouble," says she won't loan them the money, but will give them a flag she made herself "for a nonexistent country . . . the flag of a virgin land; no jerk found it before, it's the place of a so-called future." Mikhi, unimpressed by the flag, tells her that they come out of desperation:

> Listen, Lady Steel Toe, we are the generation that doesn't need to wake up in the morning. No French colonizer to fight, no road of unity to build, no Green March to walk. We are unlikely to be Berber or able to fight for our origins. Palestine is too far away. Iraq is lost. We haven't studied enough to have a sit-in in front of Parliament. Government jobs are just shit. So we are just passing through this life and moving to hell instead of moving to Europe.

In one short monologue, Mikhi describes his generation as the first in Morocco not to have a cause since independence from the French in 1956. In the relative stability and openness found in today's Moroccan society of the new millennium, cultivated by King Mohammed VI, causes such as the Green March of 1975 are events of the young men's parents' history. Thousands of Moroccans were urged by Hassan II to march to the border of the Western Sahara and cross over the line, symbolically claiming the region for Morocco from Spain. At the same time, this political act was meant to demonstrate national unity and absolute allegiance to the monarchy of King Hassan II. Even now in Morocco, where freedom of speech is increasingly exercised, the right to protest is not an option for the unskilled and the uneducated who, as Mikhi says, "cannot go before Parliament and demand jobs" like the recent university graduates one sees demonstrating in the streets of Rabat. Mikhi, Ash, and Moulay make up parts of the unseen masses; the poor who do not have "something to rely on to exist." Following the interlude with Lady Steel Toe, and out of desperation, the three hijack a bus and its passengers in order to obtain the 120 dirhams that have become symbolically attached to achieving something in a society that will not acknowledge them.

The bus, previously used as a *lieu générateur* for political commentary in Lasri's short film *Ali J'nah Freestyle*, again spawns dialogues on the ills of modern society among the protagonists, their hostages, and the police chief who comes to arrest them. The bus is another visual metaphor for the static, stuck life from which the protagonists cannot extract themselves. Although metaphorically the bus also represents the possibility of a means of motion to somewhere else, if only they could use it to get there, it ironically becomes a prison in which they are definitively trapped. Physically, the bus is wedged in the sand when one of the many police officers called to the scene shoots out its tires. It is now the no-man's-land in which the three young men, like K in *(K) reve!* as well as a whole generation of young people, are lost. This no-man's-land becomes fragile as it teeters on its blown-out tires, finally propped up by the policemen with a couple of two-by-fours in the hope of lasting long enough to bide negotiating time with Ash and Mikhi, who have violently threatened the passengers held inside.

Inspector Daoud (Hassan Badida), who "has no teeth," both literally and figuratively, is called to the scene to handle the situation. Broken down and embittered by his twenty years on the force, Daoud halfheartedly throws himself into the situation. He tries to encourage the hostage takers to give up, only his microphone doesn't work. When he tries to speak into it, only hissing and sputtering come out the other end. He is inaudible and, as he says, "just one of the fucked-up . . . in a world of fuckups" who will never be heard.

Hicham Lasri's film paints a pessimistic view of the plight of the majority of young people living in Morocco. His characters are not redeemed at the end of the film, nor do they all survive to change the course of the fate that seems to have already been meted out for them. Once Mikhi and Ash see that there is no exit, they tell mute Moulay to pretend he is one of the passengers so he won't be linked to their crime. Ash, talking one last time to his mother on Moulay's cell phone, realizes that she is having a heart attack. Mikhi decides they must run for it. He exits the bus in a hail of gunfire that kills him on the spot. The Flag of No Country, given to the men by Lady Steel Toe, is wrapped around his body. Ash decides that his only fate is suicide, since he cannot face twenty-five years in prison "in the dark." "I'm a light bug," he quips. He, too, runs outside the bus, knocks down the two-by-fours propping it up, lies down next to Mikhi, and waits for the bus to topple over. Moulay watches the bloody scene unfold behind the bus window. He, too, is a prisoner within its metallic walls. When the bus does finally roll over on its side, killing Ash and imprisoning all aboard in a pile of metal and sand, Lasri's message arrives at its end. The bus's final resting place is in the dusty neglected backdrop of the poorer areas surrounding Agadir. A town generally known for its tourist resorts, and as a popular destination for Europeans, is revealed as a place of utter destitution. "What are eyes good for if they only see despair," states Inspector Daoud as the film's "machine" comes to a grinding halt; the words "Insert Coin" flashing on the screen.

Ahmed Boulane's *Les Anges de Satan* (2007): Drugs, Sin, and Rock 'n' Roll

Like *Casanegra, Les anges de Satan* by Ahmed Boulane created quite a stir when it was released in March 2007. Based on the real events of "l'affaire des sataniques" (the affair of Satan worshippers) that took place in 2003, Boulane tells the tale of thirteen young heavy-metal band members who were tried for crimes "against Islam." The film's publicity poster aptly captures (in French) the heart of the film: "Au Maroc les jeunes sont arrêtés et jugés. Leur seule crime: aimer la musique" (In Morocco young people are arrested and judged. Their only crime: loving music).

The premiere of Boulane's most controversial film occurred on February 28, 2007, at the huge Megaramma Cinémas in Casablanca. Everyone connected to filmmaking in Morocco was present, as well as many journalists, writers, and people of the Moroccan elite (government officials, the minister of culture, etc.). The opening credits of the film are introduced by an invisible narrator who states in French that "cette histoire est inspirée de faits reels" (this story is inspired by real events) as the debut unfolds at a heavy-metal concert where the band is playing to a packed house. Are we in Morocco, Europe, or the United States? It's difficult to decipher from the noise, the screaming youths in the audience, and the heavy-metal rockers decked out in goth attire, routine for Anglo-European aficionados. For Boulane, like Marrakchi, it is important that his audience understands that, in the era of globalization, young people are basically the same no matter where one travels. They all share similar hedonistic hopes and dreams and are, after all, the future generations of the New Morocco and the globe.

Access to personal freedom of choice in contemporary Moroccan society is at the root of the 2003 events surrounding the trial and judgment of the band. "La liberté ne se conceptualise pas. Elle se vit" (Freedom isn't conceptualized. It's lived), Boulane notes in an interview (Faquihi 2007, n.p.). Almost exactly four years earlier, in February 2003, thirteen young heavy-metal rockers were incarcerated, accused of taking drugs, satanic worship, and defamation of the

Islamic faith. The fourteenth person charged was a young café owner, Mohammed Ali Kamel Abdou Youssef, originally from Egypt, who was accused of letting the band members meet in his café. Except for playing the music, none of the charges were true. The worst drug offense of which the young men were guilty was smoking hashish. They were primarily from upper-middle-class Casablancan families. The judge ruled against them based on heavy-metal T-shirts with English slogans such as "Kiss My Ass" written on them, skulls and crossbones found in the band's studio, and other goth attire and paraphernalia. The defense for three of the detainees, who were particularly harassed by the presiding judge, declared in court: "These young people have committed no crime. . . . Their only fault was to have played music in different cultural venues in Casablanca, notably at the FOL" (la Fondation des oeuvres laïques, the Foundation for Secular Works) (Chadi 2003, 5).

Boulane's film suggests that this last point is the reason for the vindictive judicial outcome against the young men by the Moroccan courts. The very notion of a secular band playing Western music at a time when the West was perceived as increasingly hostile to Islam and Muslim countries (the United States had just invaded Iraq) is explained in the film as being at the root of excessively harsh rulings against the band members. The second reason for the conservative judicial decision was the 2002 legislative elections that gave the Islamic PJD (Party for Justice and Development) a significant amount of seats in the Moroccan Parliament. These events, as *Le journal hebdomadaire* points out, were representative of a new brand of Moroccan politics that exemplified a "foi schizophrénique" (schizophrenic belief) completely counter to what the post Lead Years were supposed to represent. The first issue stemming from the "affaire," which entered public intellectual debates in French and Arabic, is represented by the questions: Was Morocco heading toward an Islamic fundamentalist state? Would the country experience what had already transpired next door in Algeria?

> Moroccan society brutally woke up with a sinking feeling, that Morocco was sliding little by little into Islamism without being able to do anything about it. Yes, certainly, we were profoundly Muslim, but the recent specter of an Algeria ravaged by a long civil war between Islamists and forces of order, with more than 100,000 deaths to consider, didn't lend

to optimism, or even more when specialists on the question
did their utmost to point out that the Morocco of the 2000s
was strongly reminiscent of the neighbor to the east during
the 1980s.[5]

Immediately after his film was released, Boulane was accused of
not accurately portraying the events as they transpired in 2003. He
interviewed only one or two of the youths detained and, as one of the
young men noted, did not inquire further into details of their ordeal:
"Ahmed Boulane discussed his scenario with some among us without ever completely consulting us, listening to what we might have
suffered during this period, without ever asking us questions." To
this accusation, Boulane remarks: "It wasn't necessary to speak with
all fourteen. . . . I'm not making a psychological film" (Semlali 2007,
n.p.). We can only wonder to what the filmmaker was referring: Psychological to what extent? When is reality not real when making a
film based on real events?

The tension between reality and fiction makes Boulane's film
somewhat conflicted in the messages it wants to portray. It becomes
basically a docudrama about an event that marked a setback for the
democratic post–Lead Years movement in Morocco. While most
events are true, Boulane embellished some that, in the end, succeeded
in discrediting his overall goals. Certain scenes in which some of
the young men are questioned by authorities and then are implied
to be tortured never happened. The roughing up of a conscientious
reporter who seeks to know the truth and organize public opinion in
support of the rockers also never happened. However, the dubious
trial did take place. One critic noted that the right-wing conservative
Islamist judge who sentenced them to prison time for the defamation
of Islam, although true, is "la réalité adaptée" (adapted reality). The
judge's comments were transcribed in an interview and printed in
newspapers across Morocco (Semlali 2007, n.p.).

Boulane's screenplay is deficient in dialogue and plot development.
Many also asked, why make a film about an event whose conclusion
we already know? The film does make a point of exposing a judicial
and law enforcement system that definitely needs scrutiny. It equally
reveals the insidious infiltration of Islamic orthodoxy into what many
had hoped, following the Lead Years, would be a secular judiciary
branch that operated independently of religious dogma. Boulane does
expose the fact that, even after the bombings in spring 2007 in Casa-

blanca, religious extremism is still prevalent in Morocco. The film also demonstrates the overwhelming support by Moroccan citizens for secular democratic reform at the time of the trials. Boulane's many scenes of the demonstrations in Casablanca and Rabat, where thousands led chants and brandished banners and posters condemning the trials as mockeries of the supposed democratic reforms taking place in 2003, remind audiences of the importance of staying vigilant in order to extract "the demons that have seized the system" (Semlali 2007, n.p.).

Boulane's film offers a sociocultural and political commentary on contemporary times. However, it does not offer any prescriptions with the hope of solving Morocco's social ills; rather, it reveals the reality facing the youth of Morocco today. *Les anges de Satan*, like *Casanegra* and the following films analyzed in this chapter, serve as visual memory documents, reminding audiences that the past still looms large in the present and, at any time, the abuses of the Lead Years could once again become a reality.

Farida Benlyazid's *Casablanca* (2002):
Corruption, Power, and Greed in the City

Farida Benlyazid's 2002 film, whose script she wrote in collaboration with Ahmed Boulane, is adapted after author and civil rights activist Rida Lamrini's novel *Les puissants de Casablanca* (The Powerful of Casablanca, 1999), which is the first installment in a trilogy entitled *La saga des puissants de Casablanca*. The filmmaker uses many of the most well-known actors working in Morocco today such as Lounis Migri (Amine) and Amal Ayouch (Talabi's wife), both of whom have played a variety of characters in film and television productions. Lamrini's saga accurately depicts a moment in Moroccan history that inevitably put the country on the road to the eventually, more democratically reformed nation of the new millennium. To understand the film, audiences need to have read the books. Therefore, Benlyazid's rendition is definitely not marketable internationally because of its plot, which follows very insular sociocultural and political events that took place in Morocco in the late 1990s. The film opens inside a car driving the streets of Casablanca at night. We see only the driver's hands, but assume the person is one of the "puissants," the powerful men who rule the streets, the banks, the police, and other institutions in Morocco.

Lamrini's trilogy begins with *Les puissants de Casablanca*, published in 1999. This first novel launches a complex story that becomes more nuanced as the narrative and its sequels progress. Each work adds more characters and plot twists. The film, like the novel, begins with Casablanca, depicted as an immense city divided along lines of class and economic wealth. The opening scene, like the novel, takes place in Derb Talian, the old colonial quarter that, at the beginning of the twentieth century, housed Italian merchant families benefiting from their economic investments in the French colonial protectorate. Today Derb Talian (*talian* is a derivative in Moroccan Arabic for *italien* in French) is inhabited by "[des] centains sinon des milliers de jeunes, avec ou sans diplômes, totalement perdus et sans avenir" (by hundreds, if not thousands of young people, with or without diplomas, totally lost and without a future) who must steal to live (Lamrini 1999, 21). It is here where Ba Lahcen (played by Mohammed Razine), a simple uneducated man who ekes out a living selling vegetables on the street, begins his journey through Benlyazid's film. Ba Lahcen is one of the "petites gens" (little people) who become victimized by the power of the mighty and their prowess in wielding it.

A nostalgia for the better times of the past, where perhaps people were more honest (although this past discounts the brutality of the colonizer), is revealed in the opening conversation between Ba Lahcen and his daughter, Aïcha. She encounters him in one of the squalid streets of Casablanca where he is gazing at an old, decrepit building constructed by the Italians in the nineteenth century. When she asks him why he is staring at the tenement, he remarks: "Looking at architecture. . . . This was a nice building before . . . The Italians were amazing builders." She responds: "During your time things were better. You had a home and a store, but since Mom died, things just get worse and worse."

The didactic prose and stilted narrative of the film are rooted in Lamrini's original novel, which is meant to instruct audiences on the ills lurking within their society. The author originally revealed that all his characters are based on real people and that none of his stories are sensationalized or invented. Audiences who screened the film in 2002 easily recognized the events occurring in Morocco during the years 1996–2003. In Lamrini's novel, these years are divided into three time periods that revolve around specific historical events: 1996–1998 (*l'assainissement,* an anti-corruption campaign); 1999–2001 (the death of Hassan II and September 11, 2001); and 2001–2003 (free-trade agreements with the

United States and Europe that have decimated Morocco's agricultural trade balance; the Casablanca bombings; and the country's ongoing struggle against Islamic fanaticism). The film, unfortunately, is much less detailed and fails to put together a timeline in a cohesive manner, although it ambitiously tries to follow the novel's plot.

In the first novel, *Les puissants de Casablanca*, Lamrini concentrates primarily on the waning years of Hassan II's reign, and on the king's campaigns of attempted "assainissement" (literally sterilization or cleansing) of the many corrupt systems in Morocco. *Assainissement* was partly due to international pressure on Hassan II to make his regime more transparent and responsible for the socioeconomic crises in Morocco that caused a rippling effect throughout the Maghreb. The International Monetary Fund (IMF) also played a role, holding the country hostage as it promised debt relief in exchange for the democratization of Moroccan institutions. In 1996–97, at the height of the "assainissement," the measures succeeded only in forcing more innocent people into prison and giving those who had power full license to wield it indiscriminately.

Lamrini himself was a victim of the government's "housecleaning." His personal experience is reified in his novel and Benlyazid's film through the character Amine, who loses his tea import business and is the victim of false accusations, which he tries to disprove in the second novel, *Les rapaces* (The Vultures). This second volume, which continues the saga of the characters from the underclass, is condensed into Benlyazid's film in order to round out the entire plot. The characters are Ba Lahcen; his daughter, Aïcha; her brother, Ali, who becomes an Islamic fundamentalist; and Amine, a small businessman who comes back to Morocco after having lived ten years in Canada (Lamrini's own story). The protagonist, Youssef, a journalist who spent twelve years in prison for having simply been in the wrong place at the wrong time during the Hassan II regime, is also a central player in Lamrini's *Saga* and the film. Youssef and Amine are from the middle class, and so is Bachir, the incorruptible police inspector who, along with them, devotes his energy to fighting the tyranny of "les puissants." These "powerful ones" are the corrupt Talabi, a member of Parliament, and his friend Yamini, the head of a bank that conducts shady deals with the French. As mentioned previously, these characters are based on real-life people, recognizable to Moroccan audiences.

Lamrini's trilogy weaves a very simple detective story with commentary on the social ills plaguing contemporary Morocco. Only some of these commentaries are highlighted in the film. Ba Lahcen's daughter, Aïcha, witnesses the murder of her friend Lamia by Jamal Yamani and his cousin Karim Talabi after she refuses to submit to Jamal's sexual advances. Both young women were picked up after being lured by the luxurious fast car and the seemingly gentlemanly airs of the rich young men. Aïcha flees and clandestinely escapes to Italy (a repeated theme in the many Moroccan novels and films that seek to draw attention to the hundreds who risk their lives every year to cross the Mediterranean in tiny boats, hoping for a better life in Europe). Although she is in Italy, eventually marries an Italian, and has a child, Aïcha never loses sight of her goal to bring her assailants to justice. She finds a human rights lawyer in France who accepts her case. Meanwhile, she contacts Amine, her former boss, who works with Bachir and Youssef to expose the corruption of Talabi and Yamani. Her mission is to put their sons, Jamal and Karim, on trial for Lamia's murder.

Lamrini's second and third novels offer the rest of the story, which, in the film, is haphazardly used to fill in missing information about the characters. Youssef,[6] the journalist trying to break the story on corruption and also reveal Yamani's and Talabi's role in the murder, is sent to jail for defamation. The two "puissants" are never brought to trial. Even though the French human rights lawyer Jupin (not in the film) is able to obtain passports and visas to France for Aïcha's father and brother, he fails in his efforts to prosecute Yamani and Talabi as well as their guilty sons, Jamal and Karim, for Lamia's death.[7]

At the end of the film, Inspector Bachir is unable to close his case and bring Yamini and Talabi to justice. Tired and ready to retire, he quips to his wife: "Luckily there's retirement . . . and we can go far away from all this noise. . . . This city is like an ogress." As for journalist Youssef, commenting on the fledgling openness of the Moroccan political system, he is skeptical, noting that "things never change." Small-time businessman Amine is absolved of the trumped-up corruption charges the government's *assainissement* program has accused him of, but he is left bitter, wondering out loud to his wife, "Should we have come back here from Canada?" Her response: "Each society has its problems and we have to educate our children to adapt to them . . . and to adapt to the values of our country."

Lamrini's saga of more than four hundred pages accurately depicts the Morocco of today as mired in the painful struggles of its transition to a more democratic society. Regrettably, due to an almost un-

Fig. 3.5. The slums of Derb Talien with La Grande Mosquée built by Hassan II in the background

intelligible plot Benlyazid's film falls short of being able to offer audiences a cogent assessment of the societal changes depicted so well in Lamrini's novels. The film does succeed on a certain level at revealing a Morocco that one still sees in the streets of Casablanca and Rabat. These cities are tainted by the disparity between class and economic strata, the tensions between modernity and traditionalism, the uneven politics of human rights and old totalitarian practices. Tensions in the film and disparities between classes are metaphorically construed in certain shots of Casablanca taken either from high up to depict actions by the "powerful," or at street level when filming scenes in the Derb Talien, the tenement area next to La Grande Mosquée. The mosque is, in the beginning of the film, half obscured by the early morning Casablancan fog. However, by the end it shines in full daylight in the backdrops of certain scenes, thus symbolically denoting the idea that perhaps corruption can be cleaned up and evil thwarted, just not at the end of this film.

Benlyazid, known for her internationally acclaimed, women-centered films *Door to the Sky* (1989) and *Women's Wiles* (1999) (discussed in chapter 5), seems to grapple with how best to render the huge saga in a two-hour film. Rida Lamrini expressed in an interview that he was disappointed in the film because he felt it only glossed over the important political events he depicts in his novels.[8] Yet, like *Casanegra, Les anges de Satan,* and *L'os de fer, Casablanca* does capture the stresses of a city and a people that are caught between the past and the present, unable to discern clearly how to proceed to the future.

The films discussed in this chapter demonstrate the overarching view that modernity in the age of globalization does not always predict a clear path to cosmopolitanism, wealth, and assurance of a better life. The city is hostile and represents a Westernized conception of social *being* that, more often than not, corrupts indigenous ways of life. These films question the paths Morocco has taken in order to encourage audiences to take a moment to ponder the price that must be paid to survive in the dystopias of the modern age.

4

Prison, Torture, and Testimony

Retelling the Memories of the Lead Years

Since 1999, filmmakers have sought to depict the terror of the Lead Years on-screen. Some of these films have been more successful (in terms of style, tightness of screenplay, and filming) than others at conveying to audiences the suffering of victims. Certain films express an urgency as they seek to rectify a past that has not been recounted but risks being forgotten by Morocco's younger generations. Plots tend to evoke the feeling that the stories had to be told as quickly as possible, lest they be forgotten. Indeed, when we consider that Morocco's population has a median age of twenty-three, the most repressive years of the Lead Years (1968–80) for the young are quickly becoming simple "bribes de mémoire" (memory snippets), passed down as oral narratives by their parents.[1] Hanane Ibrahimi, leading actress in the film version of *La chambre noire* (The black room, 2004), and twenty-four years old at the time, stressed in an interview how important it was for her to portray the events of the 1970s, the time frame of the film, because she does realize the significance of the sacrifice of the older generation: "It's thanks to the struggles and suffering of past generations that we have acquired certain rights" (Bernichi, n.p.).

Three principal films dealing with prison and torture during the Lead Years have been made in Moroccan Arabic since 1999. *Jawhara* (2003), *La chambre noire* (The black room, 2004), and *Mémoire en détention* (Memory in detention, 2004) were released in theaters over a two-year span from 2003 to 2004; all were subtitled in French. In addition to these *longs métrages* (feature-length films), a short film, *Faux pas* (False steps, 2003) by Lahcen Zinoun, narrated in French, metaphorically depicts the kidnapping of several prominent activists during the Lead Years. The film *J'ai vu tuer Ben Barka* (I saw Ben Barka get killed, 2005), which explores the abduction, torture, and assassination of Ben Barka, was a CCM-French coproduction, made by Serge Le Péron and Saïd Smihi, both residing in France. These films' themes are raw and graphic, but true to the stories of torture and abuse they seek to depict. The CCM's support attests to the more open climate and Moroccans' willingness to confront the past.

Films made about human rights abuses and the incarcerations of numerous innocents during the Lead Years have been inspired by *La littérature carcérale* (prison literature), which has become increasingly popular as Morocco delves into the egregious violations committed in its past. Since 1999, *la mémoire refoulée* (suppressed memory) of this dark period has been depicted on the screen as filmmakers have explored a past pregnant with untold stories about abductions, disappearances, and flagrant abuses of civil liberties.

Accurately documenting history is imperative in order to establish a collective conscience for Morocco that can critically interrogate how abuse of human rights has influenced the political interworking of Moroccan politics. Filmmakers who have tackled the daring texts of the muted history of Morocco are Hassan Benjelloun, Saâd Chraïbi, Lahcen Zinoun, and Jillali Ferhati. Their film texts ferret out the suppressed memories of an entire generation. These filmmakers also realize what French historian Maurice Halbwachs noted as he documented the impact of World War I trauma on collective memory in Europe: that (re)constructing the past always implies accurately recording memory that "must start from shared data or conceptions." Halbwachs emphasized that "we always carry with us a number of distinct persons" and, therefore, "our memories remain collective" (1980, 31).

Documenting suppressed memory in contemporary times through testimonies—rendered both on the screen and on the page—is an integral part of the individual's, as well as the Moroccan collective's, search for a new identity in the post Lead Years. This *travail de mémoire* (memory work) mandates "the reappropriation and negotiation that each person must do with respect to his past in order to progress in his own future individuality" (Zekri 2006). The films analyzed in this chapter are what French historian Pierre Nora defines as "memory sites," tragic representations important for linking together historical memory, the individual's remembrances, and the vitality of a nation's identity:

> Ultimately, memory constrains the behavior of individuals, and individuals alone. By defining the relation to the past, it shapes the future. This "law of remembrance" has great coercive force: for the individual, the discovery of roots, of "belonging" to some group, becomes the source of identity, its true and hidden meaning. (1992, 11)

What is interesting in Morocco is that many perpetrators of torture and abuse during the Lead Years are still in power. The collective denial, or *refoulement* (repression) of memory, which denies the Moroccan people justice and closure, also prohibits the proper construction of memory sites to begin the nation's collective healing. Therefore, conceptualizing a common belief system that accurately reflects the past remains elusive. Commenting on the government's denial of the abuse he and other inmates suffered at the hands of torturers in Tazmamart prison during the Lead Years, Ahmed Marzouki, author of *Tazmamart: Cellule 10* (2001, Tazmamart: Cell 10), notes that Moroccan officials consistently refused to acknowledge the existence of prisons, particularly Tazmamart, long after they were exposed to the international community:

> Tazmamart didn't exist and has never existed. This was the response of Moroccan parliamentarian Fayçal El Khatib when coolly answering the question posed by a Western radio station: "This supposed prison has only existed in the imagination of the enemies of our democracy." (2001, 10)

Despite the authorities' unwillingness to dredge up the past, endeavors to set records straight, particularly on human rights issues, have gained momentum in Morocco, and film has been at the forefront of reconstituting events few knew about during the Lead Years. Rectification of historical memory has been influenced by the proliferation of testimonial writing and cinematography published and produced since 1999.[2] Ahmed Marzouki's *Tazmamart: Cellule 10* was the first novel of *la littérature carcérale* to be officially recognized by King Mohammed VI and published in Morocco. Other authors and former victims such as Mohammed Raïss (*De Skhirat à Tazmamart: Retour du bout de l'enfer*, From Skhirat to Tazmamart: Return from the depths of hell), translated from Arabic in 2002, like Marzouki, also recounts the underground medieval prison located in southeastern Morocco, which, for eighteen years, was the living tomb of fifty-eight men. The imprisoned men's only crime was to have obeyed the orders of superiors who plotted to overthrow King Hassan II in two coup d'états that took place in 1971 and 1972.[3]

For almost twenty years, the prisoners fought against madness and inevitable death in tiny, cramped cells, designed as "living graves" for the purpose of assuring slow extinction. In October 1991, when they were finally released due to pressure from the international community, only thirty-one men remained alive.[4] Other authors and former victims who have taken up the pen to tell their stories include Abdelfettah Fakihani, Jaouad Mdidech, Ali and Midhat Bourequat in French, and Fatna El Bouih in Arabic. Famous exiled authors Abdelhak Serhane and Tahar Ben Jelloun have also contributed works of fiction, based on the prisoners' accounts, of what is now known as *la littérature carcérale.* These novels, like the films analyzed here, scrutinize abuse of human rights in Moroccan prisons as a hidden history, manipulated by the despots and the manipulators of Morocco's *Makhzen,* which represents the omnipotent power of the monarchy and "the system." To counter the historical manipulations and cover-ups of the Lead Years, authors and filmmakers use their voices to accurately depict what *should have been* said.

Lahcen Zinoun's *Faux Pas* (2003): A Short Interrogation of the Past

Lahcen Zinoun, born in 1944, is best known as Morocco's premier dance choreographer. His Ecole de danse (School of Dance) is the first of its kind in a country that traditionally has not embraced Western classical dance. In 1958, Zinoun entered the musical conservatory of Casablanca where he eventually was drawn to dance, much to the chagrin of his father, who shunned him thereafter because of his choice. Zinoun states in an interview, "Je me suis rendu compte que ce n'était pas simplement la danse qui dérangeait. C'était la découverte du corps, son affirmation, son utilisation" (I realized that it wasn't simply dance that bothered him. It was the discovery of the body, its affirmation, its use) (Mirabet, n.p.).

Fig. 4.1. Lahcen Zinoun, Casablanca, 2009

In 1964, he received a first prize in dance bestowed by the Conservatory of Casablanca. Yet, despite the accolades that came with the prize from the school and the authorities, Zinoun was refused a scholarship to study dance abroad. Shortly thereafter, he left anyway for Belgium, where he studied choreography with the famous Maurice Béjart. Zinoun returned to Morocco to encourage Moroccans to embrace dance, teaching for several years in Rabat and Casablanca during the 1970s. However, he realized that he "was a stranger in his own country." His efforts in 1986 to found the National Troupe of Traditional Dance and to promote the richness of traditional styles met with resistance from the monarchy of Hassan II. In an interview, Zinoun explains the hostility against him: "Le roi [Hassan II] m'a convoqué pour me dire qu'au Maroc, on ne danse pas. Que le Maroc était un pays d'hommes" (King Hassan II called me in order to tell me that in Morocco we don't dance. Morocco was a country of men) (Mirabet, n.p.).

Forbidden to dance, Zinoun suffered from depression and turned to other forms of artistic expression, primarily painting. In 1991, he began dancing again and founded a new school of dance in Casablanca in which his wife and sons, also accomplished dancers, have taught.[5] Zinoun, drawn to many artistic forms, found that cinematography was a means to blend the visual of his paintings with the corporeal movements of dance. Always a sociopolitically committed activist, Zinoun remarked in an interview that the role of the filmmaker is to be an "individualist . . . because each person is a thermometer, able to measure and reflect the politics of the time." The problem in Morocco, however, is that "there is no political support to encourage artists," and artists, filmmakers, and novelists who challenge the government are often penalized. Although the past is easier to render on the screen and in texts, Zinoun stresses that government officials usually just "give you a rope by which to hang yourself."[6] In the early 2000s, the filmmaker's shorts, *Assamt* (2001), *Piano* (2002), *Le silence* (2000), and *Faux pas* (False steps, 2003), achieved international acclaim. His 2007 feature-length film, *La beauté éparpillée* (Scattered beauty), was praised for its visual richness, evoked in period costumes and decors.

The eighteen-minute film *Faux pas* reflects Zinoun's personal experiences with repression during the Lead Years under Hassan II. The story, told from the viewpoint (and vantage point) of feet, takes on several meanings as the film unfolds. "Faux pas" in French figuratively means "error," yet in the context of the film, the term also connotes a "misplaced step" (the word *pas* literally means "step"), since the entire film is shot from the perspective of the silent characters' feet (both shod and bare, male and female). Aurally, "faux pas" sounds like "faut pas" meaning "must not"—a warning—also an underlying theme. Except for the haunting narration of the female voice that recounts the events of Evelyn Serfaty's 1952 kidnapping, torture, and subsequent imprisonment until 1956 during the waning years of French occupation in Morocco, it is the feet of men and women who tell the story of human rights abuse.

Zinoun's camerawork is visually stunning as it re-creates the horrors experienced during the Lead Years (1963–99) and during French occupation (1912–56). Two periods of historical réfoulement are contextualized, forcing audiences to think about the thousands of Moroccans who were made to "disappear" during these times; either at the hands of the French during occupation or later in the era of Hassan

II. *Faux pas* tells the countless stories of the faceless masses who were abducted, tortured, and disposed of without a trace. The film opens with an ode to Evelyn Serfaty, sister to Abraham Serfaty, Jewish by birth, but also a communist-activist fighting against the French occupiers in the 1950s. Both Serfaty and his sister were exiled to France, where they were incarcerated until 1956. Later, in the Morocco of the 1970s, Abraham Serfaty was again imprisoned, this time under Hassan II for his militant activism on university campuses across the country with the poet-author Abdellatif Laâbi. Both Serfaty and Laâbi founded the communist literary review *Souffles*, in which they published much of their ideology calling for a multiparty democratic political system. Therefore, Zinoun's film is particularly moving for Moroccan audiences who are aware of a long history of repression and the principal players who were caught up in it: "This film is dedicated to Evelyn Serfaty. A Moroccan, communist militant who suffered imprisonment from 1952 to 1956 at the hands of the French after being deported to France with her brother." The film at once denounces a repressive history and also reminds audiences of the diverse population of Moroccans (Jews, Christians, Berbers, secularists, and Muslims) who fought and died for independence and human liberty in the country. At the same time, Zinoun's anonymous feet allude to the random abductions that took place during Hassan II's reign (1963–99) and about which many victims' families still do not have information.[7]

In the opening scene, feet shod in men's black dress shoes (reminiscent of the styles worn in the 1950s) drunkenly stagger up a flight of stairs before entering an apartment. The feet stumble and we hear dripping water, which becomes louder as the feet walk unsteadily to a sofa. The drip of a faucet, reminiscent of the water torture the French used to make suspects reveal the whereabouts of insurgents, is unmistakable as it grows louder in the background. The denouement is narrated by a woman's voice that provides details in French about Evelyn Serfaty's kidnapping.

Zinoun's mastery of artistic montage relies on contrasting opposites. The struggling feet of nefarious henchmen who have broken into the apartment to abduct and torture are juxtaposed with the legs and hooves of a horse running on the beach in unfettered freedom. The feet forced under water, succumbing to torture, are contrasted with the splash of the seawater under the horse's hooves as it gallops in the waves. Water is juxtaposed to the fire used to hurriedly burn the papers of outlawed acts—the "faut pas"—of writings for justice: Serfaty's letters and poems, a picture of Che Guevara, the books of dissidents and "agitators." The brightly lit hallway in which feet are dragged down a stairwell is in stark contrast to the dark nighttime streets where feet run into nightclubs to escape in order to find compatriots with whom, and crowds in which, to hide.

Banal little everyday sounds and noises in Zinoun's film become amplified harbingers of malicious acts: a phone ringing, knocking on a door, a woman screaming, a glass shattering on flagstones. Slats in between stairwells become bars on windows looking through to the bloodied, shackled feet of the incarcerated; always anonymous and always in agony. At the beginning of the film a man's feet are taken, and at the end they are a woman's. In the last scene, feet stand on a stool before plunging toward the floor in a death by hanging. "I had to endure all this because I'm the sister of my brother," the voice recalls. In the closing credits, on a silent screen, Evelyn writes: "I call upon all members of humankind, who have a conscience, to end all persecution. Their protest will protect our women and children. [Signed by] Evelyn." Through Evelyn Serfaty's story, Zinoun notes, "tribute is paid to all Moroccan women, silenced throughout history, who fought for the dignity of humankind while risking their lives."

Zinoun's deft camerawork demonstrates the power of film to bring to light the egregious past abuses of human rights in Morocco. Yet, in 2003 when the film was made, its allusion to torture techniques such as waterboarding and wanton incarcerations of thousands in Abu Ghraib and Guantanamo without trial or access to judicial process cannot be discounted. Its relevance to today's climate of terrorism and torture makes this short silent film a testimony, documenting the human rights abuses that occur every day in countries across the globe.

Serge Le Péron and Saïd Smihi's *J'ai Vu Tuer Ben Barka* (2005): The Docurealist Film about the Lead Years

Serge Le Péron and Saïd Smihi's *J'ai vu tuer Ben Barka* is the first feature-length docurealist film to be made on the obscure past of Mehdi Ben Barka, the Moroccan socialist oppositional leader assassinated in October 1965. French Serge Le Péron and Moroccan Saïd

Smihi joined forces to reveal all the information thus far released by authorities in France and Morocco on what for more than forty years has been known as "L'affaire Ben Barka."[8] While nothing exceedingly new is disclosed in the film, Le Péron and Smihi offer audiences a unique version of the events, reconstructed from almost all the players involved. The "affaire" is not centered on Ben Barka, but rather on all those who directly or indirectly were implicated in his death: "It's not a documentary; it's a fiction film that doesn't betray reality," state the filmmakers.[9] The affair, classified as one of the most "obscure and embarrassing events of the Fifth Republic," is told in three "acts" that depict flashbacks of the events before and after Ben Barka's assassination.[10]

In 1965, the Moroccan Marxist intellectual Ben Barka roamed the world, working with the socialist leaders of the Third World Movement to rectify the socioeconomic and political ills generated by years of colonialism and Western imperialism. Ben Barka's participation in the populist movements of the 1960s led him to forge friendships with people such as Fidel Castro, Che Guevara, Amilcar Cabral, and Malcolm X. Their goal: to found unifying socialist ideologies that would benefit the developing world. His relationships with these seminal figures put Ben Barka's name on every secret-service wanted list; from France's DST to the American CIA and, according to Ben Barka's son Bachir, the Israeli Mossad.[11] As the 1959 elected leader of the UNFP (Union nationale des forces populaires) in Morocco, Ben Barka posed a threat to the monarchy of Mohammed V and, subsequently, to King Hassan II. In 1962, the opposition leader, accused falsely by the king of plotting assassinations, fled the country. In 1965 he was abducted by the French police under orders from Charles de Gaulle (close friend to King Hassan II and General Oufkir, then minister of the interior), tortured in a house in Fontenay-le-Vicomte, a suburb of Paris, and later killed. His body was never found.

Le Péron and Smihi limit the time frame of their film to the months leading up to Ben Barka's kidnapping and assassination as well as those immediately following the incident. These include highlighting the mock trial in France that supposedly revealed the culprits. In the film, Ben Barka is depicted in his 1965 true-life role as chairman of the committee planning the January 1966 Tricontinental Conference. The conference was to take place in Havana, bringing together dignitaries and leaders from three continents—Africa, Asia, and Latin America—in order to discuss strategies to combat apartheid, the preponderance of colonialism in certain regions, and economic disparity in the Third World.

On October 29, 1965, as the film depicts, Ben Barka did go to the Brasserie Lipp, Boulevard Saint Germain, Paris, to meet and discuss a documentary film with a journalist, a film producer, and a screenwriter. Their goal was to make a documentary about the national liberation movements in which Ben Barka was participating. The character Figon in Le Péron and Smihi's film describes his proposed documentary film as "la première fresque de la décolonisation" (the first fresco of decolonization) as he tries to sell the idea to Georges Franju, the chosen director for the project. According to Ben Barka's son Bachir, the appointment was a sham, used to entrap his father. Upon his arrival at the restaurant, Ben Barka was met by two French detectives who insisted that he accompany them. This was the last time the leader was seen alive.[12]

Le Péron and Smihi tell their story gleaned from history. In actual events leading up to Ben Barka's assassination, screenwriter Marguerite Duras, director Georges Franju, and the small-time bandit Georges Figon were all either directly or indirectly players in Ben Barka's untimely death. In the film, as in reality, Duras and Franju, both admirers of Ben Barka, are ignorant of the plot against him. The real-life Franju was reported as never having recovered from his involuntary implication in Mehdi Ben Barka's disappearance.[13] The film's story is told from the point of view of Figon, who, while participating in the plot to abduct Ben Barka, is small-fry next to the henchmen Boucheseiche, Oufkir, and Dlimi, historically the ultimate assassins of the opposition leader.

In 1965, small-time bandit Figon, recently released from prison after serving time for various petty crimes, tries his luck at journalism and film production. Seeking funding to make a film with Franju, Figon's "friends" in the French government put him in contact with Moroccan officials, who tell him they wish to make a documentary about decolonization. They entreat Figon to contact Ben Barka, whom they would like to act as "historical adviser" on the scenario. In January 1966, Figon ends up assassinated after selling information to a newsmagazine about what he saw at the house in Fontenay-le-Vicomte where Ben Barka was tortured and believed to have been assassinated.

J'ai vu tuer Ben Barka is particularly interesting in that it is not specifically about Ben Barka, but rather the historical events, dissemination and covering up of facts, and culpability of major political figures living in both France and Morocco in the 1960s. Le Péron and Smihi do not reveal any new information on the affair, but rather demand that the annals of history divulge all information about an event that is now more than forty years old. To date, as they stipulate at the end of the film, there are still missing documents and inexistent files that could offer closure, certainly as to what happened to Ben Barka's body. The film makes a point of drawing audiences' attention on both sides of the Mediterranean to the fact that the histories of both France and Morocco would have been exceedingly different if the famous leader had lived. The film's story line is probably very close to reality, and probes the national memories of Morocco and France to "faire éclater la vérité" (expose reality), as Figon remarks when he divulges his story to a newsmagazine under the sensationalized title "J'ai vu tuer Ben Barka."

Shot in the classical style of the French *polars* (police/detective stories) of the 1950s and 1960s, the filmmakers capture the mood of the times. Jazz music of the 1960s sets the tempo for scenes taken from real documentary footage of the era mixed with those of the film. Situating the action entirely in France points a blatant finger at French officials' culpability and collusion with Moroccan generals Oufkir and Dlimi, who wanted Ben Barka dead. The rapid scenes that present General Oufkir, Hassan II's right-hand man, who arrives at Fontenay to torture and then kill Ben Barka, allude to the fact that the entire kidnapping was orchestrated by French authorities in order to ensure the continuation of the Moroccan monarchy's hold on power at the time. The revelation of the truth, in the end, does not disclose much more than, as Marguerite Duras (played by Josiane Balasko) notes, the elimination of a man "qui était écouté aux quatre coins de la planète" (who was listened to by the four corners of the world).

It is evident that, despite the continuing refusal of French and Moroccan authorities to reveal everything about the Ben Barka affair, the more open political climate of the post Lead Years has contributed to the airing of the dirty political laundry of the past. With respect to the film itself, it most assuredly poses the question: "Is this really a Moroccan film?" Apart from the Moroccan actors—Fayçal Khiari (Oufkir), Mouna Fettou (Ben Barka's wife), and Azize Kabouche (Chtouki, member of the Moroccan secret service)—the cast is international. Ben Barka is played by the Armenian actor Simon Abkarian, since the filmmakers determined that "a Moroccan actor wouldn't have had the versatility" to play the role.[14] However, we could argue that its international cast promotes a universal commitment to human rights on a global scale.

Released in 2005, at the height of the American occupation of Iraq and the events following September 11, 2001, that generated a preoccupation with terrorism in the West, the film's theme—establishing justice for those who still must live under political oppression— seems timeless. As one critic remarked, "Ben Barka est le prototype de l'homme qu'il ne fallait pas abattre. Quand on tue Ben Barka, on se retrouve avec Ben Laden" (Ben Barka is the prototype of the man one should not kill. When men like Ben Barka are killed, we find ourselves with Bin Laden) (Gourlet, n.p.).

Jillali Ferhati's *Mémoire en Détention* (2004): Turning the Page of History?

"I wanted to make a film about a character who couldn't remember anything, but at the time, I didn't know what he shouldn't remember," states Jillali Ferhati in an interview.[15] Ferhati's film, which was distributed across Morocco in 2004, is considered to be the best and most effective of in-country produced films whose subjects dwell on recapturing the past of the Lead Years.[16] The filmmaker, also an accomplished man of the stage who for years lived in exile in Paris where he worked in various theaters, sees himself as a representative of the people and responsible for accurately depicting their past. Ferhati's films, for the most part all set in his native Tangier, include *Une brèche dans le mur* (A hole in the wall, 1978), *Poupées de roseau* (Cane dolls, 1981), and the compelling *La plage des enfants perdus* (The beach of lost children, 1991). In 1995 he made *Cheveaux du fortune* (Horses of fortune), followed by *Mémoire en détention* in 2004. Like Benjelloun, Ferhati is known for making films with engaging social messages, and *Mémoire en détention* is no exception to this rule. However, at no time does the filmmaker directly name or blame perpetrators, collaborators, or torturers. Rather, the plot's vagueness with regard to a specific time frame encourages audiences to think about freedom and human rights on a universal level, as precious and always in danger of being abused.

Ferhati not only directs but also plays the leading role of Mokhtar Alyouni, who has spent years in detention. He has been incarcerated for such a long time that he and the prison officials have forgotten why he was originally imprisoned. Little by little, we learn that his crime was political activism (presumed in the 1970s, although dates are not precise) in one of the many militant groups of the era. In prison he is befriended by a much younger prisoner, Zoubeir, who was incarcerated for car theft but whose father, also detained and tortured, died in prison for being a political activist "in the past." Zoubeir's father and Mokhtar, as later revealed, knew each other, as did the many others who were rounded up and imprisoned because Mokhtar's father revealed their names in an effort to free his son.

In the end, almost all died in prison. When Mokhtar is finally released, amnesiac and with no family to claim him, the prison warden commands Zoubeir, also freed after three years of detention, to help the elderly man retrace his steps in order to recover his memory. With only the addresses on empty envelopes from the letters Mokhtar keeps in a box, Zoubeir not only looks for people who can recognize the old man and clue him in on his past, he also seeks to find out from Mokhtar the truth about his own father. Zoubeir's last memory of his father is a violent one, captured in one childhood moment when at eight years old he saw him dragged from his home.

Complicating the plot, the prison warden tells Zoubeir that there were two Mokhtar Alyounis in prison. One was a bank executive, condemned for having siphoned millions from a bank, and the other a political activist. One Alyouni was released "years ago." And, because the prison warden claims that "we have no more political activists locked up in this country," the Mokhtar being released must be the banker. When Zoubeir protests, wondering why he should help the man, the warden tells him that Mokhtar still is an amnesiac who needs to find his family. Zoubeir is also doubtful about which Alyouni was really released years earlier and is drawn to the project by the possibility of finding out about his father's past. The mistaken/switched identity, a seemingly weak link in the script in the beginning, is later clarified when audiences are told the bank executive bribed Mokhtar the activist to "give him his identity" so that he could get out of prison. Mokhtar the activist readily agreed because of the overwhelming guilt he felt for having "betrayed" the list of names to his father, who later communicated them to the authorities.

The question then arises: Is Mokhtar faking his amnesia in order to forget the betrayal, or is he really suffering from memory loss? As the two protagonists crisscross the country (primarily the north), tracking down the few militant activists who are left, Zoubeir ferrets out the truth about his father's and Mokhtar's pasts. When Mokhtar asks Zoubeir why he cares, he replies, "I'm trying to figure out what you have in your head, but what can you expect? Our generation doesn't understand anything." Ferhati's call to the younger generations not to forget the past of the Lead Years is blatantly expressed in Zoubeir's quest for the truth in what he sees as a past that is fading into obscurity. Ferhati, like Benjelloun, Boulane, and others, impresses upon audiences that although things seem right now, the past is fragile and must be remembered. Zoubeir emphatically points out: "One day we live in fear and the next in peace . . . but I have to look for my past."

Certain symbols in Ferhati's film are understood to represent a particular era. Like many of his contemporaries, the filmmaker seeks to challenge audiences to think in universal terms about the human condition. His central message is a warning that in any society, at any time, atrocities, kidnappings, and torture could occur. These warnings are symbolically gathered and guarded in Mokhtar's cardboard box, which he constantly carries under his arm, not letting Zoubeir get near it. The letters symbolically represent the murky secrets that are still left to be uncovered, as well as the thousands whose testimonies will forever lie buried in the past unless they are opened and exposed.

Parallel to the events alluded to in the past, in the present Zoubeir reads outloud news clippings to Mokhtar that describe Morocco's ongoing efforts to rectify the abuses of the Lead Years through an "association des droits de l'homme" (human rights organization), which is not specifically named but is understood to be the Instance d'equité et de reconciliation (IER, Equity and Reconciliation Committee), formed in 2004 by Mohammed VI to document abuses of human rights under Hassan II. Zoubeir, reading outloud to Mokhtar from a French-language newspaper, announces that the task of the association will be to aid "tous les anciens détenus politiques" (all former political prisoners) to obtain reparations. The association will

> primo faire une enquête sur les abus de pouvoir dont été victimes les citoyens, arrêtés illégalement pour leurs idées politiques ; secundo, la restitution des corps des prisonniers d'opinion morts sous la torture dans les geôles ; tertio, l'indemnisation au profit des anciens détenus politiques en ayant droits.

(first conduct an investigation into the abuses of power that victimized citizens who were arrested for their political ideas; second, [it will demand] the return of the remains of prisoners who died under torture in prison; third, [it will demand] indemnities for former prisoners.)

These three items, of course, formed the driving mission of the IER, which later handed its report to King Mohammed VI in 2005. Many former victims and their families, however, have stated that the efforts of the commission were too little too late. The "too little, too late" message is interwoven into the film with snippets of scenes from the past of bodies being tortured and dark cells and long corridors. Reading in French, Zoubeir/Ferhati also invokes the many testimonial accounts that have been published in recent years by small French-language publishers operating in Morocco. These include Tarik Editions, Editions Eddif, and Editions Marsam, whose publishers have committed themselves to authors who were once also former victims and are seeking to recount their stories in order to reveal what has never been told.[17]

In an effort to unearth Mokhtar's buried past, Zoubeir takes him to an abandoned prison. Zoubeir, also an aspiring theater actor, delivers a monologue as Mokhtar wanders in the dark, abandoned halls: "They poured cold water on my head; they hurt me . . . What did they want? What did I do to them? God help me." The delivery does succeed in opening the old man's mind, from which emerge scenes of his own torture. These become more vivid when Zoubeir tells him that the abandoned prison is actually "the first prison where you were taken the first time." Ironically, he notes, "They now want to make it into a cultural center." He closes his soliloquy by poetically adding: "If only memories would die before the bodies that house them do."

Ferhati makes a point of rendering memory as a tangible thing throughout his film. Not only is Mokhtar's locked box of letters a symbol, but memory is also "experienced" as something that inhabits the body. Mokhtar's recurring bloody nose, which begins flowing at inopportune times, is a constant reminder of his past torture. In a final flashback in the schoolroom where he once taught math, the bloody nose of the present is linked to a young Mokhtar who was beaten and his head slammed against a wall before being taken away and imprisoned. The school, which is visited by Zoubeir and Mokhtar at the end of the film, becomes a *lieu de mémoire* where the old man finally regains and relives his past. It is also the place where Zahra (Fatima Loukili) comes to after a long trek home from exile. She has received Mokhtar's letters over the years and now, deciding that things are safe in present-day Morocco, decides to come home to look for him. She, too, was an activist and a teacher, once Mokhtar's lover, and eventually taken and imprisoned for unspecified political crimes.

In the end, memory is restored and broken lives are put back together. Mokhtar and Zahra, as living former detainees, rediscover each other. Others, like Zoubeir's father, are now properly remembered in the present. Yet, Ferhati's title, *Mémoire en détention* (Memory in detention, or Imprisoned memory, depending on how one prefers to translate it into English), remains a telling metaphor for an entire country held hostage to its past. It still remains to be seen how the future will continue to pay homage to those who lost their lives during the Lead Years. Like the film, the ending is left open-ended, leading audiences to the conclusion that there is much left to be written about torture and imprisonment in the annals of history.

Hassan Benjelloun's *La Chambre Noire* (2004): Uncovering the Dark Recesses of the Past

La chambre noire, by filmmaker Hassan Benjelloun, is based on Jaouad Mdidech's book of the same title. Although Mdidech collaborated on the film's screenplay, it diverges from the book by cultivating the love story between Kamal (played by Mohammed Nadif) and Najat (Hanane Ibrahimi), fiancés who are only briefly mentioned in Mdidech's autobiography. In the film, both protagonists work at the airport and seem apolitical and oblivious to the impending doom that awaits them. The 1970s, the backdrop for the film's plot, represent some of the most repressive years of Hassan II's reign, during which the hunt for and incarceration of Marxist-Leninist supporters was in its heyday. Benjelloun emphasizes the randomness of kidnappings and interrogations. From one moment to the next, people disappear without a trace. Although he left his militant student days behind him, is a respectable airport employee, and professes to be apolitical, Kamal is abducted from his place of employment and sequestered. He is interrogated about his years as a rebel at the university and his activity as a leader of the "March 23rd" Marxist-Leninist group. Without trial or access to a lawyer, he is thrown in prison at Derb Moulay Chérif (which is also the Arabic title of the film). While there, he is forced to reveal the names of his former comrades, even though he confesses not to have seen them for years.

Najat tries to find him, risking her own family's safety. When she does finally locate him in prison and secures visitation rights, Kamal tells her to "marry someone else" because he knows he will be condemned to years in prison. Subsequently, the prisoners engage in a hunger strike in order to bring attention to their plight, notably to improve conditions in the prison and demand a trial to face their accusers. Najat and Kamal are separated forever. Most of the second half of the film concentrates on revealing the unjust legal system, lawyers who refused to represent detainees, and the resulting mock trial the prisoners end up facing. The unjust outcome leads their lawyers to storm out of the courtroom, disgusted by the judge's flagrant abuse of human rights as the prisoners chant, "The road of struggle calls us."

Despite the media's support, documenting their strike and demands for their freedom in the papers, all prisoners are condemned to between fourteen (Mdidech) and twenty-two years of prison. Najat marries someone else. Years later, in the concluding scene of the film, she meets Mdidech again as he signs copies of his work, *La chambre noire*, in a bookstore. Najat, with her little girl, approaches her former lover for his signature. The film ends on a somewhat upbeat note, but also alludes to the bitter legacy of the thousands of lives of the disappeared cut short during the Lead Years.

La chambre noire, although winning the L'étalon d'argent award at FESPACO in Ouagadougou (Burkina Faso) in 2005, received mixed reviews at home. The weekly francophone newsmagazine *TelQuel* disparaged the film, emphasizing that "we learned nothing new that we didn't already know."[18] Although the work reveals few tidbits of new information, it still serves as a cinematic, documented memory that is, at least, preserved on film. Like the novel of the same title, the film demonstrates the closeness and solidarity of the prison detainees as they struggle to endure their incarceration. The masses of prisoners Benjelloun depicts in the film expose just how widespread torture and detention were during the Lead Years.

Hassan Benjelloun's retelling of history is important and, like his other films *Jugement d'une femme* and *Où vas-tu Moshé?*, serves to educate the young about the flagrant abuse of human rights during the past, particularly the Lead Years. The filmmaker inserts real footage of television clips from the Green March, a nationalist propaganda stunt orchestrated by Hassan II on November 6, 1975. Nearly 350,000 unarmed Moroccans were urged to march to the border of the Western Sahara and cross over the line, symbolically claiming the region for Morocco from Spain. The green flags waved by participants also symbolically demonstrated national unity, allegiance to the king, and faith in Islam. Supporters also waved the Moroccan flag's colors, red and green (red for freedom, green for Islam), and pictures of Hassan II, thus presenting the public's en masse approbation for the king.[19]

The Green March became the monarchy's symbol for Islam, openly countering Marxist-Leninist ideology that supported pluralist party politics and secular institutions. Hassan II, therefore, successfully suppressed the ideals of the opposition and the political enfranchisement of hundreds who sought to counter his rule. Benjelloun's depiction of the march in conjunction with the trials is daring and reveals the monarchy's flagrant abuse of power while it sought to divert attention from the human rights abuses taking place in its prisons. Audiences viewing the film in the present are reminded of just how politics and ideology can be used to manipulate, coerce, and destroy a people. These haunting facts, many believe, are still a possible reality for contemporary Morocco.

Saâd Chraïbi's *Jawhara* (2003): Prison Seen from a Child's Eyes

Saâd Chraïbi's *Jawhara* (2003) also opened to mixed reviews in Morocco. It was the first film to visually depict on-screen the incarceration of women and the abuse of their civil rights during the Lead Years. To date, *Jawhara* is the only film ever to have been made about women's lives in prison. The suffering of women during the Lead Years tends to be a subject avoided by filmmakers and activists. Authors also have been hesitant to evoke the issue. It was not until the late 1990s and the subsequent publication of Fatna El Bouhi's testimonial, *Une femme nommée Rachid* (A woman named Rachid, 2002), that women began to put voices and faces to the horror they endured. Women's accounts of prison rape and torture have been something of a mystery, since upon their release the majority preferred to remain silent about their experiences because of the stigma associated with rape. Speaking for her sisters, also detained, raped, and silenced, El Bouhi noted in a 2004 interview that women were still hesitant to speak of the past because her nation, even with the efforts of the IER, was unable to address and heal the open wounds of its past:

> Je comprends, reprend-t-elle, la pudeur des témoignages de femmes qui témoignent aujourd'hui dans le cadre des auditions de l'IER. On ne peut pas, comme cela, sans préparation, sans soutien et suivi psychologique, surgir des oubliettes, vider toutes ses tripes et retourner à l'anonymat comme si de rien n'était.

> (I understand, she remarks, the modesty of the testimonies by the women who gave evidence today in the IER sessions. We can't, just like that, without preparation, without support and psychological counseling, spring forth from oblivion, empty our guts, and return to anonymity as if nothing happened.) (Boukhari 2006, n.p.)

Ironically, former female prisoners are also viewed, because of their gender, as martyrs and, therefore, their stories are considered virtually untouchable by the public. The general societal belief is that female testimonials are still too horrific to be imparted to the public in Morocco. Former female prisoners are simply silent *gardiennes de la mémoire* (female memory keepers), the example par excellence of a purity "spoliée par le Makhzen" (stained by the Makhzen) (Zekri 2006, 205–6).[20] "Woman as the sacred heart of the nation" is still a prevalent theme in Moroccan culture. For a woman to admit that she was tortured and "spoiled," and for her to reveal that some of her sisters were even killed by men who were supposed to cherish and protect them, would mean that Moroccans themselves had sought to annihilate their own beings—their own mothers—and the lifeblood of the nation.

Moroccan feminist, psychiatrist, and author Rita El Khayat explains that the belief that women are the engenderers of national purity is still the norm in societies where "groups of kinship superior to the immediate family dominate" (2002, 56). This is true for Moroccan society as well as elsewhere in the Arab world. As stipulated in El Khayat's *Les femmes arabes* (Arab women) and, indeed, throughout her impressive oeuvre, women are never viewed as individuals or equal partners in marriage because the larger society will always take precedence over them. Therefore, for a woman to speak, and even exist as a completely self-sufficient individual, is an act of defiance in the face of society and the nation (56).[21]

Jawhara breaks with stereotype to give women a voice in the telling of their own stories of the past. The film is the account of a girl born in prison after her mother, Safia, is raped by a prison warden. Jawhara is destined to remain in prison as long as her mother's sentence is sustained. Set in the 1970s and told as a flashback by the now adult Jawhara, Safia, the girl's mother, is a member of a small amateur theater troupe that decides to put on a politically charged antigovernment play. Saïd, her lover and director of the show, is also taken by the police but escapes. He flees with tapes from the police station that contain disturbing images of torture and interrogation. Although other members of the troupe are eventually freed, Safia remains in custody, relocated to a farm detention center in the desert while police hunt for Saïd and the damning tapes. She and her daughter remain hostages there for years. The filmmaker's allusion to the historical eighteen-year imprisonment of the Oufkir family in the desert during Hassan II's reign is not lost on audiences. Safia becomes ill and dies, leaving Jawhara, who is later reunited with Saïd to fend for herself.

Jawhara blends anachronism with fantasy to weave a tale that should have made more of an impact on audiences but instead received lukewarm reception from critics. Chraïbi films scenes in present-day Casablanca, altering little to plunge the time frame back into the 1970s. The filmmaker claimed that this was done on purpose to remind audiences that the Lead Years are ever present and that prison and torture are still part of our everyday realities (Raji, n.p.). This noble cause, however, is undermined by certain scenes rendered in cartoon format. The fantastic, animated court scenes do not justly portray the reality of corrupt judges, co-opted testimony, and manipulated officials at the hands of the *Makhzen*. These abrupt transitions, between animated scenes and Jawhara and her mother in prison, are interchanged with little warning and no context for viewers. The story becomes a confused rendition of historical memory.

However, as a document that bears witness to the thousands of silenced voices of the past, the film serves as a noteworthy historical marker. Like all the films discussed in this chapter, it offers a first timid step toward depicting the Lead Years on screen. Films about incarceration have opened a cinematic dialogue about torture and human rights that continues to fuel discussion.

In general, Moroccan prison films, produced by filmmakers as survivors of the Lead Years, leave us with a lasting lesson. These film texts "demeurent" (reside) in the present as "proof . . . untenable" and as fragile, shared "secrets" between the victim and their public (Derrida 2000, 30). Moroccan filmmakers transmit to us that it is imperative for a nation seeking to construct a collective conscience in the present not to forget the events of the past. The collective *lieux de mémoire* must provide places that are "created by the interaction between memory and history, an interaction resulting in a mutual [understanding]" between the state and its people (Nora 1992, 11). Only this pact will ensure a national identity and a historical consciousness that will be equitable and accurately defined for all, guaranteeing the New Morocco's well-being for future generations.

5

Women's Voices

Documenting Morocco through Feminine Lenses

African filmmakers, male and female, particularly in the last fifteen years, have repeatedly given women central roles that "challenge the misrepresentations, preconceptions and stereotypes that abound [in the West] vis-à-vis the position and role of women in Africa" (Thackway 2003, 147). In order to understand the strength and power of African women as depicted on-screen, we only need to consider Senegalese Sembène Ousmane's entire oeuvre, notably, *Black Girl* (1968), *Ceddo* (1976), *Faat Kiné* (2001), and *Molaadé* (2005). Younger male cineastes such as Senegalese Moussa Sene Absa (*Tableau Ferraille*, 1997; and *Madame Brouette*, 2002) and Malian Abderrahmane Sissako (*Bamako*, 2006) have continued Sembene's thematic structure favoring strong women's roles through which grand social-realist messages are conveyed. Women filmmakers from West Africa also demonstrate in their films that women are the pillars of community and country in Africa. Pioneering Senegalese filmmaker Safi Faye's *Kaddu beykat* (The voice of the peasant, 1975) and her more recent compatriots, Khady Sylla (*Les bijoux*, 1997) and Fatou Kandé Senghor (*Diola Tigi*, a documentary film, 2008), have contributed significantly to the advancement of women's filmmaking in West Africa.

African Womanism on the Screen

African women filmmakers, particularly from francophone sub-Saharan Africa, promote an *Africana womanist* philosophy that is rooted in Afrocentrist ideology. Afrocentrist womanists define feminism and their roles and places in their respective societies on their own terms, irrespective of Western feminist paradigms. Africana womanism relies on the "specificity" of the African woman's condition, while contextualizing a feminism that expresses "African women's yearning [for new conceptions of themselves] as opposed to an imposed or dogmatic position" (Kolawole 1997, 22). Translating this "yearning" is a defining trait most noticeable in sub-Saharan African women's cinematography.

The heroines of African films by earlier, groundbreaking women filmmakers such as Senegalese Safi Faye and Togolese Anne-Laure Folly reflect a "transformation of consciousness" that depicts African women as "genuinely free to forge new combinations of personality traits . . . without the need . . . to imitate the model of the European," or dwell on traditional mores and customs that have hindered their active agency in contemporary African societies (Lazreg 1994, 322). Female filmmakers have promoted African womanism as an applicable ideology through which to transcribe the realities of African women's lives. The term *Africana* is meant to be inclusive of all women of the continent and in the African diaspora and therefore not defined by skin color. African womanists seek to work within the system of established African societies in order to foster change not only for women, but men too. It is a humanist approach that relies on the centrality of the African experience as promoted within Afrocentrist ideology. Women filmmakers on the continent have contended for a long time that sexual difference is but one component of their movement championing the rights of women in Africa and across the diaspora.

Early on, women filmmakers began to formulate the specificity of African life and women's roles within it on the screen. The films of filmmakers Safi Faye, Anne-Laure Folly, and the later Khady Sylla and Fatou Kandé Senghor echo the socially transformative theories promoted by scholars such as Susan Arndt, Mary E. Kolawole, and Clenora Hudson-Weems. These scholars maintain that what is essential to an Africana woman's identity and agency is very different from what white Western European and American feminists have struggled for since the inception of Western feminist movements.

Films such as Senegalese Khady Sylla's *Les bijoux* (Jewelry, 1996); Burkina Fasian Fanta Regina Nacro's *Puk nini* (1995) and *Le truc de Konaté* (Konaté's Thing, 1997); Zimbabwean Tsitsi Dangarembga's *Everyone's Child* (1996) and *Mother's Day* (2004); Togolese Anne-Laure

124 / *Women's Voices*

Folly's *Femmes aux yeux ouverts* (Women with open eyes, 1993); Senegalese Safi Faye's *Mossane* (1996); and Angolian/Guadeloupean Sara Maldoror's earlier *Sambizanga* (1972) reflect African women scholars' argument for an ideology that does not align itself with Western feminism, which is viewed by many as historically alienating women of color along lines of race and class. Yet African women filmmakers, like their sisters in the West, would agree that cinema has the power to "produce and maintain a fascinating hold on its spectator by mobilizing pleasure . . . [particularly] the unconscious desire of the [female] subject" (Flitterman-Lewis 1996, 2–3).

However, since the function of cinema in African society compels other scenarios to be written for and about women that have less to do with objectivity/desire and more with social change, women cineastes working on the continent tend not to fall into the traps of constructing uniquely feminine images in terms of sexual pleasure. African women's filmmaking tends not to ascribe to Western preconceived notions of desire, or what Laura Mulvey claimed in her groundbreaking article "Visual Pleasure" as "mainstream film [that] coded the erotic into the language of the dominant patriarchal order" (1992, 6). This being said, however, African women filmmakers do promote the idea in their films that there is "[an] alternative . . . thrill that comes from leaving the past behind without rejecting it, transcending outworn or oppressive forms, or daring to break with normal pleasurable expectations in order to conceive a new language of desire" (6). African women's lenses conceptualize desire as shared by both men and women. "Women directors have referred to African men and women's shared struggle," points out Thackway in her study. Both "make films that revalue African subjects and highlight/counter structures that oppress both sexes" in order to show audiences that "African men and women consider women's emancipation as the way forward" (Thackway 2003, 149).

Like their counterparts in sub-Saharan Africa, contemporary Moroccan women filmmakers are influencing the views and opinions of their spectators through thought-provoking films that promote Africana womanist agendas. In the last fifteen years, the films of cineastes Farida Benlyazid, Zakia Tahiri, Narjiss Nejjar, and Yasmine Kassari, among others, have documented the sociopolitical and cultural transitions taking place now with respect to the roles and place of women in Moroccan society, as well as in a larger, global context. Since 1999, particularly, women filmmakers have militantly expressed their unique experiences in today's New Morocco. While their films delve into the challenges of a country in transition, they also reveal certain universalities about the female experience in contemporary society. These include woman's capacity to persevere against the constraints of family and traditionalism and the conflicts that women face as individuals who must negotiate with the omnipotent collective that takes precedence in Moroccan society. The women filmmakers studied in this chapter demonstrate an "écriture féminine" on the screen that visually depicts the voice of Moroccan women, a voice that is diverse and, at the same time, unified in its expression of feminine *being* in contemporary times.

The Uniqueness of Moroccan Women's Filmmaking

Although they came relatively late to filmmaking, Moroccan female cineastes have set their cinematography apart from their sisters' in Algeria and Tunisia. Moroccan women's themes in the new millennium are socially engaged, thought-provoking, and, with regard to male filmmakers, more readily cast women in take-charge roles. While promoting the credo of womanist agendas, their films are less didactic than those found in sub-Saharan Africa.

Moroccan womanist films such as *Les yeux secs* (2002, by Narjiss Nejjar) and *L'enfant endormi* (2004, by Yasmine Kassari) promote the enfranchisement, socially, culturally and, to some extent, politically, of women. Yet, comparing them with recent films by Algerians Yamina Bachir Chouikh (*Rachida*, 2002) and Djamila Sahraoui (*Barakat!*, 2006) and Tunisians Nadia El Fani (*Bedwin Hacker*, 2002) and Raja Amari (*Satin Rouge*, 2002), Moroccan women's themes tend to be much more subtle and subdued, as Denise Brahimi explains: "When comparing Moroccan cinema to Algerian [we note that] . . . pain is expressed by silence, rather than by screams" (2009, 35). Moroccan women's recent films are, with the exception perhaps of *Marock* by Leïla Marrakchi, aimed at audiences to encourage social activism in the mainstream, rather than to shock cultural values. Although it is difficult to defend this subtle difference, I would argue that the militancy levels in women's films in Morocco differ from those in Algeria and Tunisia because of the historical events of the past and the present.

Algeria's and Tunisia's revolutionary movements of the late 1950s, the subsequent founding of quasi-socialist governments that used film as propaganda to promote state-building ideologies, as well as the influence of Third Cinema movements in the 1960s on filmmaking in both countries, most definitely shaped how their industries would make films in the next decades. Civil war in Algeria in the 1990s and the aggressive Arabization of society in Tunisia (particularly since September 11, 2001) also have contributed to how the industries have shaped production patterns. The civil war in Algeria virtually made filmmaking in-country impossible, as indicates Merzak Allouache, who, when making *Bab El-Oued City* (1994) had to clandestinely shoot in undisclosed locations for fear of reprisals from the Islamic fundamentalists.[1]

Filmmakers in Tunisia, known for their auteur individualism as well as their fondness for making aesthetic films, rather than the populist and epic ones favored by Morocco, have suffered declining audience attendance because there is no national film institute from which to secure investment (such as the "avance sur recettes" policy in Morocco and Algeria) or money for advertising for films produced in country. As Boughedir suggests, Tunisia "suffers from too much individualism" and, in the absence of a national cinema institution (the Société anonyme Tunisienne de production et d'expansion cinématographique does not have the same prominent place in cultural production as does the CCM in Morocco), depends too much on private investment, which has led to a decline in the number of films made each year: "Unlike Tunisia, Morocco remarkably based the organization of its audiovisual industry on solidarity. Moroccan cinema is funded by a part of the TV advertising income [of the country] and thus [has been able] to increase production."[2] These specific realities in each of the three Maghrebian countries have also influenced how and why women make their films.

A strong feminist movement came to Tunisia on the heels of Habib Bourghiba's revolution to end colonialism in the late 1950s. To date, Tunisia still leads Arab nations in the constitutional guarantees and rights given to women. For example, Tunisia is the only country in the Arab world to have constitutionally banned polygamy. Despite recent setbacks due to the rise of Islamic fundamentalism in North Africa, which have brought with it conservative values, Tunisia still remains a beacon for women's rights in the Arab world. Women filmmakers have been actively making films in the country since the late 1970s, and their films have been somewhat funded by SATPEC and by international promoters in France, Belgium, and Spain. Interestingly, the prevalence of women-made films by filmmakers such as Moufida Tlatli, Nadia El Fani, and Raja Amari have "traumatized male cineastes" who see their "loss of masculine identity" as the result of "the power and autonomy of Tunisian women . . . which have created cultural trauma" (Brahimi 2009, 59–60).

Algeria's recent history, certainly in the 1980s with the rise in power of the FIS (Front Islamique du salut, Islamic Front) party, failed elections in 1988 and ensuing riots (which killed more than five hundred youths), and the subsequent civil war in the 1990s (the violence from which particularly targeted women in the most heinous manners), has made "the category 'woman' . . . indistinguishable from the . . . purely religious and the profane" (Lazreg 1994, 129). Despite the religious fundamentalist violence waged against them in the 1990s, women have continued to be present "visibly" in Algerian society. Their noticeable physical presence in public space in postcolonial society has its roots in the Marxist revolution of 1954–62, which finally ended in liberation in 1962. The war could not have been won without the participation of women.

Contrary to women's "mantle of invisibility" in the nineteenth century, which was a product of cultural taboos as much as "colonial policies," after the war of liberation women gained modest ground sociopolitically once the colonial regime had been toppled. Although postcolonial female emancipation in Algeria was far from what Tunisian women experienced, Marnia Lazreg notes that "since 1962 . . . the entry of women into the worlds of school and work has made them singularly conspicuous, considering their past invisibility" (1994, 172). Yet, women in Algeria still have not "shared equally with men in the benefits that accrued from the independence of their country"(119). The conflicts that characterize gender polemics in the modern state in Algeria today are reified in women's filmmaking. There are only four Algerian women filmmakers actually residing in Algeria and making films: Samira Hadj Djilani, Baya Hachemi, Nadia Cherabi, and Yamina Bachir Chouikh. These four women primarily work in television.[3] Algeria's film industry, like much of its literary production, has become one primarily conceived of in exile due to political instability and violence. In recent years, the country's instability has been captured in feature-length films by men and women: *Bab El-Oued City* (Merzak Allouach, 1994); *Viva Laldjérie* (Nadir Moknèche, 2004); and *Barakat!* (Djamila Sahraoui, 2006); as well as in documentaries such as *Aliénations* (Malek Ben Smaïl, 2004).

The film industry in Morocco, as elsewhere in the East and the West, has been predominantly defined by men. Women's roles in Moroccan male filmmakers' works tend to be pessimistic, casting them often as victims of sociocultural mores, misery, and poverty. Although many of these films speak the truth about some women's reality (Hassan Benjelloun's *Judgement d'une femme*; Jillali Ferhati's *La plage des enfants perdus*), women filmmakers contend that these works do not portray all parts of the sum total of their existence.

This chapter seeks to address certain pressing questions with regard to women's filmmaking in Morocco: To what extent does women's filmmaking accurately represent the reality of the human condition in general, and the feminine condition specifically, in Morocco? And, if the filmmakers truthfully do portray women's reality, are they able to generate awareness and discussion within Moroccan society in order to advance sociopolitical change?

Kaïd Ensa (Women's Wiles, 1999), Farida Benlyazid: Women Can't Be Put in Cages

Farida Benlyazid paved the way for women filmmakers in Morocco. As early as the 1970s she began writing scripts for filmmakers such as Mohammed Abderrahmane Tazi, Jillali Ferhati, and later, Hakim Noury (Carter 2001, 344). Her most notable scripts were for the now famous films *Badis* (1988) and *A la recherche du mari de ma femme* (Looking for my wife's husband, 1993), both directed by M. A. Tazi. Benlyazid has written and directed her own films, the most known of which include: *Une porte sur le ciel* (Door to the sky, 1987) and *Kaïd Ensa* (*Ruses de femmes*, Women's Wiles).

She shoots her films primarily in Moroccan Arabic, placing women in roles where they are forced to "confront dramatic changes and problems in Moroccan society" (Carter 2001, 344). Often her works are retrospectives on women's place in society, dating from independence in 1956 to the mid-1990s. Her films are generally realistic, with perhaps the exception of *Women's Wiles*, and rarely allow for "magic solutions" that will drastically alter women's designated roles in society. Benlyazid's style draws on the tenets of social-realist filmmaking to reveal the inequalities in traditional practices that have impeded women's emancipation in contemporary society. "Benlyazid uses her storytelling," as

Fig. 5.1. Farida Benlyazid, Fez, Morocco, 2009

Carter explains, "to reveal the structures of oppression and domination, even those replicated by women themselves" (344).

In *Women's Wiles* a young contemporary girl is taken back in time to the epoch of the sultans by her mother, who tells her the story of "Lalla Aïcha: Merchant's Daughter," a well-known Arab-Andalusian fairy tale, whose main theme shows the superiority of women over men. The film portrays a Scheherazade-type protagonist, the female storyteller par excellence, who passes her tales on to other women. Lalla Aïcha, daughter of a wealthy merchant, is cloistered in her garden, where she studies flowers and music. Although set in the distant past and reminiscent of a tale from *1001 Arabian Nights*, Aïcha counters how women are supposed to behave by enjoying a close relationship with her father, who admires her tenacity and strong will to get things she wants. Her formidable personality contradicts what is viewed as women's "proper" behavior at the time (although not specified, the story seems set in the eighteenth century). Lalla Aïcha also councils and acts as a business partner to her father, who relies on her financial savvy.

One day when in her garden, the heroine realizes she is being watched by the son of the sultan next door. He has fallen in love with her and wants to make her his bride. However, she finds him impetuous. They play a series of "ruses" on each other that become increasingly vicious; including one where Aïcha dresses up as a "slave from the Sudan," complete with blackface, and enters the prince's palace. She serves him tea, slips him a potion, he falls asleep, and she shaves off his beard (the sign of a religiously pious man). He is forced to stay indoors, sequestered for seven days, in order to grow his beard back. Metaphorically, Benlyazid turns the gender tables on cloistering. As the weeks go by, neither the prince from his palace, nor Aïcha from her garden, will allow the other to get the upper hand in their tit-for-tat competition that is based on the question: "Are women more intelligent than men?"

The prince asks for Lalla Aïcha's hand in marriage, which she accepts, thinking she will be able to change him. He promptly puts her in a dungeon cell and commands her to give in and acknowledge that "the ruse of men is stronger than that of women." She refuses, inciting the prince to seek council from his confidant, a sage and bookseller in the medina. Their conversation on the wiles of women and their intelligence thematically offers a grounding dialogue for the rest of the film:

> PRINCE: Are women intelligent?
> SAGE: Of course. They are intelligent, and one must not forget that there are women sages, erudite, and even Sufis.
> PRINCE: But their intelligence isn't like men's.
> SAGE: What do you mean? Sometimes they are more intelligent than men.
> PRINCE: Of course, but only from time to time, on rare occasions.
> SAGE: Yes, a woman has children, which she must take care of and raise. That doesn't leave her a lot of time for other things. Good is Woman, and Bad is Woman, and God said: Their ruse is immense. If the truth be known, we should hope that God doesn't make them our enemies. . . .
> PRINCE: Why are they so stubborn?

To answer this question, the sage gives the prince a book by Jelaluddin Rumi, the well-known Persian poet and sage who wrote in the thirteenth century. The symbolic importance of this book is significant to Benlyazid's story. Rumi was known for promoting unconventional ideals that transcended ethnic and nationalist rhetoric as well as preached equality. He was also known for having founded the Mevlevi Order, which in Turkey is recognized for its "whirling dervishes," dancing, and music—all viewed as atypical to traditional Islam. To accentuate her point that there are many beautiful practices in Islam (many of them Sufi) that are diverse and spiritual, Benlyazid follows the conversation of the prince and the sage with a dancing scene in which the prince's cousin, a young woman dressed in the clothes typical of the dervishes, whirls around in a courtyard to Sufi music. She stumbles upon the dungeon cell of Aïcha, whom she befriends. Although the cousin shares the same opinions about women's equality, she tells her "to just give in to the Prince and admit that women are less clever at ruses than men," so that she can be freed. Aïcha, holding fast to her principles, remarks, "He must learn what women are worth."

Aïcha cleverly has her father dig a tunnel from his house to her dungeon so that she can be with her family every day. For years, she sets traps for the prince in various disguises: as a Bedouin princess who lures him into her tent, a dancing woman who performs for him on the shore of a river, and a nomadic princess who invites him to partake of her beauty. After each tryst, she asks the prince to give her a token of his love. She also gives birth after every encounter, producing three children who stay with her father as she continues to live in her dungeon cell. The ruse of all ruses remains unbeknownst to the prince, who continues to ask her, "Lalla Aïcha, the Humiliated One who Lives in the Cellar, which is the cleverer, men or women?" On the day the prince decides to marry the woman who has been chosen for him by his father the sultan, Aïcha sends her children into his courtyard. They are bearing the gifts he bestowed on her in her various disguises. Discovering the truth, he also admits that "woman is not the object of desire, but the light of God." In the end, husband and wife, as they are, come together, both acknowledging, "We are under the orders of God and he gave strength to men and the art of ruses to women."

While a seemingly banal fairy tale, Benlyazid reveals to audiences certain themes that reflect contemporary dialogues on the emancipation of women in Moroccan society. The filmmaker's goal is to demonstrate to her viewers that women have always participated actively and equally in Moroccan social history. Feminism was a part of Moroccan life before the word actually existed, as attests her constant reiteration of the fact that women were "sages, erudite, and members of the Sufi order," long before more unfavorable traditions stripped them of their rights. Like many Maghrebian women filmmakers, such as Tunisian Moufida Tlati (*Les silences du palais*, Silences of the palace, 1994) and Algerian Assia Djebar (*La nouba des femmes de Mont Chenoua*, The circle of women on Mount Chenoua, 1977), Benlyazid seeks to revisit history in order to highlight women's contributions to their societies and cultures. What on the surface seems like a banal folktale is actually a social-realist text that instructs audiences about the vital contributions of women throughout history to Moroccan society.

Benlyazid particularly focuses on the subject of spatial divisions between genders as a means to study and contradict the tenets of traditionalist Islamic cultures. On numerous occasions, she brings up the subject of female sequestration. Although the heroine admits at one moment, "We women spend our lives locked up," she never lets this state become her own. For the prince, Aïcha is perhaps locked away in the cellar, but she also constantly ruptures the gender divisions between inside and outside spaces dictated by traditional Islam. She repeatedly freely passes from the interior spaces that confine her—the prince's cellar and her father's house—to the outside world. The heroine reveals that women are clever enough to find ways to disrupt the status quo in order to live as equal citizens in society. Seemingly passive, subdued "Lalla Aïcha, the Humiliated One Who Lives in the Cellar," as the prince continuously calls her, when in outside space rides a horse through the forest and becomes a nomadic princess who, reminiscent of the Kahina, a Berber queen who fought against Arab conquerors, gives orders to her soldiers and armies.[4]

Benlyazid's film also alludes to Berber culture as being perhaps more equitable and historically offering more equality for women than the Arab culture that conquered it in eighth century AD. Whenever Aïcha is free in open, outside space, she dons traditional Berber dress, employs Berber musicians to do her bidding, and favors the abodes of large Berber tents, pitched on the banks of rivers or in the desert. The filmmaker's Berber-centric themes are not hidden, making the film a harbinger announcing the thematic trends of the post Lead Years. Unlike his father, Mohammed VI has over the past decade promoted *Berberisme* as a key contributor to the uniqueness of Moroccan identity.

Les Yeux Secs (Dry Eyes, 2002), Narjiss Nejjar: Berber Women's Voices

Narjiss Nejjar, thirty-seven years old, is one of Morocco's up-and-coming women filmmakers who delves into the pertinent issues of women's lives. "Je fais ce que je veux, j'écris ce que je veux comme je veux" (I do what I want, I write what I want like I want), the filmmaker exclaims, rebutting the criticism surrounding her first feature-length film, *Les yeux secs*.[5] As soon as the film debuted in theaters across Morocco, it was mired in controversy, primarily because the work exposed how rural women, in particular, are marginalized and how their emancipation in society is still impeded by the constraints of religious and cultural traditions and social mores. Her film exposes how men are able to wield their power over women and control their destinies. The film also criticizes certain taboos associated with sexuality and sexual relationships between men and women, not only in traditional milieus, but in Moroccan society as a whole: "Un peuple est grand quand il sait dire l'amour sans honte" (A people is great when it knows how to pronounce love without embarrassment), Nejjar exclaims in a line at the beginning of her film (Ganne 2003, n.p.)

Les yeux secs, shot in Tamizigh (one of the several Berber languages of Morocco) and Moroccan Arabic, is set in the Atlas Mountain region in the villages of Tizi N'Isly and Aghbala in the province of Beni Mellal. Tizi is inhabited entirely by women who are prostitutes. Once a month, they are visited by men in the region, but the rest of the time they live in total isolation. Indeed, the Beni Mellal region is known for its isolation, destitution, and poverty. The principal actors, Mina (Raouia) and Fahd (Khalid Benchegra), were accompanied by nonprofessional actors and extras from the region. Many played themselves and used their own names. Raouia, as the elderly Mina, tells her story upon her release from prison in Casablanca after a twenty-five-year period of incarceration. Her crime: prostitution in her remote village in the Atlas Mountains. After being picked up in a raid on the village by local authorities, she is taken to Casablanca, and forced to abandon her eight-month-old daughter, Hala.

Upon Mina's release, she decides to return to her village to reclaim her daughter's affection, though Hala has since become cold and unforgiving. Hala is now a leader, dictating the norms of the community's trade in a village inhabited solely by women who realize that prostitution is the only viable means for them to make a

living. Upon her return, Mina disguises her identity in order to find
out more about her daughter, who she knows will blame her for her
abandonment. Hala has instigated the draconian practice of abandon-
ing babies at birth in neighboring villages so that they will not be
obligated to continue their mothers' trade. The women seem to have
come to a consensus that this practice is the only hope of economic
survival and assuring that their generation will be the last to serve
as prostitutes for the men in the outlying countryside. Older women
of Mina's generation who cannot work anymore have been relegated
to the mountain caves, once used as granaries when the village was
more prosperous. As they wait to die, these mothers are basically kept
by their daughters.

Mina returns to the village with Fahd, who grew up marginalized
as an orphan, and later was a prison guard where she was incarcerated. Indeed, prisons construed physically by man and nature, as well
as metaphorically rendered as societal marginalization, are constant
symbols in the film. The feeling of being hemmed in with nowhere
to go is evoked through carefully filmed scenes of women speaking
through the barred windows of their impoverished hovels, or sequestered within the confines of villages and caves, high up in the mountains. One of the most striking symbolic prison images, marking the
division between the rural women and the rest of the outside world, is
the field of red flags Fahd and Mina encounter as they hike up to the
village on the road from Casablanca. The flags are attached to poles
stuck in the ground like an army of soldiers. In the latter part of the
film, as Fahd stands in front of the field of flags, which are also the
same color as the fields of red poppies covering the mountainsides,
Mina's voice-over tells him that they represent the virgins who had to
give themselves up to the wiles of male clients: "On the nights of the
full moon, when men came to sully us, the youngest of the adolescent
women was chosen, and the next day, before sunrise, she would hang
her red scarf on a pole . . . the scarf of virgins."

After her release, Fahd sees Mina on a street while driving a bus,
his most recent job. Mina proposes that he accompany her in his bus
as a business partner for a new moneymaking venture she has devised
for the village women. Her goal is to found a weaving cooperative
in the village to sell the women's Berber carpets in Casablanca. She
hopes that they will bring lucrative profits, enabling women, old and
young, to discard prostitution as their source of income. Fahd agrees
to help fulfill her goal, stating he has nothing to lose, although he

knows nothing about the Berbers and does not speak the language. Knowing she risks not being let back into the village with a man, Mina decides to pretend Fahd is her son.

Although Hala rejects her mother and refuses to come to terms with her, she ultimately falls in love with Fahd (who, contrary to normative masculine roles in Arab cinema, does not fall into the cinematic trap of saving Hala as a Prince Charming). Hala's desire for him overrides her belief that prostitutes cannot "love" men and that they are unable to enter into lasting relationships with them. Fahd disproves the stereotyped brutal man Hala has only known by offering a loving and caring "new man" who "loses his traditional masculinity" in order to "connect with the women of the village" (Pisters 2007, 86). Fahd explores his *devenir-femme* (a becoming-woman) as he becomes more attached to the village women and dedicated to helping them find another means to make a living.

His relationship with Zaïnba, a young girl who is presumed to be Hala's daughter, and whom he befriends even though he is unable to communicate with her, leads him to invest even more in changing the women's seemingly condemned destiny. On the night when the men come to the prostitutes, young Zaïnba is initiated into the trade. Insane with grief over her violated innocence and his incapacity to save her, Fahd, clad in woman's clothing, runs into the mountains. As he climbs higher into the snowy peaks, he strips himself to his underwear, symbolically shedding himself of his appropriated feminine identity and any possibility of bonding in solidarity with the women of the village. Stripped naked, lying in the frigid snow, he is fragile and vulnerable, not at all the overtly macho hero Hala had thought he would be. In the desolate mountains, away from the constraints of traditional mores and archaic gender roles, it is Hala, in the end, who comes to save him, followed by her mother. When she finds him, the young woman covers his naked body for warmth. It is at this point, as Fahd is treated as a vulnerable child by two mothers who seek to protect him, that social and gender power distinctions between men and women are virtually nullified. Nejjar leaves her characters before a *tabula rasa* on which to remake their identities, destinies, and gender roles. Both male and female roles are equalized as they face the challenges of building a new identity and destiny for themselves.

At the end of the film, Mina realizes that she cannot change the mentalities of the rural men toward women, but she can work to alter the prostitutes' view of themselves as victims, imprisoned in what they believe can be their only trade. She stays to found her weaving company with the older generation of mothers and sends Fahd, Hala, and Zaïnba to a new destination that is not defined in the concluding scenes of the film. The open ending, metaphorically rendered as the three ride a motorcycle out of the village over the vast southern plains of Morocco, is disconcerting. Yet, the gaping hole at the end of the film could also be read as symbolically alluding to the uncertainty of the lives of many Moroccan women who are engulfed by illiteracy, poverty, and lack of resources.

Despite the symbolic images throughout her film, the feminist messages Nejjar promotes continue to be pertinent for all Moroccan women: how to counter the judgment of others, live life as an individual who enjoys full rights in civil society, and avoid being manipulated by men. In an interview, Nejjar emphasized that "je continuerais à harceler les consciences en faisant des films . . . des films et des films . . . pour que nous (les femmes) ne soyons plus jamais de simples pantins désarticulés, rasant les murs et marchant sur la pointe des pieds, mais des citoyens à part entière" (I will continue to harass consciences by making films . . . films and films . . . so that we [women] will never again be inarticulate puppets, wallflowers walking on eggshells, but rather full-fledged citizens) (Ganne 2003, n.p.).

In addition to her feminist messages, Nejjar seeks to call attention to a minority group whose destiny in the twenty-first century is precarious within the scope of the modern state and the nation of Morocco (Pisters 2007, 86). The posts with the red flags, dotting the hills like tombs, symbolically meant to represent the lives of lost virgins, also metaphorically stand for the lost innocence of the rural Berber communities that live marginalized existences. They have been left destitute, impoverished, and illiterate, as the rest of urbanized Morocco launches ahead into the era of globalization.

Nejjar's seemingly good intentions to bring light to the plight of the Berbers were mired in controversy. Her film reified Morocco's need to address these isolated regions, still oppressed by pervasive traditionalism, tribalism, and the patriarchal status quo. Despite her perhaps good intentions, the filmmaker was accused of having duped the illiterate female villagers into thinking they were making a documentary about the widespread historical practice of prostitution across Morocco. In reality, because she focused only on Tizi and Aghbala to delve into the topic of rural prostitution, the filmmaker was accused of outing the region's secrets, and thus adversely affecting the populations living there. Although all agree that prostitution as a means of generating income to stay alive in rural areas of Morocco exists, the women of Tizi and Aghbala filed a lawsuit in 2002 against Nejjar for defamation: "Nous avons été trompées, montrées comme des semi-humains qui n'ont d'autre occupation que de forniquer, ce film n'a rien à voir avec notre région, nous ne sommes pas le bordel du Maroc" (We were duped, exposed as quasi-humans who have no other occupation other than to fornicate. This film has nothing to do with our region; we are not the whorehouse of Morocco).[6]

In a larger context, the controversy also revealed contemporary tensions between poorer Berber areas, which claim a unique heritage and rural way of life, and urban modern and more-Europeanized Moroccans. The latter group, to which Nejjar belongs, seek to strategize ways to bring people out of poverty but are often accused of not understanding the very areas they wish to help. Alluding to this complex situation, Aïcha Aït Berri, writing for *Le monde berbère*, criticizes the filmmaker, stating that her film reduces "l'identité berbère à la prostitution en qualifiant les actrices de vraies prostituées" (Berber identity to prostitution, equating the actresses to real prostitutes) (Aït Berri, n.p.).

Noufissa Sbaï, author, women's activist, the film's producer, and mother of Narjiss Nejjar, insisted in an interview that the accusations and lawsuit filed by some of the Berber women were politically motivated and the result of "une grande manipulation par les hommes de la région qui ont tenté de politiser ce film à des fins électorales" (a huge manipulation by men of the region who wanted to politicize the film in order to influence elections).[7] The lawsuit was later dropped due to the dedicated work in the region by several dynamic people who saw that the money the actors earned from the benefits of the film was genuine and would help, according to Sbaï, with "la scolarisation des filles . . . la santé et les droits des paysans . . . Un film peut contribuer au développement socio-économique et donner l'occasion aux plus démunis de se battre pour la prise de parole et de décisions" (the education of girls . . . health and the rights of country people . . . A film can contribute to socioeconomic development and generate an occasion for the most impoverished to fight for the right to speak and to make decisions).[8]

Les yeux secs remains one of the most controversial films to be made in the post Lead Years in Morocco. It forces Moroccan audiences to

Fig. 5.2. Noufissa Sbaï, film producer and feminist activist, Rabat, Morocco, 2007

discuss sensitive topics such as social disparities due to gender, race, class, ethnicity, language, and economic means. Equally important, the film represents the increasing sociocultural and political inquiries that young filmmakers, particularly women, are making in order to effectuate positive changes in their homeland.

L'Enfant Endormi (The Sleeping Child, 2004), Yasmine Kassari: The Myths of Modern Morocco

Yasmine Kassari, thirty-seven, like Leïla Marrakchi, is an MRE film-maker residing in Europe. She studied medicine in Paris before enrolling in the INSAS, the national film institute of Brussels. Kassari made several short films: *Le feutre noir* (The black pen, 1994); *Chiens errants* (Wild dogs, 1995); and *Linda et Nadia* (2000). In 2002, her documentary *Quand les homes pleurent* (When men cry), about clandestine male immigration to Spain, won critical acclaim. In 2004, Kassari completed her first feature-length film, *L'enfant endormi*, which although

Fig. 5.3. Yasmine Kassari (photo courtesy of *Cinergie*)

based on fiction, portrays many of the realities about clandestine immigration to Europe and poverty depicted in her documentary. The docurealist style of her film is also enhanced by Kassari's decision to use untrained actors. Except for Rachida Brakni, a French-Algerian actress who has won film awards for several mainstream French films (Coline Serrau's *Chaos* and *Loin* by André Téchiné), all other actors were nonprofessional and came primarily from the same village. Kassari notes that her decision was based on creating authenticity: "These people are from the same region. They all come from the same tribe. They even resemble each other physically, which is amazing." Ironically, Kassari notes, Rachida Brakni, whose Arabic was very poor, had to work the hardest to be authentic.[9]

The lavish beauty of the costumes and the unreserved camerawork used to capture the wild expansive scenery of Kassari's film attest to the generous international financial backing she obtained for her production. Despite the funding, which enabled her to make a technically advanced film in an urban setting, Kassari chose the bleak, sparsely populated desert-like landscape of northern Morocco. Her sets are minimalist, highlighting the stark and barren lives of the villagers in one of the most remote regions of the country. The nearest large town, Taourit, is twenty kilometers away. So remote and isolated is the backdrop to Kassari's film that on first glance the foreign viewer would think the story was set in an earlier century. It is only when we are able to detect in the background modern cars, cell phones, and the technical innovations found in Taourit that we realize Kassari's women are living in the present. The filmmaker depicts so accurately what contemporary Morocco is: a country that is divided between past and present, old and new, traditional and modern, rural and urban.

L'enfant endormi begins with Zeineb's wedding as she is seated, clothed in her bridal gown, and sequestered in a room full of other women. "Why can't you move?" a little girl asks her. "Because I'm the bride," she responds. This first scene exemplifies the gender divisions that are present throughout the film, as well as the confined lives women in the village must live. Women are left to fend for themselves, to persevere and endure silently while their men go off to Spain to find work. Marriage is the fragile chain that continues to link them to tradition and custom. As Hassan's blind grandmother notes disparagingly as she looks at her grand-daughter-to-be: "What a life that girl will have. They marry and he leaves. Before, we married our children so that they would go. Now we do it to ensure that they will come home."

Young women remain in a fixed space, married or as brides-to-be, watched by families and governed by mothers and in-laws. Kassari constantly reminds audiences that women's identity and ultimate being are defined as much by masculine oppression as the marginalization, poverty, and illiteracy that are the daily realities of the village. Zeineb marries Hassan the day before he is to leave clandestinely for Spain to find work, like so many others from the village. His mother urges him to think twice, "to stay here and earn your bread." His only response: "There is nothing here." Not even the song the men sing at the wedding will deter those who decide to go. The song's stanzas foreshadow the men's destiny, which will be forever bleak: "In Spain there is nothing waiting. . . . I will crisscross the continents. . . . The uneducated man should think twice. . . . Even languages will trip you up . . . and you, the one with the diploma that rots in a closet, and you who aim for anything. . . . If you really want to immigrate, divorce your lovely wife, and she will live better free."

Zeineb's wedding night leaves her pregnant. Because she is husbandless, her mother-in-law decides that it is best if the young woman puts the fetus to "sleep" with a talisman from a holy man in Touarit. The women rely on an ancient pre-Islamic belief, which later was adopted into the Islamic law that is practiced in the Maghreb and other parts of Africa. The custom circumvents biological science in order to make pregnancies legitimate for up to four or five years. In order to keep family honor intact, save face if a woman becomes widowed or pregnant out of wedlock, or if a woman needs an heir in the case of an absent husband, she may invoke the power of "the sleeping child." The custom ordains that if a woman discovers she is pregnant and her husband is "absent," for whatever reason, she may "put her child to sleep" until the appropriate time comes to wake it up. She simply folds the talisman, keeps it in a box, and when she is ready, opens it in a bucket of water and lets it sit under the stars for seven nights in order to wake the child. The four- to five-year rule gives a woman certain rights in the eyes of her community if she is widowed or repudiated by helping to explain a fatherless birth: "Contrary to what one would think, it is not a question of superstition or believing in spirits, but of an accepted and commented-on position in Islamic legislation. The belief in the 'sleeping child in its mother's womb' responds, in fact, to a social logic that differs from biological or scientific logic."[10] A woman's pregnancy thus becomes absent in her womb.

Indeed, absence—of men (fathers, brothers, sons, and husbands), prosperity, and access to modernity—defines the thematic structures of Kassari's film. Lack dictates the parameters of the lives of Zeineb and the other women of the village. After the film's first few minutes, male presence, for the most part, is off-camera. The videotapes the émigré husbands send from Spain are symbolic of the presence-absence state they represent in their women's everyday lives. Olivier Barlet notes that "men are both the hope and the obstacles, angels and demons [in the film]. Above all, they continue to hover over the women's future like a sine qua non condition for their self-fulfillment."[11] Even when they transgress the social norms, as Zeineb's friend Halima does when she considers adultery, "women remain victims of patriarchy" meted out by the older mothers and grandmothers who act like men in their absence (Barlet 2007, n.p.). Patriarchal domination is so inscribed into the very essence and existence of the village, it determines the biological rhythms of women that are deemed necessary for keeping family and tribal structures intact.

Halima is Zeineb's cousin and her opposite. She is fiery, defiant, and, when she sees that her husband, Ahmed, refuses to come home from Spain, she attempts to have an affair with Amziane, one of the few men to have returned from Europe. Amziane explains to her that there is nothing in Spain for immigrants. After both are badly beaten by Halima's husband's family upon the discovery of their indiscretions, Amziane comes to Halima's window to speak to her one last time:

HALIMA: Why didn't you stay in Europe?
AMZIANE: I didn't like it.
HALIMA: Isn't it better over there?
AMZIANE: Sure, for the people from there.
HALIMA: People do what they want there.
AMZIANE: Only the people from there.
HALIMA: As soon as Ahmed gets his papers in order, I'll go there.
AMZIANE: Halima, here you are the most beautiful woman. Over there you will be ashamed of yourself . . . of your color . . . of your dresses . . .
HALIMA: It's true, I'm illiterate.
AMZIANE: It's not that. Groveling in foreigners' countries is so different from groveling in your own.

Like many Moroccan filmmakers, Yasmine Kassari wants her audiences on both sides of the Mediterranean to understand the loss immigrants face when they make the choice to leave their homeland. Life is not easier in Europe, and risking one's life to go there does not bring the happiness and fortune so many seek. These cruel realities become more evident in the videotapes that are sent back from the men in Spain. They suffer injury, unemployment, and isolation. Their faces are marred by the bitter experience of immigration and their disillusionments stemming from what Europe has not offered.

In contrast to the camera lens from Spain that documents the defeat of the village men's lives, Zeineb and Halima's decision to borrow their neighbor's camera to videotape themselves allows the two women a defiant voice they never have had. The "cinematographic pen" they seize demonstrates that they are not duped by their illiteracy or cowed into accepting their fate in the hermetically sealed feminine space in which they have been enclosed. Previously, where the young women had been seen only in the background of the tapes made by the mothers who spoke to their sons, Zeineb and Halima now decide to directly engage the camera, speaking openly to their husbands one to one. The lens becomes their weapon of confrontation, and filming marks the first step to their emancipation.

Clad in their best clothes, made up with lipstick and mascara, hair uncovered and falling around their shoulders, Halima demands to know why Ahmed refuses to talk to her on-camera (he is seen in the videos sent by the men, but never addresses her or her family). Zeineb tells Hassan that his mother has died and that she is pregnant. The close-ups of the women's faces set them apart from the usual mass of the village's feminine collective, allowing each woman to claim her individuality, something she has never dared to do before. Emboldened by her refusal to be engulfed in the collective, feminine passivity of the village, Halima breaks with the norms of her stifling existence. She procures birth control pills, which she never uses but hides under blankets "just in case." The pills represent the modernity and freedom she so desires but cannot have and the sexual frustration she experiences due to the absence of her husband.

After her severe beating for having simply spoken with Amziane, Halima decides to demand a divorce, leave the village, and go back to her family. This decision means having to give up her children, leaving them behind to wait on a father who will never come back. When Zeineb tells her that "she will never be granted a divorce by [her] husband's family," Halima responds, "The essential thing is to ask." After her friend leaves, Zeineb goes to Taourit to have her photo taken to put into a letter to her husband in order to tell him that his mother has died and that she has had to "put to sleep" their child.

When she receives Hassan's response (read by Amziane, who is one of the few literate men in the village), she feels deceived. Hassan's reply is cold and unforgiving: "Zeineb, wake up the child and never go to Taourit again without my permission." Realizing that she can expect nothing from a husband who has become someone she does not know, the young woman tears up the talisman and throws it into the river, washing away her child, her hopes, and her dreams. This rupture with the myth of the sleeping child permits her to assert her independence over her body and her destiny. In the end, it is through the absence of patriarchy, and the women's challenge of the validity of mythical belief and its power over them, that Halima and Zeineb claim their individuality and *personhood*. Halima defies social norms, leaves her husband's family, and returns to her native village. Zeineb refuses the pregnancy, which would link her biologically to her husband, his family, and his tribe.

In an interview, Kassari notes that illegal immigration, poverty, and illiteracy are not just Morocco's problems, they are indicative of those of "three-quarters of the planet! The entire world wants to go North. . . . It's as Nietzsche said, 'One is able to philosophize when everything is going well.' But when one spends all his time looking for his bread, one does not philosophize at all! One doesn't have the time to develop relationships with other men and women." She further emphasizes that men and women in Morocco have become victims of economics. Modernity is perhaps prosperous if everyone has equal access to it. This, however, is still not the reality in Morocco.[12]

Deux Femmes sur la Route (2007), Farida Bourquia: A Moroccan *Thelma and Louise*

Farida Bourquia, sixty-one, is one of the first Moroccan women to make filmmaking a career both on the screen and in television. After studying in Moscow at the National Theatre (1968–73), Bourquia returned to Morocco and taught dramatic arts at the national conservatory in Casablanca. She has spent the major part of her career working for RTM (radio-télévision marocaine), creating programs for children and sociocultural documentaries. Her made-for-television films include *Le dernier aveu* (The last promise), *La bague* (The ring), *Je ne reviendrai pas* (I will not come back), *Le visage et le miroir* (The face and the mirror), *La boîte magique* (The magic box), and *La maison demandée* (The popular house). In 1975, in honor of the International Year of Women, she made several documentaries about Moroccan women specifically for the events surrounding this occasion.[13] These were the first documentaries solely produced and directed by a woman. Her feature-length films are *Al jamra* (Pebbles, 1982) and the recent *Tariq al Aylat* (*Deux femmes sur la route*, Two women on the road, 2007).

Two Women on the Road in many ways is a Moroccan version of the American classic female road movie, *Thelma and Louise* (1991, Ridley Scott). Bourquia's film surprisingly contains many of the same messages about women who love men too much who ultimately end up betraying them. The film opens with Amina driving alone on a desolate road on the way to Tetouan in the northeastern part of Morocco.

Her car overheats and she is stranded on the barren highway's shoulder. She is helped by a goatherd, who promises to go to a nearby village to get her a new radiator. Once in the village, she discovers after waiting hours for the new part in her broken-down car that the goat herder absconded with her 300 dirhams and her radiator.

While waiting, smoking a cigarette, Amina is approached by middle-aged traditionally dressed Rahma, who declares that the young woman owes her money for the blankets she has brought her from the market. Amina tells her she has ordered no blankets and that Rahma has mistaken her for someone else. Rahma will not budge and asks her pryingly where she is going. Amina says to Tetouan but tells her that her car has broken down and she is waiting on a part. The older woman tells her to forget it, that "the men are dishonest around here; you'll never see your radiator or the money again." She convinces Amina to spend the night with her and wait until the next day to confront the dishonest mechanics.

As she walks through the hot, dusty village, Amina, skimpily clad in tight-fitting jeans, tank top with bared shoulders, sporting stiletto heels, wearing lots of makeup and openly chain-smoking (something women, up to a few years ago, never did in public in Morocco), is an oddity. The young urban woman of the millennium generation, juxtaposed to the traditional, middle-aged Rahma of the country, who wears a headscarf and long dress, is a symbol for the schizophrenia women confront every day as they are caught between the conventional past and the uncertainties of the present.

Rahma is fat, dowdy, and walks clumsily behind the brazen Amina as they traverse the village. Yet, one thing both women have in common is that both their husbands have deserted them. They recognize that their differences are only in physical appearance. Rahma states that her husband "went back to his village and left me for a younger woman as soon as he retired." Amina reveals that she is trying to find money to pay off a judge to get her husband out of jail. Despite the young woman's emancipated ways and independence, she divulges that she, too, has been betrayed by her husband, who told her after their marriage that he "already had a wife." When Rahma asks Amina how she could marry a married man, she replies: "for money." The young woman later admits that her husband has been jailed for drug trafficking in Tetouan.

Rahma also must go to Tetouan, a city to which she has never been. She, like many mothers before her, is summoned to identify the body of her son, which washed up onshore after he embarked in a small boat for Italy. She tearfully tells Amina that "these kids don't know how to do anything except throw themselves into the sea. They tear up their papers. They don't make it there, but they aren't able to come back." Rahma's life has been defined by the men who have left her; so much so that she tells her young guest: "I decided that a woman must look for her own bread in the street." Both women realize that despite age, backgrounds, and goals in life, they have more in common than they originally thought.

Without a car, Amina agrees to accompany Rahma on the bus to Tetouan. However, they must stop in Chefchaouen (a mountain village high in the Rif mountains) where the younger woman's mother lives, a mother she hasn't seen in years. She is hesitant to go see her, telling Rahma, "I send her money on the condition that she will forget me." After convincing her that "family is family," Rahma accompanies Amina to her mother's house. The mother is cold and unforgiving. She, too, has been abandoned by her husband and cursed with two sons, "one who is an atheist and the other a fundamentalist." Like Kassari, Bourquia reveals the omnipotent power families have over their daughters' lives. To stay would mean having to live under the rule of her brothers and the domination of her mother, who loves her only for the money she brings in. Bitter, Amina leaves, throwing all the money she has at her mother. As she slams the door behind her, she screams to Rahma, "I will have nothing to do with this family anymore."

During their time on the bus, the women meet Abdeslaam, a taxi driver from Chefchaouen who has been traveling for two days trying to get over his wife's attempt to kill him with poison and her affair with his co–taxi driver and partner. He offers to take both women to Tetouan because it would be better than going home and "facing an empty house." Fragile and dejected, Abdeslaam falls in love with Amina, who refuses to have anything to do with him. "I don't need any problems in my life right now," she tells him. Nevertheless, he insists on staying in an adjacent hotel room while the women take care of their business. Rahma goes to the morgue to see if her son's body is really there. It isn't, much to both women's relief. She then waits with Amina outside the courthouse in order to pay off the corrupt judge who has assured the young woman's husband's release. The meeting, however, does not take place before Amina sees her husband coming out of the courthouse with his first wife and children. She realizes she has been duped by him. Yet, the pain of this realization is lessened by the fact that she has found Rahma, whom she now calls "Mother."

Both women's stories end bittersweetly. Although Amina is freed of the life of crime she would have had to lead if she had stayed with her dubious husband, and Rahma's son is perhaps safe and sound in Europe "somewhere," the women's ultimate destinies are unsure. As they stand out over the cliffs of the sea, Amina asks Rahma what she thinks of the ocean. The older woman replies: "It's the first time I've seen it. I like it, except it is monstrous because it eats our children." In the didactic dialogue between the women, Bourquia evokes the larger, symbolic message that the sea steals Morocco's youth. In the brief scene concluding her film, the filmmaker condemns the folly of those who choose illegal immigration and urges Moroccans to find the means to stay home. Contrasting the universality of her message, Bourquia symbolically uses the majestic cliffs on which the women are standing to represent their newfound unfettered freedom.

Bourquia's film exposes the everyday hurdles women face because of the whims and broken promises of men. The overtly "chick flick" quality of the filmmaker's story casts men as inept and made fragile by unemployment, alcohol, and poverty. They are effortlessly swayed by prospects of easy money (either by leaving the country and going to Europe or by drug trafficking) or religious dogma, as Amina's mother explains, stating that her fundamentalist son is "haunted like a possessed zombie." They do not come to the defense of women and are, in general, there only to take advantage of them. This fact is made most evident when Rahma and Amina, while waiting on a train, are hassled by two homeless men and later when the younger woman, alone and drunk in the hotel's bar, is almost kidnapped by a shady man who says he wants to "show her photos of Tetouan during colonial times." She is rescued only when Rahma notices from the hotel balcony that the young woman is about to be forced into a car. Even women who had the potential to marry happily are left alone and abandoned. Sitting in a café, Amina learns from a girlhood friend that just before her marriage the groom was hit by a truck and killed. "I could have been married in Switzerland, but he wanted to have a Moroccan wedding. We were going to live next to a lake in Switzerland. . . . I should have married a Swiss guy."

In general, Bourquia offers audiences a pessimistic depiction of contemporary women's lives, no matter their class, education, or social standing. Whether they are rural or urban, educated or illiterate, rich

Fig. 5.4. Poster for the film *Number One* (2008) by Zakia Tahiri

or poor, women all face a particular kind of feminine misery that can be caused only by men. However, the film also instructs audiences that in contemporary Morocco women can also persevere and survive on their own. Amina and Rahma drive away along a coastline that is as foreboding as it is beautiful. Unlike Thelma and Louise, they do not choose to drive over the cliffs, but to tackle the obstacles before them.

Number One (2008), Zakia Tahiri: A Comic Family Code?

The comedy *Number One* by Zakia Tahiri takes to task the reticence of Moroccan men to embrace the new prescriptions of King Mohammed VI's *Moudawana* (Family Code) of 2004. The *Moudawana* reforms of 2004 brought women out of the dark ages as far as granting them rights to divorce and increased access to the judicial system in Morocco. There have been several Moudawanas in the past,[14] but the 2004 legislation has gone the farthest in granting rights to women under Sharia law. Specifically it raised the marriage age to eighteen (for both men and women), granted women the right to contract their own marriages (no father, brother, or other male family member need be involved), granted equal authority in the family to men and women, approved greater financial rights (women have new rights to assets acquired by marriage) in cases of divorce or a husband's death, established judicial divorce (men must go to court), and stipulated that a husband's verbal repudiation is no longer valid (both husband and wife must seek divorce through the courts).

Disappointing to Moroccan feminists, polygamy was not abolished. However, with the reform, polygamy now requires a judge's authorization and the consent of the husband's first wife in court before he is allowed to take a second. Women can specify in their marriage contracts that polygamy is not an option for their future husbands. And, in general, divorce is now a prerogative that can be exercised as much by the wife as by the husband. Although men and women are now equally protected under the law, the 2004 reform did not address inheritance law, which is still based on Sharia directives (meaning that a woman can inherit only two-thirds of what a man can). The persistence of the unequal inheritance stipulations in the Sharia are still on the horizon for women's rights advocates. Needless to say, the 2004 reforms signify great gains for women in Moroccan society. The enactment of the reforms makes Morocco today one of the most women-friendly countries in the Arab world. Yet, as Tahiri's film suggests, changing laws is one thing; transforming behavior is another. Although humorous, the film acidly points out that the Moroccan male mind-set will not change overnight. It will take a generation to eradicate machismo and sexism in a country still ruled by men and functioning within the patriarchal paradigms of an overbearing monarchy that dictates the norms of society.

Zakia Tahiri is a filmmaker and also a well-known actress whose first major roles were in *Fort Saganne* (1983) with Gérard Depardieu and Cathérine Deneuve, and the later Moroccan films *Badis* (1989) and *A la recherche du mari de ma femme* (Looking for my wife's husband, 1993), both by Abderrahmane Tazi. Tahiri's roles have also included playing the heroine in the critically acclaimed *Une porte sur le ciel* (A door to the sky, 1987), by Farida Benlyazid. She has lived and worked in France with periodic stints in Morocco.

Zakia Tahiri's first feature-length film, *Number One*, was shot in dialectical Arabic and is based on her experiences as a woman who lives between two cultures, caught between the feminism of France and the traditionalism of her homeland. In an interview, Tahiri remarks, "I profoundly, viscerally, effectively, aesthetically love Morocco, but how do you talk about a country with love and lucidity? It was in Casablanca, this dense, churning megalopolis, living in a mixture of dialectical Arabic and French, that I wanted deliciously to lose myself. So, I designed Aziz, my Number One, whom I looked for, discovered, tamed. I hated him and pardoned him. He scared me, made me laugh and cry" (Chabâa, n.p.).[15]

Number One, set in 2004 in the wake of the Moudawana reform, is the story of Aziz (played by Aziz Saâdallah), who is the director of a clothing manufacturing plant called Maroc Star. It is a company that is constantly battling the encroaching Chinese who undercut Moroccan prices with cheap imports. Aziz is macho, overbearing and brutish, condescending to his female employees, and disrespectful to his cowed wife, Soraya (Nezha Rahil). His one ambition in life is to become "Number One" at the factory, which his boss, Mr. Laraki (Abderrahim Bargache), tells him will happen if he lands the French contract held by Mademoiselle Morel (Chantal Ladesou).

One day, influenced by the "air du temps" of women's emancipation broadcast on TV by newswomen touting the positive aspects of the new Moudawana, Soraya decides that Aziz needs to change. In an effort to stop his browbeating, she seeks help from the local witch, Chama, who gives her a potion to mix into Aziz's soup. The next morning he wakes up an altered man, unable to insult or treat any woman disrespectfully. His new Prince Charming personality pleases his workers and his wife alike. Soraya's good fortune becomes the envy of all her female neighbors, much to the chagrin of their husbands. Aziz remarks, "I've become a new man, freer and closer to my wife. I see her differently. The psychiatrist calls it 'the Moudawana syndrome.'"

Despite his newfound respect for women, Aziz's life at work becomes a hell as he struggles to win the contract from the "ball-crushing" feminist Mademoiselle Morel, who threatens to take her order for eighty thousand pairs of jeans to the Chinese unless Aziz can produce a quality product. Viewed by his CEO, Mr. Laraki, as having gone soft on pushing his women employees to finish the job, Aziz is fired. The employees, who now adore him, go on strike, threatening Laraki with the loss of Morel's contract and closure if he doesn't hire Aziz back. Aziz views his firing as caused by his newfound feminism, so he, too, seeks out a healer to rectify the charm. Much to his chagrin, the medicine man, living in a local slum, tells Aziz that his wife's hex is too strong, and he cannot change it. "Women today are horrible," he quips.

Soraya, although recognizing how much her life has improved due to the new "douceur" of her husband's behavior, also realizes that she changed him by false means. She returns to Chama for an antidote, again mixes it in Aziz's soup, confesses the entire story to him, and then waits for his decision. Left alone in front of his meal, he pretends to eat the antidote to make her happy, but ends up throwing it in the garbage. It is difficult to determine the moral of the filmmaker's story or her affirmation, as she claims, that men can be changed by women. In the end, all seems to be restored: Aziz gets his job back, Soraya ends up with a model husband who helps out around the house, Mademoiselle Morel gets her eighty thousand pairs of jeans, the women employees find new joy in their backbreaking, sixteen-hour-a-day labor over sewing machines, and Mr. Laraki also seems to embrace some newly found appreciation for women and babies.

From the beginning, Tahiri notes that the Moudawana, although decreed as law, still is a document that "has remained insufficiently explained to some, not understood by others, and badly interpreted by many who propagate conflicting ideas about it." The humor and frivolity portrayed gloss over the true transformative stakes for women as prescribed in the Moudawana. The fact that Tahiri is an "outsider" to her country and not really concerned with the sociocultural debates that have taken place since the reform is evident in the flippancy of her male characters. Their vapid remarks such as "We are dead with this new Moudawana," and the sentiment, as evoked by one of Aziz's friends, that there's a lot more choice "with all these new divorcees, so I'm happy," make too light issues of inequality that persist in Moroccan society despite the reforms. In a country where women are still hindered by illiteracy and traditionalism, there is little place for hilarity.

Women are disproportionately hampered by poverty and lack of access to education and means of advancement without male tutelage. Some feminist activists have noted that it will take a generation to implement the changes as prescribed in the Moudawana; transformations that must affect equitably both urban and rural women, extending across classes and social strata. The film places the responsibility of change on men who will, in fact, never change, as captured in Aziz's weak statement: "I think I should change the country." Tahiri's message, relying on "should" instead of "will," continues the sustained belief that women are obligated to wait on men, relying on the will of the masculine to transform the status quo.

This is not a feminist, socially transformative film. The filmmaker never insists that women must find the strength to stand up for themselves. Instead, Tahiri tells them that the only way they can hope to combat the prowess of men is by using potions and magic. In the end, it is Aziz who is voted "Number One," not only by his workers at the factory, but also by a leading women's magazine whose editors put him on the cover of its "Man of the Year" issue. Soraya, emancipated only insofar as her husband is now more attentive, continues to slave away as a housewife with no skills, condemned to a life of cleaning and cooking. Once again, men are advanced to "number one," while women are left behind preparing their dinners.

*****

The majority of films made in the last decade by Moroccan women ring true to the tenets of social-realist filmmaking. They instruct audiences by focusing on once taboo and controversial topics, from rural poverty and prostitution to divorce and repudiation. Womanist films delve into the arduous choices that both traditional and modern Moroccan women must make every day and how the consequences of those choices dictate their futures. Additionally, Moroccan women's filmmaking documents the changing customs, traditions, politics, and economic influences impacting women's lives in the new millennium. They promote new conceptions of female subjecthood that are both particular and universal, indicative of changes in Morocco, on the continent of Africa, and in the larger global context. Yet, these filmmakers' works still leave open-ended questions for their protagonists. Their cinematic narratives speak for all Moroccan women who, at the dawn of the new millennium, find themselves at the crossroads of modernity and tradition.

Conclusion

The Future of Moroccan Cinema?

"The future of Moroccan cinema" is a statement with an inherent question that arises any time one discusses the film industry in the country. On the one hand, the industry does have a future; however, on the other, many filmmakers and people in the business wonder what that future will be. In a special 2008 issue dedicated to celebrating the fiftieth anniversary of Moroccan filmmaking, *CinéMag Maroc*, the country's leading film magazine, notes that as they celebrate the "golden jubilee" of Moroccan filmmaking, filmmakers must also acknowledge that the film industry has been marked by "a long trajectory of trial and error, research, and long desert crossings." Equally noteworthy, the magazine emphasizes, is the fact that cinema production in Morocco has finally come into its maturity; one that has permitted the inception of "tools and strategies that allow for a national cinematographic production that is increasingly visible," recognized and appreciated throughout the world (90).

Moroccan filmmakers working at home and abroad have made significant contributions to international cinema in the last fifty years. In the same celebratory issue, Noureddine Sail, head of the CCM, explains the rich history of Moroccan filmmaking as due in part to "a cinema that has dedicated itself to prolonging inherited imagery from the literary and pictorial orientalist tradition of the nineteenth century." He emphasizes that "Moroccan cinema is sustained by a look and an esthetic of otherness where the other and his space are perceived through perceptive codes construed by the West" (90).

It is the imagery of the exotic colonial past, blended with France's conception of cinema as the Seventh Art, and Morocco's own multi-ethnic and multilinguistic identity that have made Moroccan cinema the multicultural cinema it is today. The increased presence of Moroccan films at international film festivals attests to the industry's sustainability and commitment to cinema as both an art form and a medium through which filmmakers are able to formulate meaningful social commentaries. Cineastes should be commended for seeking to develop and impart their own concept of cinema with regard to themes, the images portrayed, and the messages conveyed. In the years to come, the industry as a whole will continue to confront issues of language, shifting audiences' tastes, lagging viewership, and resources, all of which impact how a film is made.

It must be noted that the rigor and sustainability of Morocco's film industry over the last fifty years are due primarily to filmmakers' dedication to finding middle ground as they negotiate these hurdles. Since 1999, they have continued to adhere to the importance of film as a vehicle through which to send sociorealist messages that will challenge audiences to invest in positive transitions taking place currently in the country. Whether male or female, MRE or based at home, cineastes view their roles as keepers of the consciousness of Morocco's collective society. They are both generators and agents of change.

CCM: Mediating or Marketing?

Despite the progress made in the industry, certainly since the end of the Lead Years, the CCM will need to play a more aggressive role in the future in order to find solutions to funding and distribution. These two issues continue to be major obstacles to promoting Moroccan films, both internationally and at home. In an interview in 2008, Abdelhatif Laassadi, spokesman for the CCM, offered a reason for its inefficaciousness on these two fronts. Primarily, Laassadi notes, the CCM has functioned only as a "mediator" between filmmakers and the realization of their projects. "Notre rôle est intermédiare" (Our role is intermediary) has been the CCM's modus operandi, certainly for the last two decades. This is perhaps one of the leading problems with actualizing the modernization of the industry. Instead of viewing its role as a "soutien créatif" (creative support), as Laassadi suggests, the CCM would better serve the future of film and filmmakers in Morocco as a body that takes the lead in founding ways to market and distribute films both at home and abroad (Sedia 2008, n.p.). It is evident that the CCM needs to explore how better to mass-market Moroccan films on DVD in Morocco and internationally. The few grainy, low-quality, illegally copied DVDs sold for 10 dirhams (about US$1.12) in the medinas of the country, or pirated onto websites, will not ensure the future well-being of the industry, as notes Alexandra Girard, reporting for the Moroccan newspaper *Le matin*. In an article titled "Bilan mitigé pour le cinéma marocain en 2008" (Mixed outcomes for Moroccan cinema in 2008), Girard remarks:

> This cinema is rich and appreciated as much by Moroccans at home as by foreign audiences, thus prompt export is needed. Nevertheless, in order to counter the persistent illegal local film market nourished by pirated DVDs, found today on every street corner, audiences must be encouraged to go to the movies. Because, in the end, if no one pays the real price for viewing these films, death to [the] art is assured. If the CCM only concentrates on channeling crowds for a few hours, then nothing will be left of the 7th Art, important and necessary for all self-respecting societies. (Girard 2008, n.p.)

The CCM has the capacity to distribute films in DVD format both at home and abroad. Therefore, it would behoove the center to take charge of an industry that has enormous potential but no distribution network established between the CCM as a marketing institution, filmmakers, and the consumer. Even foreign-language subtitling, once thought to be a barrier, really isn't. Notably, for a few hundred dirhams per film, as filmmaker Hassan Benjelloun suggested in an interview, the CCM could easily subtitle films for international festivals abroad, taking the burden off the filmmaker.[1] At present, subtitling is the responsibility of the cineaste, who also must find international festivals in which to screen his or her film. Thus, the challenge will be how to exploit the global networks that are already available for DVD distribution and film festival attendance. Marketing films on Moroccans' own terms, without European or American intervention (or reliance on foreign distribution companies in general), will be crucial in gaining further international recognition, ensuring sustainability, and professionalizing the role of the CCM.

Cinemas and Ticket Sales

The CCM also should play a more active role in assuring viable movie theaters ("salles") for screening Moroccan films. In an article titled "Bilan cinématographique 2009: Des chiffres qui mettent à nu l'état du 7ème Art marocain" (Cinema outcomes for 2009: Numbers that lay bare the state of Morocco's 7th Art), Ouafaâ Bennani, writing for *Le matin*, notes the mixed results of a cinema caught between trying to modernize itself and the vestiges of the past, overburdened by archaic methods of organization (2010, n.p.). Reporting on a conference held in March 2009 by the CCM at the National Library in Rabat (which gathered CCM employees, filmmakers, producers, and film critics as well as a general audience of cinema aficionados), Bennani notes that the most pressing questions discussed focused on lack of movie theaters and the weak ticket sales of Moroccan films at home.

Film critic Moulay Driss Jaidi pointed out that until the number of cinemas in Morocco increases, it will be difficult to encourage cinemagoers to attend the screenings of Moroccan films. He referred to the "catastrophic decrease of theatres between 2008 and 2009," noting a decrease from 149 to about 40. The dearth of theaters has significantly hindered the development of Moroccan film. Jaidi also pointed out that, if "we rely on the statistics reported by the CCM, [our information is mixed] because it counts screens rather than 'salles' (theaters), so instead of forty cinemas, there are seventy screens" (Bennani 2010, n.p.). Thus, the CCM hypes large multiplexes as successes because they are counted as multiple screens, not single theaters, whereas small village movie houses with single screens are the norm in most regions of Morocco.

Parallel to the decline in the number of movie houses, Jaidi pointed out that ticket sales have fallen, noting that only 2,638,707 tickets for films were sold in 2009. This number marks a significant decrease from the 11,614,845 sold in 2000. The issue of ticket sales is directly linked to the decline in the number of theaters. Jaidi emphasized that the numbers for both are also unequally distributed across Morocco as 50 percent of all theaters are found in Casablanca. Others are spread out in large cities such as Rabat and Fez (which usually have three to five per city) and small towns that, on average, boast only one to three theaters. Jaidi equally brought up the question of the 150 screens that the CCM had promised to build in this decade: "Je ne sais pas comment et quand ce projet connaîtra le jour et par quels moyens, alors que nous assistons continuellement à des fermetures de salles . . . puis, quel est ce public qui va remplir ces salles ?" (I don't know how this project will see the light of day, since we constantly see cinemas which are closing . . . and, what will be the public that will fill these cinemas?). Jaidi's negative numbers, however, were countered by some positive news at the conference, which did announce new theater openings in Salé and Agdal (suburbs of Rabat), Tangier, Martil, Khouribga, and Ouarzazate (Bennani 2010, n.p.).

Teaching, Training, and Schools

Moroccan cinema is continuing in an evolutionary process that is hopeful. For example, the number of films produced per year has increased. According to the CCM, 2009 was a bumper-crop year for number of films produced (fifteen feature-length films and four shorts). Critic Mourad Lefhel noted at the conference in March 2009 that television stations, notably 2M, have invested heavily in the promotion of Moroccan cinema by regularly airing feature-length films (Bennani 2010, n.p.).

A significant hindrance to filmmaking in Morocco has been in the technical domain. The shortage of trained Moroccan technicians, cameramen, and sound people, as well as professional scriptwriters in the field who live and work exclusively in Morocco has significantly impacted the cost of film production in the country. This fact was repeatedly expressed to me in the interviews I conducted with filmmakers and producers as I toured the country.[2] For example, of the fifteen films produced in 2009, fourteen were written by the directors themselves without the aid of professional scriptwriters. While some directors have proved to be gifted screenwriters, most lack the professional eye or know-how to bring to fruition a solid script. Many film critics blame badly written scripts as part of the problem with the overall quality of Moroccan films (i.e., their lack of appeal to mainstream markets abroad) (Bennani 2010, n.p).

Furthermore, the aura of Europe as the pinnacle of perfection is still significant in the mind-set of most filmmakers. Khalid Damoun, head of the Association of Film Critics in Morocco, notes that the majority of directors and producers do not have confidence in Moroccan technicians, preferring to rely on foreign film editors and photo technicians. In their view, lack of professionals contributes to unprofessional films, notes Damoun (Bennani 2010, n.p.). However, some signs that this purview is changing do exist. In 2006, ESAV (Ecole supérieure des arts visuels de Marrakech, Advanced Education in the Visual Arts, Marrakech) was opened and touted as the first school of advanced study in cinema south of the Mediterranean. The ESAV has been hailed and supported internationally by huge names in cinema such as Martin Scorsese, Jean-Pierre Jeunet, and Abderrahmane Sissako. The school also holds partnerships with four European film schools. At present, there are 160 full-time students, ranging from seventeen to thirty years of age. The majority are Moroccan, yet the school has become international as it enrolls increasing numbers of students from all over Africa and even Europe.

Like most Moroccan schools, the model is French, so in order to be admitted students must first pass an exam at the level of the baccalaureate and then study for three to five years depending on the program. Almost all instruction is in French. ESAV remains an elitist institution since it is private and costs the equivalent of 3,000 to 4,500 euros per year, a small fortune for most Moroccans who earn less than 180 euros a month.[3] A similar school was founded in 2002 in Rabat. The ISCA (Institut, spécialisé du cinéma de l'audiovisuel) is also private, functions in French, and focuses on training students in the technical aspects of primarily television and audiovisual journalism. It has been lauded for its foresight in seeing the need to train young Moroccans in technical fields and for its pedagogy, which is multidisciplinary.

During the conference on the status of the industry in 2009, almost all attendees agreed that the future of Moroccan cinema would be in the hands of young people who see film as a way to discuss social taboos in society, explore new technical innovation, and, in general, advance the sociocultural and political dialogues of the country into the twenty-first century. Film criticism, as both a genre and a vehicle through which to contextualize meaningful commentary on society in Morocco, will also need to be sustained in order to ensure the future vitality of the industry. Attendees at the conference noted that additional platforms for discussing and forming thoughtful film criticism are needed.

Although younger film aficionados have founded blogs (as mentioned in the introduction), it remains to be seen if venues for developing and supporting future film discourse among the general public will increase. Certainly the proliferation of blogs and activity on the Internet have shifted how the dissemination of traditional film is diffused in newspapers and magazines, as notes Damoun: "Les critiques de cinéma n'ont plus de place dans les journaux ni dans les émissions de télévision et radio. Alors que la direction du CCM nous reproche de ne plus faire notre travail" (Cinema critics no longer have space in newspapers or on television and radio shows. At the same time the heads of the CCM criticize us for no longer doing our job) (Bennani 2010, n.p).

If modes of discourse must, and in some instances have, changed, then it is up to the old guard to do the same. Although confronted with hurdles such as flagging ticket sales and cinema closures, the "Report of 2009" notes that the CCM authorized filming for 29 feature-length films, 28 telefilms, 80 shorts, 7 medium-length films, 16 series, 59 documentaries, 4 sitcoms, and 44 institutional films (films made for specific corporations) (Bennani 2010, n.p.). In 2009, 2,638,707 Moroccans went to see films in theaters! Perhaps this attests to the fact that as film language becomes more accessible, the masses become more used to the idea of film as an integral part of everyday society and culture. The fine line that must be walked, according to most filmmakers, is how to make their films entertaining enough to draw crowds, but still true to "les sujets dans la réalité" (subjects in the reality) of everyday Morocco (Girard 2008, n.p.).

Film Language and Communication
In and Outside Morocco

Film critic Mustapha Mesnaoui emphasizes that film can indeed play a role in "bridging gaps" as a "langue de communication" (language of communication) in contemporary society. The "7th Art," he declares, has the potential to unite modernists and traditionalists by offering them a cinema that is inclusive of all views and debates, encouraging them to reflect on the reality of multicultural Morocco (Ziane 2005, n.p). Film is a medium through which contemporary issues, which might not otherwise be available to large audiences who lack access to literature, can be vetted and discussed. Festivals in Tangier, Fez,

Rabat, and Casablanca have provided mediating spaces in which communication is founded, not only between filmmakers and their audiences, but also among classes, genders, and ethnicities. The language of Moroccan film is all-inclusive, carving out a multifaceted milieu that is at once Berber/Arab/French, rural and urban, traditional and modern.

Today, Moroccan cinema acts as a mirror for a society that is remaking itself. Like literature, the press, and other forms of media that are invested socioculturally and politically in the dynamics and debates currently taking place in the country, cinema is a key element in the documentation of past history and present realities. It provides a forum through which to analyze, reflect, and discuss the contemporary issues that are present in society and that contribute to the shaping of the contours of the New Morocco.

Notes

Preface

1. "Nous ne voulons pas faire du cinéma subversif . . . il s'agit avant tout de faire du cinéma un moyen adéquate de dénonciation, et non une arme à la quête d'une subversion folle et insoutenable" (my translation).
2. However, one cannot be blindly optimistic about transparency, certainly in the press. As recently as September 2009, journalists writing for several newspapers and newsmagazines, such as *TelQuel* and the arabophone journal *Akhbar al youm* (published by the company Media 21 and owned by Baoufik Bouachrine, who is also the editor), were incarcerated and issues of both publications were seized by the police. *Akhbar al youm* has been shut down indefinitely. According to the Minister of the Interior, the newsmagazine is guilty of publishing a cartoon of Prince Moulay Ismaïl next to a partial six-pointed star instead of the five denoted on the Moroccan flag. The Ministry of the Interior stopped short of anti-Semitic language, but did fault the cartoonist, Khalid Gueddar, for "defacing the national flag of the Kingdom of Morocco."

A communiqué from the Ministry of the Interior affirmed that "l'utilisation de l'étoile de David dans la caricature suscite par ailleurs des interrogations sur les insinuations de ses auteurs" (use of the Star of David in a cartoon brings to light the authors' insinuations); (reported on *TelQuel*'s website: http://www.telquel-online.com/392/edito_392.shtml. See also http://entrenousmarocains.blogspot.com/2009/09/lactualite-du-jour-le-prince-moulay_29.html.

In July 2009, during the celebrations marking the tenth anniversary of Mohammed VI's reign, journalists were hoping for a brighter, more transparent future in the saga of the free press in Morocco. However, this was not to be the case. Further disappointments and setbacks occurred. The Committee to Protect Journalists, an international organization designed to protect the integrity of the free press, reported that "on August 1, 2009, authorities destroyed more than 100,000 copies of *Nichane* (permanently shut down in 2010), an Arabic-language weekly, and *TelQuel*, its French-language sister, both of which carried a public opinion poll in which 91 percent of respondents said they viewed the king favorably. Three days later, the government banned an issue of the French daily *Le Monde* that also carried the poll results." The site stresses that royal authorities condemned the entire survey process: "Conducting a survey, the main focus of which is to ask the citizens to give their thoughts on the king's actions, is in itself a violation of the principles and the foundation of the royal system." The minister of communication, Khalid Naciri, told reporters: "In Morocco, the monarchy cannot be the object of a debate, even through a survey." See http://www.cpj.org/2010/02/attacks-on-the-press-2009-morocco.php.

3. Some of the blog websites dealing with Moroccan film currently (as of June 2010) include: *Blog Riad*, http://riad-aguerzame.com/blog/balade-dans-le-sud-marocain/; *Blog Rachid Naim*, http://naim.over-blog.org/article-10119409.html; *Bladi Net*, http://www.bladi.net; *Save Cinemas in Morocco*, http://www.savecinemasinmorocco.com (articles in French and English); *Le Blog Nadif* (by Mohammed Nadif, actor and director), http://www.pointinfo.org/nadif/.

4. Valérie Ganne, "Tizi, le village des prostituées," Afrik.com (May 22, 2003), http://www.afrik.com/article6113.html.

Introduction: Moroccan National Cinema

Epigraph: Hassan Benjelloun, in discussion with the author, May 29, 2009.

1. General Lyautey was a career colonial officer. He dedicated his life's mission to securing Morocco for French interests. His policy for contact with indigenous people relied on a "divide and conquer" method of operation, wherein tribesmen were kept at bay in order to maintain French domination in the country.

2. We have only to think of the "dark" heroines of "foreign" origins: Emma in *Madame Bovary* (Gustave Flaubert) and the eponymous heroine of *Thérèse Raquin* (Emile Zola); the encounter with otherness in Algeria, as depicted in *Une année dans le Sahel* (A Year in the Sahel, Eugène

Fromentin), and Turkey and the Congo, as described in André Gide's *La marche turque* (The turkish march) and *Voyage au Congo* (Travels to Congo).

3. Marabouts are traditional holy men and women who are responsible for healing and providing talismans. The marabout continues to be a popular figure in literature and does still exist in traditional villages across Morocco and other regions in Africa.

4. See Frank Ukadike, *Black African Cinema* (Berkeley: University of California Press, 1994). This is also one of the reasons that in the former British colonies the development of the video and television industries is much more apparent than in francophone West Africa. The Nigerian video market is rivaled by none other on the continent.

5. The first presentation of film in Egypt was made in January 1896 by Brunio (a Lumière photographer), who was there shooting film for the Lumière brothers. A Lumière camera and film program were used. The first film produced in Egypt in 1912 was *Dans les rues d'Alexandrie* (In the streets of Alexandria, M. de Lagarne); the first feature film more than one hour in length was Koubla Fil Sahara'a *Ibrahim lama*, made in 1927; and the first "talkie" was *Onchoudet el Fouad*, made in 1932. See http://www.learnaboutmovieposters.com/newsite/INDEX/COUNTRIES/Egypt/EgyptianHistory.asp.

6. In 1985 the prestigious IDHEC was restructured by then Minister of Culture Jack Lang. FEMIS now includes seven departments for direction, screenwriting, picture, sound editing, production, and set design. Courses in script and film distribution were also added in the 1992. In 2002, a European production training program was founded with an affiliate program in Germany. FEMIS is now a public institution administered by the Ministry of Culture and Communication.

7. Ksikes emphasized this fact in a February 2007 symposium held by journalists at the annual Salon de Livre in Casablanca.

8. Interview with Kamal Mouline, June 1, 2009, Centre cinématographic marocain, Rabat, Morocco.

9. According to Ghareeb, the films *Love in Casablanca* and *Searching for My Wife's Husband* sold more than 150,000 tickets each in Casablanca alone.

10. In 2005, 150,000 people flocked to see *Marock* when it first opened in theaters: "autant qu'en France" (as many as in France), attests a *TelQuel* feature article on the filmmaker.

11. Funding is assured by a tax added to all electricity bills in Morocco. This tax, known as "la taxe audiovisuelle" (media tax) is levied to fund primarily the CCM and 2M (the national television channel). Interview with Kamal Mouline, June 1, 2009, Rabat, Morocco.

12. Interview with Kamal Mouline, CCM, June 1, 2009, Rabat, Morocco.

13. Rachid Chenchabi notes in an article from 1984 that Férid Boughedir, notable Tunisian film critic and filmmaker, humorously characterized the three Maghrebian national cinemas as follows: Algerians are known for "la dignité de l'humilié" (the dignity of the humiliated) and always bend to the power of their government; Tunisians fight for "l'exigence de la vérité" (claiming truth) and rely on a liberty of expression unlike anywhere else in the Arab world, so "they speak," but succumb to the diversity of their freedom and are, therefore, "Un orphelin qui cherche son visage" (an orphan who seeks his face); and the Moroccans live in the perpetual "plainte silencieuse . . . j'étouffe, j'étouffe" (silent complaint . . . I'm suffocating, I'm suffocating). Rachid Chenchabi, "Le cinéma maghrébin, une dimension francophone?" *Franzosisch heute*15, no. 2 (1984): 224–33.

14. On average, the CCM awards about US$400,000 per film. Filmmakers compete on an annual basis for these funds,which are distributed through the "avances sur recette" (advance estimate of ticket sales) program. Interview with Kamal Mouline, June 1, 2009, Rabat, Morocco.

15. I repeatedly asked him if there was "an agenda" in his use of language (i.e., Does the use of French evoke a different meaning for audiences than Arabic?). He said not really and that the French dialogues in *Tabite*, and indeed all his films, are used to "fit the mood" or the place of the action. Interview, February 2007.

16. The premiere was held at the Mohammed V Theater in downtown Rabat to a packed audience on February 20, 2007. Although Lahlou is considered "fou" (crazy) by everyone I talked to, his films, even the most bizarre, still find audiences.

17. However, after spending some months in Tunisia, I would say that this is now less the case. Arabization has been successful in transplanting many of the French dailies and print media as well as diminishing French language use in Tunisian cinema, although French films made in France are still widely distributed in Tunisian theaters.

Chapter 1: Theories and Polemics

1. Algeria is known as the "People's Democratic Republic of Algeria," although since 1962 it has been ruled by one party, the FLN, a single military and political power in the country. The party holds "elections" to elect presidents, who are usually cadres from the military. Tunisia touts a republic presidential system that is parliamentary and includes a Chamber of Representatives and a Chamber of Advisers. Zine El Abidine Ben Ali declared himself "president for life" in 1987 after wrenching the office

from Habib Bourguiba, whom Ben Ali and his medical experts deemed was mentally unfit to function further in office.

2. Lynn Teo Simarski, "Through North African Eyes," *Saudi Aramco World*, last accessed February 5, 2009, http://www.saudiaramcoworld.com/issue/ 199201/through.north.african.eyes.htm.

3. Even today, Ben Barka remains "the most notorious symbol of Morocco's ongoing difficulties with kidnapping and disappearance" (Slyomovics 2005, 49). Ben Barka's kidnapping in Paris and subsequent execution in France (details of which are revealed in Ali Bourequat's 1993 testimonial *Dix-huit ans de solitude*, Eighteen years of solitude) are not new subjects in contemporary Moroccan discourse. However, the ghost of Ben Barka still haunts the conscience of Moroccan society, and his story remains a symbol of flagrant state-sanctioned torture and abuse. Even though there is an avenue named after him in Rabat, and his role in opposition party politics in the 1960s has been well documented (most recently on the screen in the French-Moroccan film *J'ai vu tuer Ben Barka* (I saw Ben Barka get killed, by Serge Le Péron and Saïd Smihi, 2005), Ben Barka endures as the quintessential martyr of the abusive Lead Years.

The truth that has been uncovered thus far reveals that he was a victim, not only of his own government, but also of the complicity of an international ring of cohorts and spies with associations ranging from the French Interpol to the American CIA. The sheer power of the omnipotent *Makhzen* (the secretive side of the state, the monarchy, and the elites who have held the real power of Morocco since the time of the sultans) wielded against the opposition leader explains why so many people were frightened into silence. In a presentation at Georgetown University (March 17, 2009), Ahmed Herzenni, head of the Conseil consecutive des droits de l'homme (CCDH, Consultative Council on Human Rights), noted that, while many dossiers filed for reparations due to human rights abuse during the Lead Years were acknowledged and action on them has been taken, Ben Barka's would remain closed because "the affair implicates parties other than Moroccan." This means that until France owns up to the role it played in the capture, torture, and assassination of the opposition leader, the details of the "affair" will remain obscure.

4. It is important to note the distinction between Third Cinema and Third World Cinema. "Third Cinema is an aesthetic and political project which is guided by certain principles in order to challenge power structures." However, Third Cinema films "are generally produced by filmmakers located within the Third World regions of Africa, Asia, and Latin America and intended for audiences in these regions. . . . Third Cinema can also include films made by filmmakers located in the so-called First or Second Worlds, as long as they adhere to the guiding principles and

are made in support of the Third World perspective." *The Battle of Algiers* by Italian Gillo Pontecorvo is a classic example of a Third World perspective promoted in a film made by a First World filmmaker. See http://thirdcinema.blueskylimit.com/thirdcinema.html.

5. See http://thirdcinema.blueskylimit.com/thirdcinema.html.

6. Third Cinema (in Spanish known as *Tercer Cine*) began in the 1960s. Its goals included to challenge neocolonialism and capitalist systems as well as the Hollywood model of filmmaking, which produced films for pure entertainment. The manifesto *Towards a Third Cinema*, written in the late 1960s by Argentine filmmakers Fernando Solanas and Octavio Getino, members of the Grupo cine liberación, theoretically conceptualized the genre. Other filmmaker-theorists, genres, and groups included Raymundo Gleyzer and his Cine de la base, the Brazilian Cinema nôvo and revolutionary cinema from Cuba.

Chapter 2: Issues, Contexts, and "Culture Wars"

1. This was repeatedly a subject of contention for Sembène Ousmane, who stated that West African filmmakers were always held over a barrel by France when they accepted funding.

2. There are of course exceptions. *L'enfant endormi* (The sleeping child, 2004), a Moroccan-Belgian coproduction taking place in northeastern Morocco, is based on a traditional Moroccan story.

3. These statistics were sent by Kamal Mouline, general counsel of the CCM, on May 26, 2010. Mr. Mouline also indicated that foreign cineastes who made films in Morocco have invested a total of US$406 million into the country's filmmaking industry in the last six years (particularly in the region of Ouarzazate, known as the "Hollywood" of Morocco due to the large soundstages that have been built in the town). The top-grossing films made in Morocco by American filmmakers include *Prince of Persia* (Mike Newel, 2010); *Green Zone* (Paul Greengrass, 2010); *Body of Lies* (Ridley Scott, 2008); *Kingdom of Heaven* (Ridley Scott, 2005); and *Sahara* (Breck Eisner, 2005).

4. Al Arabiya newschannel, http://www.alarabiya.net/articles/2007/12/13/42889.html, 13 December 2007.

5. Hicham Houdaïfa and Fedoua Tounassi, "*Marock le vrai débat,*" *Le journal hebdomadaire*, May 27–June 2, 2006: 18–25, 18.

6. Ahmed Benchemsi, "*Les 50 qui feront le Maroc de demain,*" *TelQuel: Le Maroc tel qu'il est*, December 2006: 38–55, 50.

7. A *TelQuel* article comments on the openness both on the set and behind the scenes during the shooting of *Marock*. Despite the emotionally, socially and even politically charged subject matter of the film, the

shooting of *Marock* came off in harmony among the technical team. The sincerity of the subject meant a lot to the team, as witnesses this technician: "It's certain that the film could have proposed clashes among us. All these question concerning religious, sexual, and linguistic rifts. But everyone understood that the film wasn't seeking to establish absolute truths but to transcribe, above all, certain realities that are useless to ignore. On the scene, Muslims, Jews, and Christians cohabited perfectly; some didn't hesitate to practice their religious rites during filming" (my translation). "Marock. Le film de tous les tabous," *TelQuel*, http://www. telquel-online.com/223/couverture_223_1.shtml.

8. Amin Rboub, *L'economiste*, http://www.leconomiste.com/print_article.html?a=67765 Mohamed Hassan El Joundy, general secretary of the Dramaturge Guild, was the most vocal critic.

9. Ibid.

10. Houdaïfa et al., 22.

11. Ibid., 66.

12. "Le Grand Voyage," http://www.worldcinemashowcase.co.nz/GRANDVOYAGE.html.

13. See http://worldcinemashowcase.co.nz/GRANDVOYAGE.html.

14. Ahsma Mouhib, http://asmaamb.over-blog.com/article-10381606.html.

15. Youssouf Elalamy informed me in an e-mail sent on May 27, 2010: "Nizar est un prénom arabe et Tayf peut être soit un nom de famille soit Tayf comme le participe passé du verbe Taafa qui veut dire tourner en procession autour de la Kaaba. Tayf voudrait donc dire 'qui a effectué le rituel de la procession autour de la Kaaba.' Au sens figuré, Tayf peut également signifier 'qui a tourné,' 'que l'on a fait tourner en bourrique.'"

16. Olivier Barlet, "la Symphonie Marocaine," review, http://www.africultures.com/php/index.php?nav=article&no=4451.

17. See http://www.comlive.net/La-symphonie-marocaine,81521.htm.

18. The Makhzen is "le pouvoir occult" (parallel, hidden power of the monarchy). It is a behemoth that has run the country through oppression, torture, and corruption since the time of the sultans. Members of the Makhzen are the elite who possess all the power in Morocco.

19. Interview with Hassan Benjelloun at his studio, May 29, 2009, Casablanca, Morocco.

20. See http://jewishrefugees.blogspot.com/2008/03/moroccan-film-focuses-on-mass-jewish.html.

21. Ibid.

22. Interview with Hassan Benjelloun, May 29, 2009, Casablanca, Morocco.

23. Ibid.

Chapter 3: Bad Boys, Drugs, and Rock 'n' Roll

1. Author's italics.

2. As cited in Brinda Bose, "Modernity, Globality, Sexuality, and the City: A Reading of Indian Cinema," *Global South*, vol. 2:1: 35–58.

3. Citation from Lakhmari's official website for the film linked to Facebook.

4. Translated roughly as: Tears of joy the day of Zamzam and teeth-clenching depression on a battlefield cleaned with Clorox, or the legend of Ash's eleventh finger.

5. "Foi schizophrénique," *Le journal hebdomadaire*, http://www.lejournal-hebdo.com/article.php3?id_article=4909.

6. In the second novel, Yousouf the journalist runs for city office on the platform of "no-corruption"; however, he loses. While on the campaign trail and writing articles against Moroccan corruption for his newspaper *La missive*, whose slogan is "L'information, sans complaisance, sans restriction" (Information without complicity or restriction), he meets Yasmina, a doctor and social activist for poor children in the slums of Casablanca (Lamrini 2000, 68). They fall in love and marry; however, their happy marriage is overshadowed by the fact that Yasmina is a Talabi, and therefore from a family that represents the corrupt elite—the very entity against which Youssef is writing and fighting his cause. The final tome, *Le temps des impunis*, published in 2004, ends on an uncertain note, thus accurately mirroring the socioeconomic and cultural climate of contemporary Morocco. Youssef is sent to prison for the damaging articles he has written. In prison, he undertakes a huger strike to draw attention to the lack of freedom of press in Morocco.

7. The last few pages of the third novel, *Le temps des impunis*, which are not included in the film, describe "un certain printemps en 2003" (a certain spring in 2003) when three bombs went off in Casablanca. The event is now considered Morocco's September 11.

8. Interview with Rida Lamrini, May 30, 2009, Casablanca, Morocco.

Chapter 4: Prison, Torture, and Testimony

1. The *CIA World Fact Book* lists the following breakdown for the Moroccan population: 0–14 years old, 32.1 percent; 15–64, 63 percent; 65 years and older, 5.1 percent. The median age: 24.3 years (24.8 years female; 23.8 male); total population as of 2007: 33,241,259, https://www.cia.gov/library/publications/the-world-factbook/geos/mo.html#People.

2. Titles of testimonial prison literature in Arabic include the novels *Ufoulu al-layl: Yawmiyat Lm'arif wa Ghbila* (The extinction of night: Journal of Lm'arif and Ghbila) by Tahar Mahfoudi (published by Dar Al-Qarawiyine, 2004), which recounts the suffering of prisoners in two detention centers in Casablanca; and *Hadit al-'atama* by Fatna El Bouih (A woman named Rachid, Le Fennec, 2001), which affirms the resistance of women who were tortured in prisons. (See Zekri 2006, 205.)

3. These coups took place in Kénitra in 1971 and in the air when generals Oufkir and Dilimi, powerful in the king's military apparatus, tried to force the royal Boeing 747 down and take over the government in 1972. Both coups failed and Hassan II assassinated the generals.

4. According to Mohammed Raïss, twenty-seven of these men are in Morocco, the three Bourequat brothers are abroad (Ali resides in the United States and Midhat and Bayazid live in France), and M'barek Touil is in the United States. (See Raïss 2002, 389.) This number, however, varies depending on the text and also when it was written, since many of the former prisoners are elderly and dying.

5. Zinoun lost his oldest son, Chems, in an auto accident in November 2008.

6. At the time of my interview with Lahcen Zinoun, he had been waiting for weeks on the Ministry of Culture to summon him to its offices to see if his proposal for several endeavors in the arts would be accepted and funded. He underscored the fact that for every two steps forward an artist takes, he must take three backward. Interview, June 11, 2009, Casablanca, Morocco.

7. Susan Slyomovics, in *The Performance of Human Rights in Morocco* (Philadelphia: Pennsylvania University Press, 2005), explains that during the years 1963–73 more than thirteen thousand people went missing. This is an official estimate, but some feel the number is much higher. The tally also does not account for the years from 1973 forward, during which many disappeared of whom families are still awaiting information.

8. The film is a Franco-Marocain-Spanish production.

9. Staff writer, *TelQuel*, http://www.telquel-online.com/194/sujet5.shtml.

10. Staff writer, *Le monde*, http://www.lemonde.fr/web/article/0,1–0@2–3476–705421,0.html.

11. See the interview with Bachir Ben Barka dated November 1999, http://www.marxist.com/appeals/ben_barka/pictures.html.

12. Ibid.

13. Ibid.

14. Staff writer, *TelQuel*, http://www.telquel-online.com/194/sujet5.shtml.

15. "Cinéma: Entretien avec Jilali Ferhati, réalisateur de Mémoire en détention," *TelQuel*, December 4, 2005, http://www.yabiladi.com/article.php?cat=culture&id=221.

16. *TelQuel*, no. 203, http://www.telquel-online.com.

17. These testimonial novels include Ahmed Marzouki's *Cellule 10: Tazmamart* (2001); Abdelfettah Fakihani's *Le couloir: Bribes de vérité sur les années de plomb* (2005); Mohammed Raïss's *De Skhirat à Tazmamart: Retour du bout de l'enfer* (2002); Fatna El Bouih's *Une femme nommée Rachid* (2002); and Aziz Binebine's *Tazmamart* (2008). For complete analyses of these testimonials, see Valérie Orlando's *Francophone Voices of the "New Morocco" in Film and Print: (Re)presenting a Society in Transition* (Palgrave Macmillan, 2009).

18. Anonymous author, http://www.telquel-online.com/124/arts_124.shtml.

19. Some have said that supporters marching in the Green March were paid by the monarchy for their support. I cannot, however, verify this information.

20. The Makhzen is the "system" in Morocco, run by the rich and powerful directly associated with the monarchy. It has been in place since the time of the sultans, before French colonial rule.

21. In particular see her works *Les femmes arabes* (Casablanca: Editions Aïni Bennaï, 2002) ; *La liaison* (Casablanca: Editions Aïni Bennaï, 2002, first published under the pseudonym Lyne Tywa, Paris: L'Harmattan, 1989) ; and *Le Maghreb des femmes: Les défis du XXIème siècle* (Rabat: Marsam, 2001).

Chapter 5: Women's Voices

1. *Days of Fear: A Booklet about the Making of Bab el Oued City*, 1997. Interview with Allouache included with the DVD.

2. See http://www.tiburonfilmfestival.com/eventInfo.php?event_id=144.

3. Samira Hadj Djilani is a producer and former director of the first private Algerian TV channel, "Khalifa TV" (which no longer exists). She has also worked for several years at the Ministry of Culture and Communication. She is a member of the "Algerian Businesswomen's Club" and also works and teaches in Spain. Currently she is working on a film about an Algerian martyr of the revolution, Aissat Idir. Baya Hachemi is a specialist in TV serial stories. Nadia Cherabi is also a filmmaker and a producer. She is a teacher at the Audiovisual School in Algiers. Cherabi, Hachemi, and Yamina Chouikh (*Rachida*, 2002) are members of the Women Film-

makers and Producers, an association that supports women making films in Algeria. (Special thanks to Margaret Braswell for this information via e-mail, September 30, 2009.)

4. The Kahina was also known to be a priestess and is thought to have reigned in Berber lands (primarily the Aurès Mountains in Algeria), in the region of Dihiya, during the seventh and eighth centuries AD. Some have also been called by the names Dihiya and Dîyya and might have been part of the Djerawa tribe, which, according to Ibn Khaldûn, were primarily Jewish. She led armies into battle to combat the invading Arabs.

5. "Polémique: Les Yeux humides d'Aghbala," *TelQuel*, no. 125, May 7, 2004, http://www.telquel-online.com/125/sujet5.shtml.

6. *TelQuel*, http://www.telquel-online.com/125/sujet5.shtml.

7. Noufissa Sbaï, e-mail correspondence, July 4, 2007.

8. Sbaï emphasizes that all the actors were paid 60DH (about US$7.50) a day, which is an enormous amount in a region where jobs are scarce and resources limited.

9. Pierre Duculot, *Cinergie*, http://www.cinergie.be/entrevue.php?action=display&id=38.

10. Joël Colin, "L'enfant endormi dans le ventre de sa mère," *Histoire et sciences sociales*, 1999 (15): 260–63, http://www.lenfantendormi.be/pdf/289.pdf.

11. See http://www.africultures.com/index.asp?menu=revue_affiche_article&no=6688&lang=_en.

12. See http://www.cinergie.be/entrevue.php?action=display&id=38.

13. See http://www.bladi.net/farida-bourquia.html.

14. The First Moudawana, decreed in 1957 by Mohammed V and later upheld by Hassan II, was based on Sharia law and the Maleke school of thought. Because the laws were religious-based, any change was viewed as a direct attack on Islam. In 1957 there was still no constitution or Parliament; the king had absolute say in all legal rulings.

In 1993, Hassan II enacted the First Reform of the Moudawana under pressure from the increased activism of women's groups that started questioning the validity of the Moudawana. At this time, the king gave Parliament control over more civil laws and "faith-based" laws. He, in a sense, accepted some parliamentary competency on affairs linked with faith, which normally fell in his jurisdiction alone as "Commander of the Faithful."

In 2004 (February), the Second Reform was decreed by Mohammed VI. Again, the reform was due to increased activism among women's groups, NGOs, and national and international associations. The reform raised the age of marriage to eighteen (for both men and women); gave women the right to contract their own marriages (no father, brother, or other male family member involved); gave equal authority in the family to men and women; granted greater financial rights (women have new rights to assets acquired by marriage); established judicial divorce (men must go to court); verbal repudiation is no longer valid; polygamy was not abolished *but* now requires a judge's authorization. Women can stipulate in their marriage contracts that polygamy not be an option. Divorce is now a prerogative that can be exercised as much by the husband as by the wife. Men and women are now equally protected under the law; however, the 2004 reform did not address inheritance, which is still based on Shari'a.

15. "J'aime le Maroc profondément, viscéralement, effectivement, esthétiquement Mais comment parler de ce pays avec amour et lucidité? C'est à Casablanca, mégapole dense, grouillante, vivante dans un mélange d'arabe courant truculent et de français que j'ai voulu me perdre avec délices. Alors j'ai dessiné mon Aziz, mon number one, je l'ai cherché, découvert, apprivoisé. Je l'ai détesté, je lui ai pardonné. Il m'a fait peur, rire, pleurer," http://www.yabiladi.com/article-culture-744.html; Qods Chabâa , *Le Soir Echos.*

Conclusion: The Future of Moroccan Cinema?

1. Hassan Benjelloun described the lack of "soutien" (aide) he received from the CCM for the distribution of his films at international film festivals. All subtitling he has assured himself, but he did indicate that the cost is minimal. Interview, May 29, 2009, Casablanca, Morocco.

2. It is certainly an issue for Hassan Benjelloun, Lahcen Zinoun, and Nabyl Lahlou, all of whom told me that making films with technicians from abroad disproportionately squeezed their already small budgets. A European technician or cameraman will demand to be paid almost three times more than a Moroccan. This is also the case for actors. Most Moroccan actors are paid very little, sometimes nothing for starring in films, and have "day jobs" on which they must rely for their primary sources of income.

3. For more information, see http://www.rfi.fr/contenu/20100522–1-une-ecole-cinema-maroc-reportage-haiti.

Selected Filmography of Moroccan Feature-Length Films: 1999–2008

(Adapted from *Cinéma marocain filmographie: Longs métrages 1958–2008*, an annual publication of the Centre cinématographique marocain (CCM). This particular issue celebrates fifty years of postcolonial filmmaking in Morocco.)

1999

Ali zaoua, Nabyl Ayouch
Les amis d'hier (Friends of yesterday), Hassan Benjelloun
Mabrouk, Driss Chouika
Ruses de femmes (Women's wiles), Farida Benlyazid

2000

Ali, Rabia et les autres (Ali, Rabia and the others), Ahmed Boulane
Amour sans visa (Love without a visa), Najib Sefrioui
Du paradis à l'enfer (From paradise to hell), Saïd Souda
Elle est diabétique, hypertendue et elle refuse de crever (She's diabetic, hypertensive, and she refuses to die), Hakim Noury
Histoire d'une rose (A story of a rose), Abdelmajid R'chich
Jugement d'une femme (A woman judged), Hassan Benjelloun

L'homme qui brodait des secrets (The man who embroidered secrets), Omar
   Chraïbi
Soif (Thirst), Saâd Chraïbi
Tresses (Braids), Jillali Ferhati
Yacout, Jamal Belmajdoub

2001

Au-delà de Gibraltar (Beyond Gibraltar), Taylan Barnan and Mourad Boucif
Le cheval de vent (Wind horse), Daoud Aoulad Syad
Les amours de Hadj Mokhtar Soldi (The love affairs of Hadj Mokhtar
   Soldi), Mustapha Derkaoui
Les années de l'exil (Years of exile), Nabyl Lahlou
Les lèvres du silence (Lips of silence), Hassan Benjelloun
Mona Saber, Abdelhai Laraki
Tayf Nizar (Nizar's ghost), (Kamal Kamal)

2002

Casablanca, Farida Benlyazid
Et après . . . (And after . . .), Mohammed Ismaïl
Histoire d'amour (Story of love), Hakim Noury
Le paradis des pauvres (Paradise of the poor), Imane Mesbahi
Le pote (The mate), Hassan Benjelloun
Les amants de Mogador (The lovers of Mogador), Souheil Ben Barka
Les yeux secs (Dry eyes), Narjiss Nejjar
Une minute de soleil en moins (One less minute of silence), Nabyl Ayouch

2003

Casablanca by Night, Mustapha Derkaoui
Face à face (Face to face), Abdelkader Lagtaa
Jawhara, Saâd Chraïbi
Les fibres de l'âme (The sinews of the soul), Hakim Belabbes
Les voisines d'Abou Moussa (The women neighbors of Abou Moussa), Ab-
   derrahmane Tazi
Mille mois (A thousand months), Faouzi Bensaïdi

Parabole (Satellite dish), Narjiss Nejjar
Rahma, Omar Chraïbi
Réveil (Waking), Mohammed Zineddine

2004

Casablanca Day Light, Mustapha Derkaoui
Casablanca, les anges ne volent pas (In Casablanca, angels do not fly), Mohammed Asli
Ici et là (Here and there), Mohammed Ismaïl
L'enfant endormi (The sleeping child), Yasmine Kassari
La chambre noire (The black room), Hassan Benjelloun
Le grand voyage (The long journey), Ismaïl Ferroukhi

Les bandits (Crooks), Saïd Naciri
Mémoire en détention (Memory in detention), Jillali Ferhati
Tarfaya, Daoud Oulad Syad
Tenja, Hassan Lagzouli

2005

J'ai vu tuer Ben Barka (I saw Ben Barka get killed), Serge Le Péron and Saïd Smihi
Juanita de Tanger (Juanita of Tangiers), Farida Benlyazid
La symphonie marocaine (The Moroccan symphony), Kamal Kamal
Le gosse de Tanger (The boy of Tangiers), Moumen Smihi
Le regard (The gaze), Noureddine Lakhmari
Les portes du paradis (Heaven's doors), Sohael and Imad Noury
Marock, Leïla Marrakchi

2006

Abdou chez les Almohades (Abdou at the Almohades' house), Saïd Naciri
Le jeu de l'amour (The game of love), Driss Chouika
Quel monde merveilleux (What a wonderful world), Faouzi Bensaïdi
Tabite or Not Tabite, Nabyl Lahlou
Wake Up Morocco!, Narjiss Nejjar

2007

Adieu mères (Good-bye, mothers), Mohammed Ismail
Argana, Hassan Rhanja
Deux femmes sur la route (Two women on the road), Farida Bourquia
En attendant Pasolini (Waiting for Pasolini), Daoud Oulad Syad
L'os de fer (The iron bone), Hicham Lasri
La beauté éparpillée (Scattered beauty), Lahcen Zinoun
Les anges de Satan (Satan's angels), Ahmed Boulane
Où vas-tu Moshé? (Where are you going, Moshé?), Hassan Benjelloun
Yasmine et les hommes (Yasmine and men), Abdelkader Lagtaa

2008

Amours voilés (Veiled loves), Aziz Salmy
Casanegra, Noureddine Lakhmari
Française (French girl), Souad El Bouhati
Itto Titrit, Mohammed Oumouloud Abbazi
Kadisha, Jérôme Cohen-Olivar
Number One, Zakia Tahiri
Sellam et Dimitan, Mohammed Amin Benamraoui
Tamazight oufella, Mohammed Mernich
Two Lakes of Tears, Mohammed Hassini
Whatever Lola Wants, Lola Gets, Nabyl Ayouch

Bibliography

Affaya, Noureddine, and Driss Guerraoui. *Le Maroc des jeunes*. Rabat: Ara (Association de recherche audiovisuelle), 2006.

Aït Berri, Aïcha. "Les Yeux secs: Tare ou œuvre d'art ?" *Le monde berbère*. http://www.mondeberbere.com/rebonds/20040514_yeuxsecs.htm.

Alaoui, Abdellah Mdarhri. *Aspects du roman marocain (1950–2003)*. Rabat: Editions Zaouia, 2006.

Al-Zahi, Farid. "The 'Possessed' or the Symbolic Body in Moroccan Cinema." Translated by Tahia Khaled Abdel Nasser. *Alif: Journal of Comparative Poetics* 15 (1995): 267–71.

Armes, Roy. *Postcolonial Images: Studies in North African Film*. Bloomington: Indiana University Press, 2005.

———. *Third World Filmmaking and the West*. Berkeley: University of California Press, 1987.

Arndt, Susan. *The Dynamics of African Feminism: Defining and Classifying African Feminist Literatures*. Trenton: Africa World Press, 2002.

Bakhtin, Mikhail M. *The Dialogic Imagination*. Austin: Texas University Press, 1981.

Barlet, Olivier. "L'Enfant endormi by Yasmine Kassari," 2007. http://www.africultures.com/index.asp?menu=revue_affiche_article&no-6688&lang=_en.

Beau, Nicolas, and Catherine Graciet. *Quand le Maroc sera islamiste*. Paris: La Decouverte, 2006.

Bennani, Ouafaâ. "Bilan cinématographique 2009: Des chiffres qui mettent à nu l'état du 7ème Art marocain." *Le Matin* (March 14, 2010), http://

www.lematin.ma/Actualite/Journal/Article.asp?idr=115&id=129674.

Bernichi, Loubna. "Un Amour de plomb." Interview with Hanane Ibrahimi. *Le journal hebdomadaire.* http://www.maroc-hebdo.press.ma/MHinternet/Archives-601/html_601/amour.html.

Bessière, Jean. *Les écrivains engagés.* Paris: Librairie Larousse, 1977.

Bose, Brinda. "Modernity, Globality, Sexuality, and the City: A Reading of Indian Cinema." *Global South* 2, no. 1 (2008): 35–58.

Boukhari, Karim. "Cinéma. La symphonie (inachevée) marocaine" (February 11, 2006). http://www.telquel-online.com/211/arts3_211.shtml.

Bourakkadi, Mustapha. "L'os de fer." *Le matin* (December 24, 2007). http://www.infosdumaroc.com/modules/news/articles-2663-le-realisateur-marocain-hicham-lasri-tourne-l-039-.html.

Bourdieu, Pierre. *The Field of Cultural Production.* New York: Columbia University Press, 1993.

———. *Language & Symbolic Power.* Third Printing. Cambridge: Harvard University Press, 1994.

Brahimi, Denise. *50 Ans de cinéma maghrébin.* Paris: Minerve, 2009.

Carter, Sandra. "Farida Benlyazid's Moroccan Women." *Quarterly Review of Film and Video* 17, no. 4 (2001): 343–69.

———. "Moroccan Cinema, What Cinema?" *Maghreb Review* 25, nos. 1–2 (2000): 66–97.

———. "Moroccan Cinema, What Moroccan Cinema?" PhD Dissertation. Unpublished. U of MI Microfilms, University of Texas, Austin, 1999.

———. *What Moroccan Cinema? A Historical and Critical Study, 1956–2006.* Lanham: Lexington Books, 2009.

Césaire, Aimé. *Discours sur le colonialisme.* Paris: Présence africaine, 1955.

Chabâa, Qods. *Le Soir Echos.* http://www.yabiladi.com/article-culture-744.html.

Chadi, Taïbi. "La Tentation du diable." *Le Maroc hebdomadaire,* no. 547 (February 28–March 6, 2003): 4–6.

Chenchabi, Rachid. "Le cinéma maghrébin, une dimension francophone?" *Franzosisch heute* 15, no. 2 (1984): 224–33.

CinéMag: Magazine du cinéma et de l'audiovisuel au Maroc (Oct./Nov./Dec. 2008).

Cinéma marocain filmograpie générale: Longs métrages, 1958–2005. Publication of the CCM. Rabat, Morocco, 2005.

Daoud, Zakya. *Les Années Lamalif: 1958–1988, trente ans de journalisme au Maroc.* Casablanca: Tarik Editions, 2007.

Derrida, Jacques. *Demeure: Fiction and Testimony*. Stanford: Stanford University Press, 2000.

Diawara, Manthia. *African Cinema: Politics and Culture*. Bloomington: Indiana University Press, 1992.

Dib, Mohammed. *L'Incendie*. Paris: Seuil, 1956.

Dwyer, Kevin. *Beyond Casablanca: M. A. Tazi and the Adventure of Moroccan Cinema*. Bloomington: Indiana University Press, 2004.

————. "'Hidden, Unsaid, Taboo' in Moroccan Cinema: Abdelkader Lagtaa's Challenge to Authority." *Framework* 43, no. 2 (Fall 2002): 117–33.

Edmonds, Lisa. "Cities on the Edge of Forever: Urban Images of the Future in Film." *Society for the Interdisciplinary Study of Social Imagery* (January 2003): 22–25.

Edwards, Brian. *Morocco Bound: Disorienting America's Maghreb, from Casablanca to the Marrakech Express*. Durham: Duke University Press, 2005.

El Ghissassi, Hakim. *Regard sur le Maroc de Mohammed VI*. Paris: Michel Lafon, 2006.

El Khayat, Rita. *Les femmes arabes*. Casablanca: Editions Aïni Bennaï, 2002.

El Mazouari, Saïd. 2007. http://www.jeunesdumaroc.com/article2983.html.

Fanon, Frantz. *Les damnés de la terre*. Paris: La Découverte, 1961. First printing Paris: Maspéro, 1965. Translation: *The Wretched of the Earth*. New York: Grove Press, 2002.

Faquihi, Faiçal. "Quand les 'sataniques' font leur cinéma!" *L'economiste* (March 7, 2007). http://www.bladi.net/116660-satanistes-cinema.html.

Flitterman-Lewis, Sandy. *To Desire Differently: Feminism and the French Cinema*. New York: Columbia University Press, 1996.

"Foi schizophrénique." *Le journal hebdomadaire*. http://www.lejournal-hebdo.com/article.php3?id_article=4909.

Gabriel, Teshome. "Towards a Critical Theory of Third World Films." In *Questions of third Cinema*. Edited by Jim Pines and Paul Willemen. London: British Film Institute, 1991.

Ganne, Valérie. "Tizi, le village des prostituées." Afrik.com (May 22, 2003). http:// www.afrik.com/article6113.html.

Ghareeb, Shirin. "An Overview of Arab Cinema." *Critique* (Fall 1997): 119–27.

Girard, Alexandra. "Bilan mitigé pour le cinéma marocain." *Le matin* (January 2, 2008). http://www.yabiladi.com/article-culture-633.html.

Gontard, Marc. "Francophone North African Literature and Critical Theory." *Research in African Literatures* (Winter 1992): 35–38.

———. *La Violence du texte.* Paris: Editions L'Harmattan, 1981.

Gonzalez, Ed. *Slant Magazine* (2005). http://slantmagazine.com/film/film _review.asp?ID=1480.

Gourlet, Loïc. *Le Quotidien du cinéma.* http://ww.lequotidienducinema.com/critiques/benbarka_critique/critique_jai_vu_tuer_ben_barka.htm.

Halbwachs, Maurice. *The Collective Memory.* New York: Harper & Row, 1980.

Haynes, Jonathan. "Nollywood in Logos, Logos in Nollywood Films." *Africa Today* 54, no. 2 (Winter 2007): 130–50.

Hayward, Susan. *French National Cinema.* London: Routledge, 1992.

Houdaïfa, Hicham, and Fedoua Tounassi. "Marock: le vrai débat." *Le journal hebdomadaire* (May 27–June 2, 2006): 18–25.

Hudson-Weems, Clenora. *Africana Womanist Literary Theory.* Trenton: Africa World Press, 2004.

Jakobsen, Janet, and Ann Pellegrini, eds. *Secularisms.* Durham: Duke University Press, 2008.

Kaye, Jacqueline, and Abdelhamid Zoubir. *The Ambiguous Compromise: Language, Literature and National Identity in Algeria and Morocco.* New York/London: Routledge, 1990.

Khatibi, Abdelkébir. *Amour bilingue.* Montpellier: Fata Morgana, 1983.

———. *Le Roman maghrébin.* Paris: Maspéro, 1968.

Kolawole, Mary E. *Womanism and African Consciousness.* Trenton: Africa World Press, 1997.

Lamrini, Rida. *Les puissants de Casablanca.* Rabat: Marsam, 1999.

———. *Les rapaces.* Rabat: Marsam, 2000.

———. *Le temps des impunis.* Rabat: Marsam, 2004.

Lasri, Hicham. *(K)rêve! L'haïtiste.* Rabat: L'Union des écrivains au Maroc, 2006.

———. *Larmes de Joie un jour de Zamzam et crissement de dents de cafard dans un champs de bataille passé à l'eau de javel ou La légende du 11ème doigt de Ash.* Vitry-sur-Seine: Les Editions de la Gare, 2007.

———. *Stati: Roman à facettes.* Casablanca: Editions de la croisée des chemins, 2009.

Lazreg, Marnia. *The Eloquence of Silence: Algerian Women in Question.* New York: Routledge, 1994.

Magharebia. "Hicham Lasri Talks about Becoming a Screenwriter and Director." February 27, 2007. http://www.magharebia.com/cocoon/awi/xhtml1 /en_GB/features/awi/features/2007/02/27/feature-02.

Marzouki, Ahmed. *Tazmamart: Cellule 10.* Paris: Gallimard, 2001.

Megherbi, Abdelghani. *Les Algériens au miroir du cinéma colonial.* Algiers: SNED, 1982.

Memmi, Albert. *Portrait du colonisé précédé de portrait du colonisateur.* Paris: Gallimard, 1957.

Mernissi, Fatima. *Beyond the Veil: Male-Female Dynamics in Modern Muslim Society.* Bloomington: Indiana University Press, 1987.

———. *Les sindbads marocains: Voyage dans le Maroc civique.* Rabat: Marsam, 2004.

Mezran, Karim. *Negotiation and Construction of National Identities.* Boston: Martinus Nijhoff, 2007.

Mirabet, Ayla. "Danse avec les images." www.telquel-online.com/ 314/ artsl_314.shtml.

Mulvey, Laura. "Visual Pleasure and Narrative Cinema." Reprinted in *The Sexual Subject: A Screen Reader in Sexuality.* New York: Routledge, 1992.

Najeb, Meriem. "Ali n'Productions annonce le tournage de L'Os de fer." *Jeunes du Maroc* (July 28, 2008). http://www.jeunesdumaroc.com/article2008.html.

Nora, Pierre. *Les lieux de mémoire.* Translation: *Realms of Memory.* Edited by Lawrence D. Kritzman. New York: Columbia University Press, 1996.

Oha, Obododimma. "The Visual Rhetoric of the Ambivalent City in Nigerian Video Films." *In Cinema and the City: Film and Urban Societies in a Global Context.* Edited by Mark Shiel and Tony Fitzmaurice. New York: Blackwell, 2001, 195–205.

Pfaff, Françoise, ed. *Focus on African Film.* Bloomington: Indiana University Press, 2004.

Pile, Steve. *The Body and the City: Psychoanalysis, Space and Subjectivity.* New York: Routledge, 1996.

Pisters, Patricia. "Refusal of Reproduction: Paradoxes of Becoming-Woman in Transnational Moroccan Filmmaking," in *Transnational Feminism in Film and Media.* Edited by Katarzyna Marciniak. New York: Palgrave Macmillan, 2007.

Raïss, Mohammed. *De Skhirat à Tazmamart: Retour du bout de l'enfer.* Casablanca: L'Afrique orient, 2002.

Raji, Hicham. "Jawhara, prison girl." http://babelmed.net/index. php?menu= 166&cont=716&lingua=en.

Rosen, Miriam. "The Uprooted Cinema: Arab Filmmakers Abroad." *Middle East Report* (July–August 1989): 34–37.

Saïd, Edward. *Humanism and Democratic Criticism.* New York: Columbia University Press, 2004.

———. *Orientalism.* New York: Vintage, 1979.

Schalk, David. *The Spectrum of Political Engagement: Mounier, Benda, Nizan, Brasillach, Sartre.* Princeton: Princeton University Press, 1979.

Sedia, Giuseppe. "Centre cinématographique marocain: Entretien avec Abdelhatif Laassadi." *Clap noir: Cinémas et audiovisuels africains* (October 11, 2008). http://www.clapnoir.org/spip.php?article269.

Sefrioui, Kenza. "Nabyl Lahlou: Dans les méanders de conscience." *Le journal hebdomadaire* (December 21, 2006). http://www.lejournal-hebdo.com/sommaire/culture/dans-les-m-andres-des-consciences.html.

Semlali, Aïda. "Cinéma: Nouveauté, Boulane et ses Hells Angels." *Le journal hebdomadaire* (March 15, 2007). http://www.lejournal-hebdo.com/sommaire/content/ view/2972/35/.

Shafik, Viola. *Arab Cinema: History and Cultural Identity.* Cairo: American University of Cairo University Press, 2007.

Shiel, Mark, and Tony Fitzmaurice. *Cinema and the City: Film and Urban Societies in a Global Context.* New York: Blackwell, 2001.

Slavin, David Henry. *Colonial Cinema and Imperial France, 1919–1939: White Blind Spots, Male, Fantasies, Settler Myths.* Baltimore: Johns Hopkins University Press, 2001.

Slyomovics Susan. *The Performance of Human Rights in Morocco.* Philadelphia: University of Pennsylvania Press, 2005.

Tebib, Elias. "Panorama des cinémas maghrébins." *Notre librairie* 149 (2000): 60–66.

Thackway, Melissa. *Africa Shoots Back: Alternative Perspectives in Sub-Saharan Francophone African Film.* New York: James Curry, 2003.

Tizourgni, Ahmed, and Nabyl Guennouni. "De la fable des 'sataniques' au 'tsunami' en passant par les actes terroristes." *L'Etendard* 53 (February 11–17, 2005).

Ukadike, Frank. *Black African Cinema.* Berkeley: University of California Press, 1994.

Vermeren, Pierre. *Le Maroc en transition.* Paris: La Découverte, 2002.

———. *Le Maroc. Idées reçues.* Paris: Le Cavalier Bleu, 2007.

Watson, Sophie, and Katherine Gibson, eds. *Postmodern Cities and Spaces.* Oxford: Blackwell, 1995.

Zekri, Khalid. *Fictions du réel. Modernité romanesque et écriture du réel au Maroc: 1990–2006.* Paris: L'Harmattan, 2006.

Ziane, Nadia. "Mustapha Mesnaoui: 'Nous n'avons pas de cinéma marocain.'" *Le matin* (August 22, 2005). http://www.lematin.ma.

Index